The American Poetry Anthology

The American Poetry Anthology

Edited by
Daniel Halpern

Routledge
Taylor & Francis Grou
LONDON AND NEW YORK

First published 1975 by Westview Press

Published 2018 by Routledge
52 Vanderbilt Avenue, New York, NY 10017
2 Park Square, Milton Park, Abingdon, Oxon OX14 4RN

Routledge is an imprint of the Taylor & Francis Group, an informa business

Library of Congress Cataloging in Publication Data
Main entry under title:

The American poetry anthology.

"Published in cooperation with Avon Books."
1. American poetry--20th century. I. Halpern, Daniel, 1945-
PS615.A4 . 811'.5'08 75-27439

ISBN 13: 978-0-367-02053-8 (hbk)
ISBN 13: 978-0-367-17040-0 (pbk)

Acknowledgments

AI: "Everything: Eloy, Arizona, 1956," "Why Can't I Leave You," "Cuba, 1960," and "Hangman" reprinted from *Cruelty* by permission of Houghton Mifflin Company. Copyright © 1970, 1973 by Ai. Copyright © 1971, 1972 by Florence Anthony.

ANDERSON, JON: "Years," "John Clare," and "In Autumn" reprinted from *In Sepia* by Jon Anderson by permission of the University of Pittsburgh Press. Copyright © 1974 by the University of Pittsburgh Press. "The Parachutist" and "The Photograph of Myself" reprinted from *Death and Friends* by Jon Anderson by permission of the University of Pittsburgh Press. Copyright © 1970 by the University of Pittsburgh Press. "The Blue Animals" reprinted from *Looking for Jonathan* by Jon Anderson by permission of the University of Pittsburgh Press. Copyright © 1968 by the University of Pittsburgh Press.

BELL MARVIN: "Acceptance Speech" reprinted by permission of Marvin Bell. Copyright © 1975 by Marvin Bell. "Here," "Impotence," and "Residue of Song" reprinted from *Residue of Song* by Marvin Bell. Copyright © 1971, 1972, 1973, 1974 by Marvin Bell. Reprinted by permission of Atheneum Publishers. "Treetops" and "The Perfection of Dentistry" reprinted from *A Probable Volume of Dreams* by Marvin Bell. Copyright © 1968, 1969 by Marvin Bell. Reprinted by permission of Atheneum Publishers.

BENEDIKT, MICHAEL: "The Grand Guignols of Love," "Divine Love" and "The European Shoe." Copyright © 1968 by Michael Benedikt. Reprinted from *The Body* by Michael Benedikt, by permission of Wesleyan University Press. "The Death of the Human Particle" by Michael Benedikt. First published by *The Partisan Review*, 1974 (Vol. XLI, #2). Reprinted by permission of Michael Benedikt. Copyright © 1974.

BIDART, FRANK: "Herbert White," George Braziller, Inc., from *Golden State* by Frank Bidart. Reprinted with the permission of the publisher. Copyright © 1973 by Frank Bidart.

BROWNE, MICHAEL DENNIS: "The Roof of the World," "Power Failure" and "Iowa, June" by Michael Dennis Browne are reprinted by permission of Charles Scribner's Sons from *The Wife of Winter*. Copyright © 1970 by Michael Dennis Browne. "Hallowe'en 1971" by Michael Dennis Browne reprinted by permission of Bantam Books, Inc., 666 Fifth Avenue, New York, New York, 10019. Copyright © 1973 by *American Review, #17*. "Paranoia" by Michael Dennis Browne reprinted by permission of *Antaeus*. Copyright © 1973 by *Antaeus*.

CLIFTON, LUCILLE: "In Salem" and ("the thirty eighth year") reprinted from *An Ordinary Woman* by Lucille Clifton. Copyright © 1974 by Lucille Clifton. Reprinted by permission of Random House, Inc. "Miss Rosie" and "Good Times" reprinted from *Good Times* by Lucille Clifton. Copyright © 1969 by Lucille Clifton. Reprinted by permission of Random House, Inc.

CONYUS: "The Great Santa Barbara Oil Disaster" reprinted by permission of the author. Copyright © 1970.

COOLEY, PETER: "Vanishing Point" reprinted by permission of *Antaeus.* Copyright © 1975 by *Antaeus.* "Alternatives" reprinted by permission of Peter Cooley. Copyright © 1975. "The Confession" reprinted by permission of Peter Cooley. Copyright © 1975.

DACEY, PHILIP: "The Obscene Caller" reprinted by permission of *The Massachusetts Review.* Copyright © 1973. "Form Rejection Letter" reprinted by permission of the Editors of *Shenandoah:* The Washington & Lee University Review. Copyright © 1973. "The Birthday" reprinted by permission of Guy Owen, editor, *Southern Poetry Review.* Copyright © 1972.

DOVE, RITA: "The Boast" by Rita Dove from the book *Intro 6* edited by George Garrett. Copyright © 1974 by Associated Writing Programs. Reprinted by permission of Doubleday & Co., Inc. "Nigger Song: An Odyssey" and "Adolescence II" reprinted by permission of *Antaeus.* Copyright © 1975 by *Antaeus.* "This Life" reprinted by permission of the author. Copyright © 1975. "Adolescence II" and "The Boast" also appeared in *Eating the Menu.* Copyright © 1974 by Bruce E. Taylor. By permission of Bruce E. Taylor.

DOW, PHILIP: "The Duck Pond at Mini's Pasture, A Dozen Years Later" reprinted by permission of the author. Copyright © 1975. "The Life" reprinted by permission of *Choice,* Milton Kessler, co-editor. Copyright © 1967. "Twilight in California" reprinted by permission of *Choice,* Victor Perl, co-editor. Copyright © 1969.

DUBIE, NORMAN: "Pastoral" reprinted by permission of the author. Copyright © 1975. "Balalaika" reprinted by permission of the author. Copyright © 1975. "The Killigrew Woods" and "The Dressing Stations" reprinted from *Alehouse Sonnets* by Norman Dubie by permission of the University of Pittsburgh Press. Copyright © 1971 by the University of Pittsburgh Press. "In the Dead of the Night" reprinted by permission of the author. Copyright © 1975.

DUNN, STEPHEN: "Looking for a Rest Area," "On Hearing the Airlines Will Use a Psychological Profile to Catch Potential Skyjackers," and "Day and Night Handball" reprinted from *Looking for Holes in the Ceiling* by Stephen Dunn by permission of the University of Massachusetts Press. Copyright © 1974.

EDSON, RUSSELL: "Children" from *The Clam Theatre.* Copyright © 1972 by Russell Edson. Reprinted from *The Clam Theatre* by Russell Edson by permission of Wesleyan University Press. "The Childhood of an Equestrian," "A Performance at Hog Theatre," "In All the Days of My Childhood," and "The Retirement of the Elephant" reprinted by permission of Harper & Row, Publishers, Inc. From *The Childhood of an Equestrian* by Russell Edson. Copyright © 1973 by Russell Edson.

FELDMAN, SUSAN: "Sea Legs" reprinted by permission of *Antaeus.* Copyright © 1975 by *Antaeus.* "Lamentations of an Au Pair Girl" reprinted by permission of the author. Copyright © 1975. "How the Invalids Make Love" reprinted by permission of the author and *The New Yorker.* Copyright © 1974, The New Yorker Magazine, Inc. "How the Invalids Make Love" appeared in *The New Yorker,* September 2, 1974. "Intruder" reprinted by permission of the author. Copyright © 1975.

FORCHÉ, CAROLYN: "Taking Off My Clothes" reprinted by permission of *Antaeus.* Copyright © 1975 by *Antaeus.* "Kalaloch" reprinted by permission of *Antaeus.* Copyright © 1975 by *Antaeus.* "Burning the Tomato Worms" reprinted by permission of the author. Copyright © 1975.

FRASER, KATHLEEN: "Poems in Which My Legs Are Accepted" reprinted from *The Young American Poets* by permission of Big Table Publishing Company, Chicago. Copyright © 1968 by Follett Publishing Co. "What You Need" reprinted by permission of Kathleen Fraser and Dennis Koran of Panjandrum Press. Copyright © 1974. "Casa de Pollos" reprinted from *What I Want* by Kathleen Fraser by permission of Harper & Row, Publishers, Inc. Copyright © 1974 by Kathleen Fraser.

GALLAGHER, TESS: "The Horse in the Drugstore" and "Kidnaper" reprinted by permission of *Antaeus* and The Penumbra Press. Copyright © 1973, 1974. "Stepping Outside" reprinted by permission of *American Poetry Review* and The Penumbra Press. Copyright © 1974. "Breasts" reprinted by permission of The Penumbra Press. Copyright © 1974 by Tess Gallagher. "Breasts" reprinted by permission of the author and *The New Yorker.* Copyright © 1973 by The New Yorker Magazine, Inc.

GILDNER, GARY: "First Practice" reprinted from *First Practice* by Gary Gildner by permission of the University of Pittsburgh Press. Copyright © 1969 by the University of Pittsburgh Press. "Digging for Indians" and "Meeting the Reincarnation Analyst" reprinted from *Digging for Indians* by Gary Gildner by permission of the University of Pittsburgh Press. Copyright © 1971 by the University of Pittsburgh Press. "The Life of the Wolf" reprinted from *Nails* by Gary Gildner by permission of the University of Pittsburgh Press. Copyright © 1975 by the University of Pittsburgh Press.

GLÜCK, LOUISE: "The Garden" reprinted by permission of *Antaeus.* Copyright © 1975 by *Antaeus.* "Gretel in Darkness," "All Hallows" and "The School Children" reprinted from *The House on Marshland* by permission of The Ecco Press. Copyright © 1975 by Louise Glück "The Racer's Widow" and "Phenomenal Survivals of Death in Nantucket" reprinted by permission of the author. Copyright © 1968 by Louise Glück.

GREGG, LINDA: "The Girl I Call Alma" reprinted by permission of *Antaeus.* Copyright © 1975 by *Antaeus.* "Sigismundo" reprinted by permission of the author. Copyright © 1975. "The Beckett Kit" reprinted by permission of *The New Yorker* and the author. Copyright © 1975. "We Manage Most When We Manage Small" reprinted by permission of the author. Copyright © 1975.

HACKER, MARILYN: "After The Revolution" reprinted from *Ambit* (U.K.) by permission of the author. Copyright © 1975. "Presentation Piece," "Before the War," "Villanelle," and "*Aube Provençale*" reprinted from *Presentation Piece* by Marilyn Hacker by permission of The Viking Press, Inc. Copyright © 1971, 1972 by Marilyn Hacker.

HALPERN, DANIEL: "Street Fire," "Summer, 1970" and "The Landing" from *Street Fire* by Daniel Halpern. Copyright © 1974, 1975 by Daniel Halpern. Reprinted by permission of The Viking Press, Inc. "The Ethnic Life" from *Traveling on Credit* by Daniel Halpern. Copyright © 1970, 1972 by Daniel Halpern. Reprinted by permission of The Viking Press, Inc. "The Ethnic Life" appeared originally in *The New Yorker.* "Fish" reprinted by permission of the author. Copyright © 1975 by Daniel Halpern.

HARPER, MICHAEL S.: "Dear John, Dear Coltrane," "We Assume: On the Death of Our Son, Reuben Masai Harper," "A Mother Speaks: The Algiers Motel Incident, Detroit," and "Deathwatch" reprinted from *Dear John, Dear Coltrane* by Michael S. Harper by permission of the University of Pittsburgh Press. Copyright © 1970 by the University of Pittsburgh Press. "*Bird Lives:* Charles Parker in St. Louis" reprinted from *History Is Your Own Heartbeat* by permission of The University of Illinois Press. Copyright © 1971 by Michael S. Harper.

HARRISON, JIM: "Suite to Fathers" and "Locations" reprinted from *Locations,* by Jim Harrison, by permission of W. W. Norton & Company, Inc. Copyright © 1968 by James Harrison. "Sketch for a Job Application Blank" reprinted from *Plain Song* by James Harrison by permission of W. W. Norton and Co., Inc. Copyright © 1965 by James Harrison.

HASS, ROBERT: "In Weather," "The Return of Robinson Jeffers," "Fall," and "Song" reprinted by permission of Yale University Press from *Field Guide* by Robert Hass. Copyright © 1973 by Robert Hass. "Against Botticelli" reprinted by permission of Robert Hass. Copyright © 1975. "Songs to Survive the Summer" reprinted by permission of *Antaeus.* Copyright © 1975 by *Antaeus.*

HEYEN, WILLIAM: "The Snapper" and "Dog Sacrifice at Lake Ronkonkoma" reprinted from *Noise in the Trees: Poems and a Memoir* by William Heyen by permission of the publisher, Vanguard Press, Inc. Copyright © 1967, 1968, 1969, 1970, 1971, 1972, 1973, 1974 by William Heyen. "The Spirit of Wrath" and "I Move to Random Consolations" reprinted from *Depth of Field* by William Heyen by permission of the Louisiana State University Press. Copyright © 1970.

INADA, LAWSON FUSAO: "Plucking Out a Rhythm" and "From Our Album" from *Before the War* by permission of William Morrow and the author. Copyright © 1971.

JAMES, THOMAS: "Hunting for Blueberries," "Mummy of a Lady Named Jemutesonekh XXI Dynasty," "Letter to a Mute," and "Letters to a Stranger" reprinted from *Letters to a Stranger* by permission of Houghton Mifflin Company. Copyright © 1972, 1973 by Thomas James.

JENSEN, LAURA: "Sleep in the Heat" reprinted by permission of *Antaeus.* Copyright © 1973 by *Antaeus.* "In the Hospital" reprinted by permission of the author and *The New Yorker.* Copyright © 1975. The New Yorker Magazine, Inc. "Talking to the Mule" and "After I Have Voted" reprinted by permission of Gemini Press, Seattle. Copyright © 1972. "Indian" reprinted by permission of *Antaeus.* Copyright © 1975 by *Antaeus.*

JONG, ERICA: "The Man Under the Bed" from *Fruits & Vegetables* by Erica Jong. Copyright © 1968, 1970, 1971 by Erica Mann Jong. Reprinted by permission of Holt, Rinehart and Winston, Inc. "The Wives of the Mafiosi" first appeared in *Poetry.* "Seventeen Warnings in Search of a Feminist Poem" and "Alcestis on the Poetry Circuit" from *Half-Lives* by Erica Jong. Copyright © 1971, 1972, 1973 by Erica Mann Jong. Reprinted by permission of Holt, Rinehart and Winston, Inc.

KLAPPERT, PETER: "The Lord's Chameleon" reprinted by permission of Peter Klappert. Copyright © 1974 by *Counter/Measures.* "The Invention of the Telephone" and "Poem for L. C." reprinted by permission of Yale University Press from *Lugging Vegetables to Nantucket* by Peter Klappert. Copyright © 1971 by Yale University.

KROLL, JUDITH: "Dick and Jane," "Not Thinking of America" and "Sestina" are reprinted from *In The Temperate Zone* by Judith Kroll by permission of Charles Scribner's Sons. Copyright © 1973 by Judith Kroll.

KUZMA, GREG: "The Pelican" from *Good News* by Greg Kuzma. Copyright © 1971 by Greg Kuzma. Reprinted by permission of The Viking Press, Inc. "The Monster" reprinted by permission of *Zeitgeist.* Copyright © 1969 by *Zeitgeist.* "Journal of the Storm" from *Song for Someone Going Away* reprinted by permission of Ithaca House. Copyright © 1971. "The Young Man Who Loved the Girl Who Took Care of Her Aging Father" reprinted by permission of Hearse Press and the author. Copyright © 1972 by Hearse Press.

LEE, AL: "Weathering the Depths," "The Lie," "Among Sharks," "Poem for the Year Twenty Twenty," and "Karl Marx" from *Time* by Al Lee. Reprinted by permission of The Ecco Press. Copyright © 1974 by Al Lee.

LEVINSON, FRED: "poem," "no more than five," "a poem," "a poem against rats," "a translation from," and "sharks in shallow water" reprinted by permission of *Antaeus.* Copyright © 1970, 1971, 1972 by *Antaeus.*

LEVIS, LARRY: "The Poem You Asked For," "Bat Angels" and "Fish" reprinted from *Wrecking Crew* by Larry Levis by permission of the University of Pittsburgh Press. Copyright © 1972 by the University of Pittsburgh Press.

LIBBEY, ELIZABETH: "Concerning the Dead Women" reprinted from issue #20 of *The American Review* by permission of Bantam Books, Inc. Copyright © 1974. "To Her Dead Mate, Montana, 1966" reprinted with permission from *The American Poetry Review,* Vol. III, Number 4. Copyright © 1975. "Marceline, To Her Husband" reprinted by permission of the author. Copyright © 1975. "Before the Mountain" reprinted by permission of the author. Copyright © 1975.

LUX, THOMAS: "Lament City" reprinted by permission of the author. Copyright © 1975. "History and Abstraction" reprinted by permission of the author. Copyright © 1975. "If You See This Man" and "The Midnight Tennis Match" from *Memory's Handgrenade* reprinted by permission of Pym-Randall Press and Thomas Lux. Copyright © 1972 by Thomas Lux. "This is a Poem for the Fathers" reprinted by permission of the author. Copyright © 1975.

MATTHEWS, WILLIAM: "The Penalty for Bigamy is Two Wives" reprinted by permission of William Matthews and *The Ohio Review.* Copyright © 1973. "Oh Yes" reprinted from *Ruining the New Road,* by William Matthews by permission of Random House, Inc. Copyright © 1969 by William Matthews. "The Cat," "Directions," and "Praise" reprinted from *Sleek for the Long Flight* by William Matthews by permission of Random House, Inc. Copyright © 1971, 1972 by William Matthews.

McCABE, ANGELA: "Back," "From Lois in London," "Inside History," "Blind Adolphus," and "Bloom Street" reprinted from *The Keeper of Height* by permission of Barlenmir House, Publishers. Copyright © 1974.

McELROY, DAVID: "Dragging in Winter," "Report from the Correspondent They Fired" reprinted by permission of *Antaeus*. Copyright © 1972 by *Antaeus*. "Spawning in Northern Minnesota" reprinted by permission of *The Nation*. Copyright © 1970 by *The Nation* and the author. "Making It Simple" reprinted by permission of Milton Kessler, co-editor of *Choice*. Copyright © 1973 by *Choice*. "Ode to a Dead Dodge" reprinted by permission of the author. Copyright © 1975.

McHUGH, HEATHER: "Catch" reprinted by permission of Bantam Books, Inc. Copyright © 1974 by *American Review*, #22. "Corps d'Esprit" reprinted by permission of the author and *The New Yorker*. Copyright © 1974 The New Yorker Magazine, Inc. "Note Delivered by Female Impersonator" reprinted by permission of Ira Sadoff, editor of *Seneca Review*. Copyright © 1974 by Hobart William Smith College Student Association.

McMICHAEL, JAMES: "The Village of the Presents" reprinted by permission of the author. Copyright © 1975. "The Inland Lighthouse" first appeared in *Poetry* June 1972. Copyright © 1972 by the Modern Poetry Association and is reprinted by permission of the editor of *Poetry*. "The Great Garret, Or 100 Wheels" first appeared in *Poetry* May 1973. Copyright © 1973 by the Modern Poetry Association and is reprinted by permission of the editor of *Poetry*. "Lutra, The Fisher" reprinted by permission of *Hawaii Review*. Copyright © 1973. "The Cabin North of It All" from *Against the Falling Evil* reprinted by permission of The Swallow Press. Copyright © 1971.

McPHERSON, SANDRA: "His Body" and "Elegies for the Hot Season" reprinted from *Elegies for the Hot Season* by permission of Indiana University Press. Copyright © 1970. "Marlow and Nancy," "Sisters," "Seaweed," and "Wanting a Mummy" reprinted from *Radiation* by permission of The Ecco Press. Copyright © 1973 by Sandra McPherson.

MEZEY, ROBERT: "In the Soul Hour," "Night on Clinton," "Back," and "A Confession" from *The Door Standing Open*, published by Houghton Mifflin Co. Reprinted by permission of Robert Mezey. Copyright © 1970 by Oxford University Press.

MONETTE, PAUL: "Bathing the Aged" reprinted from *The Carpenter at the Asylum* by Paul Monette, by permission of Little, Brown and Co. Copyright © 1971 by Paul Monette. "Degas" reprinted from *The American Review*, #20, by permission of Bantam Books, Inc. Copyright © 1974. "Into the Dark" reprinted by permission of *Antaeus*. Copyright © 1975 by *Antaeus*.

MUSKE, CAROL: "Hyena" reprinted from *Eating the Menu* by permission of Bruce E. Taylor. Copyright © 1974 by Bruce E. Taylor. "Found" reprinted by permission of *Antaeus*. Copyright © 1974 by *Antaeus*. "Child with Six Fingers" reprinted by permission of *Antaeus*. Copyright © 1972 by *Antaeus*.

"Rice" reprinted by permission of *Mundus Artium*. Copyright © 1974 by *Mundus Artium*, Ohio University, Ellis Hall, Athens, Ohio. "Swansong" reprinted by permission of *Esquire Magazine*. Copyright © 1974 by Esquire, Inc.

MYERS, JACK: "So Long Solon," "Mirror for the Barnyard," "When I Held You To My Chest, You Fit," and "The Apprentice Painter" reprinted by permission of *Antaeus* Copyright © 1973 by *Antaeus*.

ORR, GREGORY: "Two Lines from the Brothers Grimm" and "Gathering the Bones Together" from *Gathering the Bones Together* by Gregory Orr. Reprinted by permission of Harper & Row, Publishers. Copyright © 1973, 1974, 1975 by Gregory Orr. "Poem" from *Burning the Empty Nests* by Gregory Orr. Copyright © 1973 by Gregory Orr. Reprinted by permission of Harper & Row, Publishers. "The Doll" From *Intro #3*. Copyright © 1970 by Bantam Books, Inc. Also from *Burning the Empty Nests* by Gregory Orr. Copyright © 1973 by Gregory Orr. Reprinted by permission of Harper & Row, Publishers.

PAPE, GREG: "October" and "For Rosa Yen, Who Lived Here" published by *Antaeus*. Copyright © 1975 by *Antaeus*. "La Llorona" and "Mercado" reprinted by permission of the author. Copyright © 1975.

PECK, JOHN: "The Ringers," "Cider and Versalius," "The Watcher," "Spring Festival on the River," and "Colophon for Lan-t'ing Hsiu-Hsi" from *Shagbark*. Copyright © 1972 by John Peck. Reprinted by permission of the publisher, The Bobbs-Merrill Company, Inc.

PLUMLY, STANLEY: "Out-of-the-Body Travel" reprinted by permission of *The Ohio Review*. Copyright © 1974 by the editors of *The Ohio Review*. "After Grief" reprinted by permission of *The Nation*. Copyright © 1974. "Fungo," "Giraffe," and "Heron" reprinted from *Giraffe* by permission of Louisiana State University Press. Copyright © 1973. "The Iron Lung" published originally in the December 28, 1974 issue of *The New Yorker* and reprinted by permission of the author and *The New Yorker*. Copyright © 1974, The New Yorker Magazine, Inc.

RAAB, LAWRENCE: "Visiting the Oracle" reprinted by permission of the author and *The New Yorker*. Copyright © 1975 The New Yorker Magazine, Inc. "Pastoral" reprinted by permission of *Antaeus*. Copyright © 1975 by *Antaeus*. "The Assassin's Fatal Error" reprinted from *The American Scholar*, Volume 44, Number 1, Winter, 1974–75. Copyright © 1974 by The United Chapters of Phi Beta Kappa. By permission of the publishers. "Attack of the Crab Monsters" reprinted by permission of *Berkshire Review*. Copyright © 1974. "Voices Answering Back: The Vampires." Copyright © 1969. Reprinted from the book *Mysteries of the Horizon* by Lawrence Raab by permission of Doubleday & Co., Inc.

REISS, JAMES: "The Breathers," "The Green Tree," "A Slight Confusion," "On Hot Days," and "¿Habla Usted Español?" reprinted from *The Breathers* by permission of The Ecco Press. Copyright © 1974 by James Reiss.

ROSEN, KENNETH: "Abstinence," "An Act," "Confab," and "Girls" from *Whole Horse* by Kenneth Rosen. Reprinted with the permission of the publisher, George Braziller, Inc. Copyright © 1973 by Kenneth Rosen.

RYAN, MICHAEL: "Prothalamion," "Letters from an Institution III," "Barren Poem," "This Is a Poem for the Dead," and "Speaking" reprinted by permission of Yale University Press from *Threats Instead of Trees* by Michael Ryan. Copyright © 1974 by Michael Ryan.

SADOFF, IRA: "Poem After Apollinaire" reprinted by permission of the author. Copyright © 1975. "A Concise History of the World" reprinted from *Settling Down* by permission of Houghton Mifflin Company. Copyright © 1975 by Ira Sadoff. "My Father's Leaving" reprinted by permission of the author. Copyright © 1975. "The Fifties" reprinted by permission of *Antaeus.* Copyright © 1975 by *Antaeus.*

SCHMITZ, DENNIS: "The Mole" reprinted by permission of *Field.* Copyright © 1970. "The Name of Our Country" reprinted by permission of *The North American Review.* Copyright © 1968 by the University of Northern Iowa. "The California Phrasebook," an excerpt reprinted by permission of *Stand: A Quarterly of the Arts.* Copyright ©1972 by Stand. "Sir Francis Drake's Circumnavigation" (Now "California Phrasebook, Part I") reprinted by permission of *Field.* Copyright © 1971 by Oberlin College. "The California Phrasebook," an excerpt, reprinted by permission of *Ironwood.* Copyright © 1972. "Goodwill, Inc." reprinted by permission of *The Iowa Review:* The University of Iowa. Copyright © 1970. "Chicago: Near West-Side Renewal" reprinted by permission of *Field.* Copyright © 1970. "Poke-Pole Fishing" reprinted by permission of *Antaeus.* Copyright © 1973 by *Antaeus.*

SEIDMAN, HUGH: "Tale of Genji" and "The Making of Color" reprinted by permission of Yale University Press from *Collecting Evidence* by Hugh Seidman. Copyright © 1970 by Hugh Seidman. "The Making of Color." Copyright © 1968 by Hugh Seidman. Originally from *Intro* #1, edited by R. V. Cassill. Copyright © 1968 by Bantam Books, Inc. Reprinted by permission of Bantam Books, Inc. "Science As Art" reprinted by permission of *Antaeus.* Copyright © 1971 by *Antaeus.* "The Great Nebula in Andromeda." Copyright © 1973 by *Antaeus.* "Drop the Wires." Copyright © 1970 by The Nation Associates, Inc. Reprinted from the book *Blood Lord* by Hugh Seidman by permission of Doubleday & Co., Inc.

SIMIC, CHARLES: "The Bird" and "Brooms" from *Return to a Place Lit by a Glass of Milk* by Charles Simic. Reprinted with the permission of the publisher, George Braziller, Inc. Copyright © 1974 by Charles Simic. "Butcher Shop," "Psalm," "Bestiary for the Fingers of My Right Hand," and "Fork" from *Dismantling the Silence* by Charles Simic. Reprinted with the permission of the publisher, George Braziller, Inc. Copyright © 1971 by Charles Simic.

SPEAR, ROBERTA: "August/Fresno 1973" reprinted by permission of the author. Copyright © 1975. "The Bat" and "A Sale of Smoke" reprinted by permission of *Antaeus*. Copyright © 1975 by *Antaeus*.

SPIVACK, KATHLEEN: "Visions." Copyright © 1969 by Sumac Press. "But You, My Darling, Should Have Married the Prince." Copyright © 1970 by *Antioch Review*, Inc. "Private Pain in Time of Trouble" and "A Child's Visit to the Biology Lab," reprinted by permission of *Antaeus*. Copyright © 1973 by *Antaeus*. "The Mad Girl With Secret Dreams." Copyright © 1973 by The Nation Associates, Inc. All by Kathleen Spivack from her book *Flying Inland*. Reprinted by permission of Doubleday & Company, Inc. Copyright © 1973 by Kathleen Spivack.

STANTON, MAURA: "Judith Recalls Holfernes," "The All-Night Waitress," "Journal of Elisa," and "Letter to Kafka" reprinted by permission of Yale University Press from *Snow on Snow* by Maura Stanton. Copyright © 1975 by Yale University.

ST. JOHN, DAVID: "For Lerida" and "Slow Dance" reprinted by permission of *Antaeus*. Copyright © 1975 by Antaeus. "Poem" reprinted by permission of George Hitchcock, editor of *Kayak*. Copyright © 1974.

STOKES, TERRY: "All Morning," "Crimes of Passion: The Phone Caller," "Crimes of Passion: The Slasher," and "Travis, the Kid Was All Heart" from *Crimes of Passion* by Terry Stokes. Reprinted from *Crimes of Passion* by Terry Stokes. Copyright © 1970, 1971, 1972, 1973 by Terry Stokes. Reprinted by permission of Alfred A. Knopf, Inc.

SWANN, BRIAN: "Desert in the Sea" reprinted by permission of the author. Copyright © 1975. "Quiet" reprinted by permission of *Antaeus*. Copyright © 1972 by *Antaeus*. "Year of the Bird" reprinted by permission of *The Nation*, where the poem appeared May 21, 1973, and the author. Copyright © 1973. "Paradigms of Fire" reprinted by permission of Robert Boyers, editor of *Salmagundi*. Copyright © 1975.

TATE, JAMES: "The Distant Orgasm," "Deaf Girl Playing," and "The Soup of Venus" from *Absences and New Poems* by James Tate by permission of Little, Brown and Co., in association with the Atlantic Monthly Press. Copyright © 1970, 1971, 1972 by James Tate. "The Blue Booby" and "Coda" from *The*

Oblivious Ha-Ha by James Tate by permission of Little, Brown and Co., in association with the Atlantic Monthly Press. Copyright © 1967, 1968, 1969, 1970 by James Tate.

WAKOSKI, DIANE: "Justice is Reason Enough" and "Wind Secrets" from the book *Trilogy*. Copyright © 1962, 1966, 1967, 1974 by Diane Wakoski. Reprinted by permission of Doubleday & Co., Inc. "The Mechanic" reprinted by permission of Simon and Schuster from *The Motorcycle Betrayal Poems*. Copyright © 1971 by Diane Wakoski. "Smudging" reprinted by permission of Black Sparrow Press, P.O. Box 25603, Los Angeles, Calif. 90025, publishers of *Smudging* by Diane Wakoski, where this poem originally appeared. Copyright © 1972 by Diane Wakoski.

WALKER, ALICE: "Burial." Copyright © 1972 by Alice Walker. "Expect Nothing," and "Black Mail." Copyright © 1973 by Alice Walker. All reprinted from her volume, *Revolutionary Petunias*, by permission of Harcourt Brace Jovanovich, Inc.

WEINGARTEN, ROGER: "Blue Bog Children," "Ethan Boldt," "Her apron through the trees," and "These Obituaries of Rattlesnakes Being Eaten by the Hogs," from *Ethan Benjamin Boldt*, by Roger Weingarten. Copyright © 1975 by Roger Weingarten. Reprinted by permission of Alfred A. Knopf, Inc.

WELCH, JAMES: "Plea to Those Who Matter" by James Welch, from *Intro #1*, edited by R. V. Cassill. Copyright © 1968 by James Welch. Reprinted by permission of Bantam Books, Inc. "Visit," "The Only Bar in Dixon" (originally appeared in *The New Yorker*), "Lady in a Distant Face," and "In My First Hard Springtime." Copyright © 1971 by James Welch. Reprinted from *Riding the Earthboy 40*, by James Welch by permission of Harper & Row, Publishers, Inc.

WILD, PETER: "Snakes" reprinted from *New & Selected Poems* by permission of New Rivers Press. Copyright © 1973 by Peter Wild. "Riding Double." Copyright © 1973 by Peter Wild. "Thomas and Charlie." Copyright © 1972 by the University of Manitoba Press. "Dog Hospital." Copyright © 1973 by Peter Wild. Reprinted from the book *Cochise* by Peter Wild by permission of Doubleday and Co., Inc.

WRIGHT, CHARLES: "Delta Traveler" reprinted from *Bloodlines* by Charles Wright, by permission of Wesleyan University Press. Copyright © 1974. "Chinoiserie." Copyright © 1973. "The Fever Toy." Copyright © 1973. "Yellow." Copyright © 1973. "Dog Creek Mainline." Copyright © 1972. Reprinted from *Hard Freight* by Charles Wright by permission of Wesleyan University Press. Copyright © 1972, 1973 by Charles Wright. "Chinoiserie," "The Fever Toy," and "Dog Creek Mainline" first appeared in *Poetry*.

YOUNG, DAVID: "The Boxcar Poem," "Thoughts of Chairman Mao," "The Death of the Novel," and "Mandelstam" reprinted from *Boxcars* by permission of The Ecco Press. Copyright © 1973 by David Young. "August at the Lake" reprinted from *Sweating Out the Winter* by David P. Young by permission of the University of Pittsburgh Press. Copyright © 1969 by the University of Pittsburgh Press.

My special thanks go to the following people, without whose help the publication of this book would have been impossible:

Robert Bly
Hayden Carruth
Donald Hall
Richard Hugo
Stanley Kunitz
Philip Levine
Howard Moss
Leonard Randolph
Gail Rosenblum
Mark Strand

Contents

Introduction

DANIEL HALPERN

Everywhere one looks, there is excitement over the proliferation of poets and poetry. There has never been such wide-ranging interest in poetry—creative writing workshops have sprung up overnight around the country; thousands of new magazines are now in existence, with as many poets supplying their material. Some of these magazines receive over 3,000 poems a month. Submissions to first-book awards have doubled and redoubled—the Yale Series of Younger Poets competition, which ten years ago drew only a couple of hundred manuscripts, now receives four to five times that many. The Walt Whitman Award for a first book of poems received over 1500 manuscripts its first year in existence. Nearly four-hundred books of poetry are published every year.

From this blossoming of talent, I have attempted to gather a selection that represents the diversity and richness of poems written by poets under forty, many of whom have written poetry that stands beside the best poetry written in the past decade—as Robert Frost wrote in his introduction to *New Poets of England and America*, "All poets I have ever heard of struck their note long before forty . . . The statistics are all in favor of their being as good and lyric as they will ever be."

Many of the poems appear here for the first time—some by poets who have published over a dozen books of poetry, some by poets who have published in only one or two literary magazines. What they have in common is, in part, the basis for my selection. All were born after 1934, into a generation that has not been comprehensively anthologized, although a few of the poets included here have appeared in such well-known anthologies as *The Contemporary American Poets*, edited by Mark Strand, Hayden Carruth's *The Voice That Is Great Within Us*, and even *The Norton Anthology of Modern Poetry*.

These poets also share a sophistication—that combination of sureness of technique, depth of feeling, and sense of commitment—that promises to evolve, with continued effort and risk, a new and powerful poetic idiom. The range and diversity of their work rise from their confrontation with the myriad forces present, or at least still lingering, in their coming of age: the New Critics of the forties; then the fifties, an era of formalism and technical virtuosity by poets such as Stanley Kunitz in his exemplary *Selected Poems 1928–1958*, Richard Wilbur, Elizabeth Bishop, Howard Nemerov, and Louis Simpson. Also beginning in the fifties, and moving with vigor into the sixties, were the Black Mountain Poets, the Beats, the New York Poets, and the Confessional Poets (Lowell's *Life Studies* was published in 1959). By 1970 the poetic line had, in a fast twenty years, been polished by the elegant hand of Wilbur, expanded by the generous hand of Ginsberg, sliced and pared by Creeley, and had its syntax shaken soundly by Merwin in his influential collections *The Moving Target* and *The Lice*. Another important force that began to take on momentum in the late fifties and early sixties was the influence of translations, brought to the attention of American poets in magazines such as Robert Bly's *The Fifties* (later *The Sixties* and *The Seventies*), and the Texas-based *Delos*. One can detect in the poetry of this anthology roots in the literature of South America, France, Spain, Germany, Russia, etc.—Neruda, Vallejo, Borges, Parra, Apollinaire, Michaux, Char, Desnos, Jarry, Trakl, Mayakovsky, Voznesensky, Alberti, Lorca, and others. Mark Strand calls it the "growing internationalism of American poetry." The influence of twentieth-century British poets seems less important, with the exception of Yeats, Auden, Thomas, and more recently, Ted Hughes. It should also be mentioned that two significant anthologies appeared which presented, when placed together, the full spectrum of American poetry in 1960. They both had great impact on younger poets in the early sixties. The first was *New Poets of England and America* (1957), edited by Donald Hall, Robert Pack, and Louis Simpson. It embraced most of the formal poetry being written during the fifties. The second was *The New American Poetry: 1945–1960* (1960), edited by Donald M. Allen. This selection brought together for the first time those poets who, under the guidance of Pound and Williams, rejected the qualities typical of academic verse. Allen wrote in his preface, "These poets have already created their own tradition, their own press, and their public." He broke them into five groups: the Black Mountain Poets, the San Francisco Renaissance, the Beat Generation, the New York Poets, and a group with "no geographical definition . . . younger poets who have been associated with and in some cases influenced by the leading writers of the preceding groups."

The oldest poets in my anthology were fifteen when the fifties got under way. The youngest was not yet born. By the mid-sixties, some of the poets had already published first books, while the younger poets were still learning reading and writing skills in grammar school. By the seventies, many of the poets had already produced work that placed them in anthologies alongside A. R. Ammons, John Ashbery, Robert Bly, Robert Creeley, Donald Justice, Galway Kinnell, Richard Howard, Maxine Kumin, Philip Levine, James Merrill, W. S. Merwin, Frank O'Hara, Sylvia Plath, Adrienne Rich, Anne Sexton, Gary Snyder, Mark Strand, and James Wright—all born in the decade preceding 1935. The youngest poets, in 1970, were finishing college and beginning to make their way into the dense forest of literary magazines—still the best place to read *current* poetry. The poets born between 1940 and 1945 were publishing, or about to publish, their first books. This group was probably less directly influenced by the formal, academic verse of the fifties than the poets born the previous five years, and relied more heavily on the poetry of the sixties—on Whitman, Stevens, Pound, Williams, Eliot, Yeats, and the poetry from other languages.

The early temptation to categorize the poetry presented here, according to a group aesthetic, was quickly abandoned. In fact, the distinguishing characteristic of this poetry is its heterogeneity, in terms of form, attitude, and treatment of content. Unlike the period from 1950 to 1965, when one could recognize with little trouble the groups mentioned above, the past ten years has produced a poetry that takes nourishment from a variety of camps. This crossbreeding creates an admixture that makes grouping impossible. Nevertheless, labeling is always in fashion, and it is fashionable to label poets who have, for example, attended the Writers' Workshop at The University of Iowa. One could then tag the neo-surrealists and put them aside. A clever observer could make a case for a West Coast school, as well as a Roethke-oriented poetry in the Northwest. The *neo*-New York Poets, as defined by *An Anthology of New York Poets*, compose an East Coast pocket, although there has been a mini-migration from the Big Apple to Bolinas. As I say, a clever observer could wrap it all up and we'd have a "contemporary poetry scene." Difficulties arise for our observer when his readers begin to trace the origins and influences of the poets, and discover that they won't stay put. The ensuing shuffle results in the amalgam that contemporary is. Putting aside the idea of groups, I have ordered the poets alphabetically.

My method of selection was simply to write nearly 150 poets whose work impressed me. I then wrote to older poets around the country who were in touch with younger poets, asking them to suggest new poets I might not know. The names of a hundred or so poets came back. In my letter to the poets I considered, I asked to see all their work, both published and unpublished, and for them to select the five poems that they would most like included in an anthology. The point was to arrive at an understanding of how each conceived of their own work through the poems they considered their best. After deciding on the poems I wanted to use, I checked the poet's choices. Sometimes we agreed, sometimes we did not.

Now comes that part of the introduction which, by convention, becomes apologetic—that statement modestly put about an anthology being a personal, and thus limited, selection of poems. Could it be otherwise? I have not kept track of how the anthology breaks down in terms of race, sex, and geographical location. Those interested in statistics can do the mathematics. I am content in my belief that this selection is the best I could make from the vast treasury of contemporary poetry. There are many poets of excellence writing today, and this narrowing to even seventy-six poets is as unfair as it is inevitable. The poetry that follows speaks for itself. I am merely the momentary gatherer—the gatherer, then, of the moment, of a particular day, of a particular mood. My preferences will make themselves known in short order. There is nothing in this collection that does not in some way engage and please me, but "it ought not to be supposed," as W. Taylor wrote at the beginning of the nineteenth century, "that any anthologist can strip the garden of its flowers."

—Daniel Halpern
January 1, 1975

AI

Everything: Eloy, Arizona, 1956

Tin shack, where my baby sleeps on his back
the way the hound taught him;
highway, black zebra, with one white stripe;
nickel in my pocket for chewing gum;
you think you're all I've got.
But when the 2 ton rolls to a stop
and the driver gets out,
I sit down in the shade and wave each finger,
saving my whole hand till the last.

He's keys, tires, a fire lit in his belly
in the diner up the road.
I'm red toenails, tight blue halter, black slip.
He's mine tonight. I don't know him.
He can only hurt me a piece at a time.

Why Can't I Leave You?

You stand behind the old black mare,
dressed as always in that red shirt,
stained from sweat, the crying of the armpits,
that will not stop for anything,
stroking her rump, while the barley goes unplanted.
I pick up my suitcase and set it down,
as I try to leave you again.
I smooth the hair back from your forehead.

I think with your laziness and the drought too,
you'll be needing my help more than ever.
You take my hands, I nod
and go to the house to unpack,
having found another reason to stay.

I undress, then put on my white lace slip
for you to take off, because you like that
and when you come in, you pull down the straps
and I unbutton your shirt.
I know we can't give each other any more
or any less than what we have.
There is safety in that, so much
that I can never get past the packing,
the begging you to please, if I can't make you happy,
come close between my thighs
and let me laugh for you from my second mouth.

Cuba, 1962

When the rooster jumps up on the windowsill
and spreads his red-gold wings,
I wake, thinking it is the sun
and call Juanita, hearing her answer,
but only in my mind.
I know she is already outside,
breaking the cane off at ground level,
using only her big hands.
I get the machete and walk among the cane,
until I see her, lying face-down in the dirt.

Juanita, dead in the morning like this.
I raise the machete—
what I take from the earth, I give back—
and cut off her feet.

I lift the body and carry it to the wagon,
where I load the cane to sell in the village.
Whoever tastes my woman in his candy, his cake,
tastes something sweeter than this sugar cane;
it is grief.
If you eat too much of it, you want more,
you can never get enough.

Hangman

In the fields, the silos open their mouths
and let the grain dribble down their sides,
for they are overflowing.
The farmers swing their scythes, brows dripping blood.
They have had the passion ripped out of their chests
and share no brotherhood with the wheat,

while far across the open land,
the Hangman mounts an empty scaffold.
He slides his hands over the coarse-grained cedar
and smells the whole Lebanese coast
in the upraised arms of Kansas.
The rope's stiff bristles prick his fingers,
as he holds it and lifts himself above the trap door.

He touches the wood again.
This will be his last hanging
and anyway he has seen other fields,
workmen nailing brass spikes into the scaffolds
and rope which coiled and uncoiled
in the laps of farm women.
He places his foot on the step going down
and nearby, a scarecrow explodes,
sending tiny slivers of straw into his eyes.

JON ANDERSON

The Blue Animals

When I awoke this morning
they were there, just as blue
as the morning, as calm
as the long green lawn

they grazed upon, turning
their delicate heads. You
would have said: No harm
shall befall us. But you were gone.

So these two opened my morning
gracefully wide and blue
as the morning sky. Their calm
mouths moved over the lawn,

and as I was turning
to call out again for you,
I saw there was no harm
at all, though you were gone.

The Photograph of Myself

Surely in my eyes that light is now lost,
or has deepened; and my hand, which
in the photograph seems tense
and strong, is less sure.
                                        Is it
the right hand? Yes, it is still
lean, and larger now;

enough to hold this small, boy's hand
within it, like a son's,

perhaps to reassure him, as I do not
my own sons, who are not yet born.
   Across the grey garden

stand some men; I do not know them.

Nor, I think, does he. But they stand firm,
   a terrible simplicity
which will disappear. So, too, the other,
unknown, as far from him

as my living self, who again
clicks the shutter.
   He did not know it would reach this far.

   But it's not real, the boy,
myself, looking out at me but not seeing,

and the garden, which never grows.
      Good friend, believe me,
here I am, perhaps your best intention;

my hand can hold now your entirely small body.
   I can love you;
you are the friend's son, myself,

to whom I speak and listen.

The Parachutist

Then the air was perfect. And his descent
to the white earth slowed.
                                             Falling
became an ability to rest—as

the released breath
believes in life. Further down it snowed,

a confusion of slow novas
which his shoes touched upon, which seemed
as he fell by

to be rising. From every
small college and rural town:
  the clearest, iced blossoms of thought,

but gentle.
                    Then the housetops
of friends, who
he thought had been speaking of his arrival,
withdrew, each from another.

He saw that his friends
lived in a solitude they had not ever said aloud.

Strangely he thought this good.

    The world, in fact,
which in these moments he came toward,

seemed casual.
Had he been thinking this all along?
  A life
where he belonged, having lived with himself

always, as a secret friend.

A few may have seen him then. In evidence:
the stopped dots
of children & dogs, sudden weave

    of a car—
acquaintances, circling up
into the adventure they imagined. They saw him drop

through the line breaks
and preciousness of art

down to the lake
which openly awaited him.
Here the thin
green ice allowed him in.

Some ran, and were late.
These would
forever imagine tragedy

(endless descent,
his face floating among the reeds,
unrecognized), as those

who imagine the silence of a guest
to be mysterious, or wrong.

John Clare

I know there is a worm in the human heart,
In its wake such emptiness as sleep should require.

Toward dawn, there was an undirected light the color of
steel;
The aspens, thin, vaguely parallel strips of slate,
Blew across each other in that light.
I went out
Having all night suffered my confusion, &
Was quieted by this.
But the earth
Vegetable rock or water that had been our salvation

Is mostly passed now, into the keeping of John Clare,
Alive,
        whose poetry simplified us—we owe the world
          ourselves—
Who, dead or sleeping, now reads the detail leaf & stone
Passing, until it will finally be memorized & done.

I know the heart can be hard, & from this
Misgiving about itself, will make a man merciless.
I know that John Clare's madness nature could not
  straighten.

If there is a worm in the heart, & chamber it has bitten
  out,
I will protect that emptiness until it is large enough.
In it will be a light the color of steel
& landscape, into which the traveler might set out.

In Autumn

At day's light
I dressed my cold body & went out.
Calling the dogs, I climbed the west hill,
Threw cut wood down to the road for hauling.
Done, there was a kind of exultation
That wanted to go on; I made my way
Up through briars & vines
To a great stone that rises at the hill's brow,
Large enough to stand on. The river
Below was a thick, dark line.
My house was quaint.
I sat, not thoughtful,
Lost in the body awhile,
Then came down the back way, winding
Through stands of cedar & pine.

I can tell you where I live.
My grief is that I bear no grief
& so I bear myself. I know I live apart.
But have had long evenings of conversation,
The faces of which betrayed
No separation from a place or time. Now,
In the middle of my life,
A woman of delicate bearing gives me
Her hand, & friends
Are so enclosed within my reasoning
I am occasionally them.

When I had finally stood, high above
The house, land, my life's slow dream,
For a moment I was required
To turn to those deep rows of cedar,
& would have gone
On walking endlessly in.
I understand by the body's knowledge
I will not begin again.
But it was October: leaves
In the yellowed light were altered & familiar.
We who have changed, & have
No hope of change, must now love
The passage of time.

Years

Sometimes in weariness I stop.
Because I've been lucky
I think the future must be plain.
Over the trees the stars are quite small.

My friends talk quietly
& we have all come to the same things.

Now if I die, I will
Inherit awhile their similar bodies.

Now if I listen
Someone is telling a story.
The characters met.
They enchanted each other by speech.

Though the stories they lived
Were not the same,
Many were distracted into love,
Slept, & woke alone, awhile serene.

MARVIN BELL

Treetops

My father moves through the South hunting duck.
It is warm, he has appeared
like a ship, surfacing, where he floats, face up,
through the ducklands. Over the tops
of trees duck will come, and he strains
not to miss seeing the first of each flock,
although it will be impossible to shoot one
from such an angle, face up like that
in a floating coffin where the lid obstructs
half a whole view, if he has a gun.
Afterlives are full of such hardships.

One meets, for example, in one's sinlessness,
high water and our faithlessness,
so the dead wonder if they are imagined
but they are not quite.

How could they know we know
when the earth shifts deceptively
to set forth ancestors to such pursuits?
My father will be asking, Is this fitting?
And I think so—I, who, with the others,
coming on the afterlife after the fact
in a dream, in a probable volume, in a
probable volume of dreams, think so.

Residue of Song

You were writing a long poem, yes,
about marriage, called "On Loneliness."

Then you decided not to.
There was a certain inconsolable *person.*
You felt you had to discover who.
You would be shocked to discover it was
not yourself. Yourself!, yourself!,
as if the whole world were but glass
for your splendid insights, put softly.
Who was it walked the length of the lawn,
crossed over into a brilliance you knew came
from another world, but from where?
She was out walking, and you were afraid for the
  children!
Had she taken out a knife? Had she
pledged her return though nothing changed?
Had she even realized how *wilful* all this was:
hysteria, dry heaving, the throat crawling
with sounds ground down from expectation,
because you lied to her about—was it
other women? No. Because you told the truth,
of course that was a kind of weeping
as if unto Mother, for approval and pointers.
Yes, yes, you expected understanding
and refreshed company, since you were the lonely.
It was as if you had been waiting on the corner,
with who knows what exploits seemingly on your
  lapels,
when *she* walked by: not forked prey, but a friend!
You brought her your past; she wept.
She brought you her future; you mislaid it,
later you squeezed until it uttered, *piano,*
"Where are we? Where, for that matter, were we
when we met? I was out walking, and you,
coming from shadow, postured like the children
we agreed upon. Amidst wickedness, we were the age,
if the age was wicked, but safe on the surface.
Suddenly, we were responsible for discourse, whereas,
years earlier, we had been held only by the moon.

What did you tell the others then, over your shoulder,
calling me to stop you—that you would never?
One appointment leads to another in these soft days.
A photograph of flowers the skin remembers,
a bowl of leaves before the kitchen screen,
is to this life as you are to mine. Your cries,
for ecstatic madness, are not sadder than some things.
From the residue of song, I have barely said my love
  again,
as if for the last time, believing that you will leave me."

The Perfection of Dentistry

Guanajuato, Mexico

Here I am, an industry without chimneys,
looking for an alternative
to abandoning privilege,
looking out from my long floral porch
which is not a porch but an expatriate
way of life (he hates her, she hates
him, but they can't leave), leaning
over the intricate stone railing,
over the caretaker asleep on the ground,
toward the haciendas on the opposite hill
which seems so luxurious without cactus.

Surviving "turistas," the physics of the fiesta
and the intimacy of our schizophrenia,
we have arrived, not without mercy,
to render unto trees and flowers and hills
our unnatural, filling-laden homage.
Across the way, they may be watching,
mineral water in hand, the spectacle-clad vermin.
But we do not think ourselves unhealthy,
if afflicted. We do not think ourselves visited

but visitors, without undue recompense.
If the trees bow slightly, that is alright. And

if the flowers bloom indiscriminately,
we can accept such favors. We knew before coming
we must restore to its altar the spine of the tree,
and the ebullient blooming to its rightful position.
We knew before coming that notoriety was wrong
everywhere, though trusting the wealthy North
  American.
But the causes of suffering are like impure water,
which one must walk beside and ingest
until one is covered completely in the sweaty afternoon.
And the momentum of the rains is like the momentum
of the bells, penetrating and cleansing the lush cover.

Here, every workday is part of a pilgrimage
for which the church tolls the approximate hours.
It's true, we have paid too much attention to our
  mouths.
We have the expression, "like pulling teeth";
we have words for the cabinets of our emotions.
But the caretaker has pulled his bad tooth
without fuss, and now weathers his senses in sleep.
And we, compensating witnesses, lead his concurrent
lives, take place in the garden of his salvation,
in the hierarchy of anonymity, and in
the masterful units of his siesta, and always did.

Impotence

Suddenly her breast has never been larger.
All night she's been on your back.
How can you tell her your testicles have fallen off?

It's serious alright. It's just the beginning.
(When the balls go, can the penis be long behind?)
Soon you'll be left with nothing but scar tissue
where once you were the cock of the walk.
Soon you'll be the laughing stock of Niagara Falls.
It's no delight you've got yourself over this barrel.
You knew how far down it was from the beginning.
All those years you were combing it out of your hair,
the hair itself was falling out. If now you're exposed
as the foolish romantic, why that's what you deserve,
Foolish Romantic. You wanted orgasm and repose.
You wanted love without memory. You earnestly desired
beautiful women in bondage, their feelings held hostage,
and for a while there, you were right in the thick of it.
Now you have the lowest membership of all.
Now you are nothing anyone would love.
Now you are a figure of total submission.
So what if you could do anything once.
(Why are you even bringing up these matters of taste?)
Now the end is near. Now you limp along.
Goodbye, A. Goodbye, B. Don't hate me, C. Farewell, D.
I'm not letting you go. Just turning you over for a while.

Acceptance Speech

My friends,
I am amazed

to be Professor
in a University

seven times larger
than my home town

and all because
I went away. Meanwhile,

the roots of the ivy
just went on crawling

in the dirt in the dark,
the light that was Brady's

and Gardner's during
our Civil War

became the blaze
in Southeast Asia

and soon everywhere
men lay down

without their women
which is what can happen

when people like me
leave home hoping

to be promoted
and end up promoted

to the rank of Captain
and discharged honorably

just before
whatever new war

we should always have known
was always coming

out of torn pockets and salt
from needles and patches of flowers

out of places for lost birds
night fog and a dying moon

from the work we do yea
(death being

what we don't do).
So to be at work

offending death
which others welcomed

who left home too
and no differently

seems to me half
of a famous story

I have never read
even in school.

Here

on Venus, time passes slowly because
we are all preoccupied with love.
The trees build up like sponges,
the crust under us accumulates like coral,
we begin to feel the long pressure
the jewel feels, if the jewel feels,
and, although this is suspicious belief,
we welcome the illusion with that thrill
formerly reserved for the profane.
His hands are under her buttocks;
her legs are bent on his shoulders;

their extensions are the piping for
"the best that has been thought or said."
The image is of a brain for all space.
The universe, remember, is a ribbon
where we follow back to the beginning
and so meet that one of whom you were thinking
when you mistook being here for being there.

MICHAEL BENEDIKT

The Death of the Human Particle

I was just sitting here at my desk quietly reading and, I thought, minding my own business, when I came upon an article containing the fact that the cells in my body are dying by the millions every few minutes—3,128,422 every three minutes was the exact figure. Also, the piece said that even should we just ever so slightly touch something, the poor things become bruised by the billions. Of course, it also explained, the body keeps replacing the extinguished cells, or otherwise each individual, such as the reader, would instantly begin to dwindle away and disappear. That was certainly a comforting thought, I thought, but still, it was somewhat disconcerting to learn that even when I wave hello to my loved one as she approaches, by inviting her to wave back, I cause her to kill a million of her particles by accelerating the pressures of the air; should I greet her with a big kiss and a hug, I murder an entire generation; and should it fall out that we fuck, we practically commit utter cellular genocide. What kind of humanists are we anyway, we human beings whose existence keeps on producing such tragedy with even the most sympathetic of our gestures? And what kind of moralists are we, too? How can we go on after finding out a thing like this about ourselves, except by telling ourselves that we needn't worry, that since the body contains such a great number of individuals, this decreases the importance of each one; or worse, perhaps we will justify our future slaughter by saying that it doesn't matter in the least how many cells we kill, since in a healthy person each dead individual cell is instantly replaced, and therefore no individual cell has any importance whatsoever. No, no, every man of true feeling knows that human life is an absolute; every man of true feeling knows also that whenever a single cell dies, it is appropriate that all mankind cries; that to be decent the mourning ought to be general and universal, and the funeral home crowded to capacity; that the line of honorary pallbearers should stretch as far as the furthermost horizon, while entire peoples get drunk at the wake; and as if by some earnest song or poem on one of the many serious subjects relating to the welfare of all mankind, the whole world be deeply touched.

The Grand Guignols of Love

for Louis Simpson and Milton Gilman
for their suggestions on the verse

"The generosity of her love provides
Me with practically all edibles.
It is like coming constantly to table.
If only we were not in our underwear, or bare,
It would be ideal dining."

He thought he might tie his lady
Up, to a chair, to amuse them that day;
Once fixed, he would tickle mercilessly.
She arrived panting, and was soon
Attendant in her underthings
His hideous plan, upon a chair.
Then he thought: no rope there!
"Does the executioner's victim
Supply her own weapon of destruction?" she inquired.
"It would have been thoughtful,"
He replied, as yet undaunted.

"Wait," he said. "I have thought
A marvelous entertainment:

I will beat you with these chains
While you dangle from this ceiling by the foot."

She, imagining the benefit
Straightway consulted her tinted wardrobe.
The array of costumes was endless
Once they started upon them.
He never knew what she would be
And she, for her part, never knew.
Courtesan, faun and fireman they ranged
And down through mythologies and classes
They plunged, then surfaced and lay gasping.

Sitting late at table that night
Solemnly, yet not without an undertone
Of joy, they concurred
That they were lucky to have encountered.
In a world fraught with indifference and danger
Here each had come upon the rare "oral" type.
Carefully, hand in hand, they would sail away
With a sharpened sense of *savoir-faire.*

And sometimes their thoughts would travel together
To lands of such gentle events
That they would look at one another.

Divine Love

A lip which had once been stolid, now moving
Gradually around the side of the head
Eye-like
The eye twisted on the end of somebody's finger and
  spinning
Around the sun, its ear,

And the brain aloft over the lake of the face—
Near the cataract of the body—
Like a cumulus cloud enlarged before a rainstorm:

A sound
That grows gradually in the East
Driving everything before it: cattle and rainbows and
 lovers
Swept on
To the table of the body at which five men and two
 women are casually sitting down to eat

The European Shoe

The European Shoe is constructed of grass and reed, bound up and wound around so that it may slip easily over the wearer's head.

In case you are an aircraft pilot, you must take care that the European Shoe does not creep off your foot, and begin to make its way carefully along the fuselage.

The European Shoe pressed against the fugitive's nose, preventing it from imminent departure.

The European Shoe spends summers in delightful ways. A lady feels its subtle and unexpected pressure the length of her decolletage. (It winters in pain.)

That time I lent you my European Shoe you departed with a look of grandeur, and in total disrepair.

The European Shoe knocks on the door of the carefree farmerette. "The harvest has been gathered in, ha, ha," it says, moving shyly forth along the edge of the couch.

I pointed to the European Shoe. I ate the European Shoe. I married the European Shoe.

Tears fall from the eye of the European Shoe as it waves goodbye to us from the back balcony of the speeding train.

It helps an old lady, extremely crippled and arthritic, move an enormous cornerstone. It invents a watch, which, when wound up tightly, flies completely to pieces.

It was a simple and dignified ceremony, distinguished for its gales of uncontrollable laughter, in which I married the European Shoe.

If it rains, the European Shoe becomes very heavy. I failed to cross the river, where thousands of European shoes lay capsized.

And so we lived alone, we two, the envy of our neighborhoods, the delight of our lively hordes of children.

I saw a flightful of graceful swallows heading to distant, half-forgotten islands over the distant seas; and in the midst of that annually questing company, I saw the European Shoe.

It never harmed anyone, and yet it never helped anyone.

Gaily it sets out into the depths of my profoundest closet, to do battle with the dusts of summer.

MICHAEL BENEDIKT

FRANK BIDART

Herbert White

"When I hit her on the head, it was good,

and then I did it to her a couple of times,—
but it was funny,—afterwards,
it was as if somebody else did it . . .

Everything flat, without sharpness, richness or line.

Still, I liked to drive past the woods where she lay,
tell the old lady and the kids I had to take a piss,
hop out and do it to her . . .

The whole buggy of them waiting for me
                                        made me feel good;
but still, just like I knew all along,
                                    she didn't move.

When the body got too discomposed,
I'd just jack off, letting it fall on her . . .

—It sounds crazy, but I tell you
sometimes it was *beautiful*—; I don't know how
to say it, but for a minute, *everything* was possible—;
and then,
then,—
        well, like I said, she didn't move: and I saw,
under me, a little girl was just lying there in the mud:

and I knew I couldn't have done that,—
somebody *else* had to have done that,—

standing above her there,
in those ordinary, shitty leaves . . .

—One time, I went to see Dad in a motel where he was
staying with a woman; but she was gone;
you could smell the wine in the air; and he started,
real embarrassing, to cry . . .
He was still a little drunk,
and asked me to forgive him for
all he hadn't done—; but, What the shit?
Who would have wanted to stay with Mom? with
bastards
not even his own kids?

I got in the truck, and started to drive,
and saw a little girl—
who I picked up, hit on the head, and
screwed, and screwed, and screwed, and screwed, then

buried,
in the garden of the motel . . .

—You see, ever since I was a kid I wanted
to *feel* things make sense: I remember

looking out the window of my room back home,—
and being almost suffocated by the asphalt;
and grass; and trees; and glass;
just *there*, just *there*, doing nothing!
not saying anything! filling me up—
but also being a wall; dead, and stopping me;
—how I wanted to see beneath it, cut

beneath it, and make it
somehow, come alive . . .

The salt of the earth;
Mom once said, 'Man's spunk is the salt of the earth . . .'

—That night, at that Twenty-nine Palms Motel
I had passed a million times on the road, everything

fit together; was alright;
it seemed like
        everything *had* to be there, like I had spent years

trying, and at last finally finished drawing this
                                        huge circle . . .

—But then, suddenly I knew
somebody *else* did it, some bastard
had hurt a little girl—; the motel
                              I could see again, it had been
itself all the time, a lousy
pile of bricks, plaster, that didn't seem to
have to be there,—but *was,* just by chance . . .

—Once, on the farm, when I was a kid,
I was screwing a goat; and the rope around his neck
when he tried to get away
pulled tight;—and just when I came,
he *died* . . .
    I came back the next day; jacked off over his body;
but it didn't do any good . . .

Mom once said:
'Man's spunk is the salt of the earth, and grows kids.'

I tried so hard to come; more *pain* than anything else;
but didn't do any good . . .

—About six months ago, I heard Dad remarried,
so I drove over to Connecticut to see him and see
if he was happy.
                    She was twenty-five years younger than him:
she had lots of little kids, and I don't know why,
I felt shaky . . .

                    I stopped in front of the address; and
snuck up to the window to look in . . .
                                        —There he was, a kid
six months old on his lap, laughing
and bouncing the kid, happy in his old age
to play the papa after years of sleeping around,—
it twisted me up . . .
                    To think that what he wouldn't give me,
                    he *wanted* to give them . . .

                    I could have killed the bastard . . .

—Naturally, I just got right back in the car,
and believe me, was determined, determined,
to head straight for home . . .

                                        but the more I drove,
I kept thinking about getting a girl,
and the more I thought I shouldn't do it,
the more I had to—

                    I saw her coming out of the movies,
saw she was alone, and
kept circling the blocks as she walked along them,
saying, 'You're going to leave her alone.'
'You're going to leave her alone.'

                                        —The woods were scary!
As the seasons changed, and you saw more and more

of the skull show through, the nights became clearer,
and the buds,—erect, like nipples . . .

—But then, one night,
nothing *worked* . . .
                                        Nothing in the sky
would blur like I wanted it to;
and I couldn't, *couldn't,*

get it to seem to me
that somebody *else* did it . . .

I tried, and tried, but there was just me there,
and her, and the sharp trees
saying, 'That's you standing there.
                                                        You're . . .
                                                                            just you.'

                                        I hope I fry.

—Hell came when I saw
                                            MYSELF . . .
                                                              and couldn't stand
what I see . . ."

MICHAEL DENNIS BROWNE

The Roof of the World

He is making love with his wife on the roof,
that's all right.
But sixteen years . . .
The cattle wait around as long as they can,
then go off, like grenades.
The neighbors get heated over breakfast,
but they won't come down,
there's no legal loophole.
If a man wants to spend as much time as that
on the roof of his house with his wife,
that's all right by the law,
there's nothing improper in that.
Sometimes they noticed the grass beneath them,
and the woods around that, change
in their colors, the summer's
thin strokes, the slow
flood of fall blood, and the townspeople
that lay down and died like ticks,
but they didn't care.
That was sixteen years well spent,
he said, she said, as both
at last came down,
to the gold of garbage,
to the piano an oak again,
the television a camera,
the dog a frog,
and the huge children they had forgotten about
waiting around minutely, in baskets,
to be born again.

Power Failure

Morley's light went out.
All of a sudden, with a plunk of silence.
And so Morley discovered the moon.
Yellow & enormous, it was glowing
just over the black ridge; Morley
had not noticed it.

The whole valley below him
went dark. And he saw the shaky
light of candles in his nearest
neighbors' house, through the trees.
Not only Morley's lights then,
but the lights of all.

How good to rediscover the moon
thought Morley, blacked out on his ridge.
How quiet the flames sway! While the
meat cooks. "I shall have to baste the meat by flashlight"
his guest's wife said. "Yes" thought Morley.

Out in the snow, did the fox stop
when the human houses went dark? Like the lungs
of a man who hear the great heart
cease, and wonder, waiting for orders.
Is the whole body closing down?

Morley's lights went out. & the valley's
with him. And many men's, who sat
in the dark like he. Friends of the dark,
thought Morley, be in your houses & wait.

The cat wants to go into the fireplace.
The friends wish to gather, but the dark forestalls them,
such dark, thinks Morley, in its own failure.

MICHAEL DENNIS BROWNE

And ah the power fails,
ah the failure of it.
The guest's wife shines
the flashlight, while the guest & friend
makes the fire.
It is Roy doing it, & Margaret shining.

Feverishly the officials are working
to find the failure. In my veins,
thinks Morley, in my veins. Orchards
darken; each in his own
landscape leaks. And a great moon rises
in the brain, in the mind of man & of Morley,
& its yellowness tells him
it is here to stay.
We must be brave in our dark.

Hallowe'en 1971

I carve my first head. Then I carve another.
Now I have two Vietnamese
children on my table.

I place a candle in each of them, & light it.
The heads are still wet inside. I've put
the seeds in a brown bag.

I take one head to the window.
The other I put on my stair, with the front
door open. By it, a bowl of candy.

II

Down the block,
round the neighborhood,

all over this darkened country,
the hollow yellow heads
burning in windows, & tiny
American ghosts running toward them
through the dark, with open hands.

Iowa, June

From my front wheels the scared rabbits
sprouting. The ditches

piled with bleached squirrels. The sky's
slow tumescence, the dark
delivering its flowers.

Who now a house has
must lie there in silence.
Who now a wife has
must guard her unbreathing beside him
in the house,
                                        the tower of the house,
as the nettles pass the window,
dryly tapping, and the stunned

moths plummet past the drifting
fireflies, trailing their
                                        canyons of gas, into
the dark grass. In the far
pasture a foal noses the oak's

growing shadow.
                                        Fathers
are losing their sons this night. Your wife,
O keep her, in the dead sea
of your own sweating as your dream

blazing and loaded lifts off
from the light-wet runway, to where
no tower of her touch may recall you,
where your sons are finally
grasslands waving unduly
                                        beneath you. She is there
for you still, in the drift of branch
in the dark, enter her as the sea
from the shore of yourself, hold
to her still through the vast
anchors of sand, rising.

In the house, the tower of the house.

Paranoia

When you drive on the freeway, cars follow you.

Someone opens your mail, two hands
that come out of your shirt-sleeves.

Your dog looks at you, he does not like you.

At the driving test the cop is tired. He has sat up
all night, screening your dreams.

If you go to the zoo, be sure to take your passport.

Everywhere you go, the dog goes with you. Beautiful
   women
come up to you and ask for the dog's telephone number.

You go to teach; everyone who passes you in the
   corridor

knows you never finished *Tristram Shandy.*
You are the assistant professor no one associates with.

At the yoga class you finally get
into the lotus position.
You are carried home.

When you close your eyes in meditation, all you see is
breasts.

When you turn the refrigerator to defrost, the TV drips.

Across the street, the pigeons call softly to each other
like the FBI on a stakeout.

When you walk to the post office and see the flag at
half-mast,
you know you have died.

LUCILLE CLIFTON

Good Times

My Daddy has paid the rent
and the insurance man is gone
and the lights is back on
and my uncle Brud has hit
for one dollar straight
and they is good times
good times
good times

My Mama has made bread
and Grampaw has come
and everybody is drunk
and dancing in the kitchen
and singing in the kitchen
oh these is good times
good times
good times

oh children think about the
good times

Miss Rosie

When I watch you
wrapped up like garbage
sitting, surrounded by the smell
of too old potato peels
or
when I watch you

in your old man's shoes
with the little toe cut out
sitting, waiting for your mind
like next week's grocery
I say
when I watch you
you wet brown bag of a woman
who used to be the best looking gal in Georgia
used to be called the Georgia Rose
I stand up
through your destruction
I stand up

In Salem

to Jeanette

Weird sister
the Black witches know that
the terror is not in the moon
choreographing the dance of wereladies
and the terror is not in the broom
swinging around to the hum of cat music
nor the wild clock face grinning from the wall,
the terror is in the plain pink
at the window
and the hedges moral as fire
and the plain face of the white woman watching us
as she beats her ordinary bread.

---

the thirty eighth year
of my life,

plain as bread
round as a cake
an ordinary woman.

an ordinary woman.

i had expected to be
smaller than this,
more beautiful,
wiser in Afrikan ways,
more confident,
i had expected
more than this.

i will be forty soon.
my mother once was forty.

my mother died at forty four,
a woman of sad countenance
leaving behind a girl
awkward as a stork.
my mother was thick,
her hair was a jungle and
she was very wise
and beautiful
and sad.

i have dreamed dreams
for you mama
more than once.
i have wrapped me
in your skin
and made you live again
more than once.
i have taken the bones you hardened
and built daughters
and they blossom and promise fruit

like Afrikan trees.
i am a woman now.
an ordinary woman.

in the thirty eighth
year of my life,
surrounded by life,
a perfect picture of
blackness blessed,
i had not expected this
loneliness.

if it is western,
if it is the final
Europe in my mind,
if in the middle of my life
i am turning the final turn
into the shining dark
let me come to it whole
and holy
not afraid
not lonely
out of my mother's life
into my own.
into my own.

i had expected more than this.
i had not expected to be
an ordinary woman.

CONYUS

The Great Santa Barbara Oil Disaster OR:

1

we ride down the coast hwy through the rain
to a beach that sits in a rocky cove
  hidden from the eye.

i sit far in the rear of the bus
where the shadows pass warmly
  over the metal walls
looking through steamed windows
  at the disheveled scenery.

a mexican girl stands in the muddy debris
of her home rummaging through the mud;
  the river passed suddenly two days
ago & shifted the geography.

the clouds mount overhead,
  prostituting themselves
in small squalls & we turn left

off the freeway into the spent community
  of carpinteria like a funeral procession
on a saturday in the march winds.

beyond the border of the thin sidewalks
  sit the bleached out houses on paper stilts
with their blinds moving in pale blue motion.

we walk beneath the dingy sky
single file to the beach,
   everything around us is a bloody womb.

2

all day we work behind the sea breaker
   in the black sand, shoveling straw
into the mouth of the skip loader,
   while the cat skinner rides high
in the seat with a hole for his eye.

in the window of an opulent club
   a servant appears to sway
in the breeze like a feather
coolly emerging from his dream.

i sit on a concrete wall
   swinging my legs over the ice plants,
touching the crushed sandwich beneath my work shirt.

after lunch we return with rakes & hip boots,
throwing sand upon the oily rocks
   & wading through the tide
that dissolves the tracks of feet.

   i turn my back to the ocean
& pull the rain jacket tight,
   looking over my shoulder at the horizon.
in the distance, someone is singing a song
   that i can hardly hear.

3

the children come to the beach
with their dogs barking happily
at a safe distance.

they watch us rake the debris
with magnetism in huge piles
for the cat skinner.

sunlight filters the surf
about our feet with blood
& birds & invincible powers.

the children run into the ocean
with granite blocks of ice,
  & symmetrically the night descends.

4

the women
of santa barbara
watch us carry
the driftwood
across the clover field,
then go home to husbands
& kill babies
in the morning
with a small pill
while we sleep.

5

green frogs croak in the rain pond;
dawn drizzling through the mist.

a white gull
floats face upward
in the greasy water.

i watch the tide
push the gull

against the rocks
in my silence.

6

pearl crack
the dawn is leaking,
quiet patterns
on the street.

cool winds
their thin flagellation,
fragilely
soars across my face.

the sun set
on the ocean
& there wasn't
any confusion.

7

the citizens of santa barbara
brought rags for us to wipe

our oily black hands on.
i found a red one

& wore it around my neck,
this is called love.

8

crickets
          in
the vacant field

sing loudly
when the sky
devours the land
in its blackness

of caskets
&
beautiful
cadillacs.

9

poem to the girl seen walking
below my window at 4:00 A.M.

i see you there
walking on the freshly
cut grass
uncertain
about your decision
to either
drown
the shadow or melt
the ambivalent
rose.

10

—for koyono

all
night
i
touched
your
breast
kissed

your
thighs
letting
the
long
black
hair
cover
me
thickly
&
when
i
awoke
alone
with
only
a
love
stain
on
the
sheet
i
fell
in
love
with
dreaming

11

all these men
were standing

at various levels
of confession shouting

at each other
about incarceration

for many years   for many years
for many thousands
of years

hiding and laughing
hiding and laughing
hiding and laughing

the hatred
the hatred
the explosion

beneath breast
laughing
coughing
away their
lives

12

wednesday.
the rain
fell heavily
& the beach
is specked
with piles
of straw & driftwood.

in the afternoon
we throw cans
of gasoline
onto the piles
& watch them
evaporate

like the happiest
years of your life.

13

we pick up the sky
& move the ocean
like a giant anaconda's
head;
        they sit on the beach
watching us . . .

we place a hot badger's claw
in the cool ashes;
   they watch & move their lips slowly.

we part the sand
& bury ourselves
in a canal of lilies;
   they turn to face each other
   in awe, pretending they don't see us.

14

beneath the houses
the shadows escape
till
   dawn
comes walking with death
on her arm
putting out lights
that burn too low

15

the chinese girl
                    served us

in cellophane gloves
the paper
tasting food at 7:00 A.M.
across the glossy counter.
the sky
was just beginning
to show traces of aurora
in
the east
& a continent
lowered its battled head.

later,
on the beach
cleaning oil
from the spume
& beach furniture,
i ate the apple
she had given me
& thought of her
in that
christian
white uniform.

thought
that she probably
felt
that she was ugly
because she wasn't white
& had
slanted eyes
& so
i took
another bowl of corn flakes
& told her that
i didn't
want the meat.

do you think
she understood
that i
loved her?

16

the 1st. night we arrived
the girls in the
dormitory
across from us
paraded before
their window in
bras & panties
being friendly.

the people
came to watch us work
& some said,
"my! don't they look almost human?"

sometimes the
children's ball
bounded in our area
& we smiled.
(everyone laughed a lot the first day.)

the sun/set

& we watched its dying legions

instruct the children to play
beyond the ring of flowers
& watch the red flags
be
cause the sky would
fall if they harbored
ambitions in our minds.

& so
we didn't laugh
anymore, or smile
                    at all
from then on
                  we just worked
slowly with our
heads keeping low
& our eyes on the ground
  so the sky wouldn't fall
& the people wouldn't know.

17

damp mist in the cool monday dawn
we board the bus with packs on our backs
in silence for a strategic location,

heading north out of santa barbara
in the wake of working nine to five/ers;

passing through small towns
where old men sit in bleached overalls
beneath dusty hats & nondescript daughters

& we pass like a shadow
of death
        to them.

18

in morgan hill
sitting next to
the fence post
with gray clouds
clipping the mountains
reminded me of freedom

& i thought that i was flying
& i thought that i was free

19

they unpacked us here
in dimly lit rooms
with dust & wax on the mantel,

some of us get stored in cardboard
& others in canvas
until next year
when xmas comes again
or the Great Santa Barbara Oil Disaster/ OR:

PETER COOLEY

Vanishing Point

He hears the summer at a distance
arrange itself inside him:
there, the sky recedes, heat lightning
strikes the last frost out of his gums.

Here, someone is lining the trees up
row to row, a theater of echoes,
moss the ants parade or now crickets
his limbs, their strings in this air
an architecture offstage
amazing to even the stones.

Later there will be rain
peeling the night back through his faces,
graftings, while the birds come down
to plant the small black fruit of his eyes.

Tell him: some morning he'll rise,
a tiny god shaking the lights
their disciples off his skin, all miracles
this ambiguous, naked
to find himself ready
already, masked, moving out.

The Confession

You have just come in the door
from having one,

the first time you tell me
with any priest in eight years
we've been married.

The storm door holds you,
closing yourself against it,
that wind where green shoots lift
my bed of crocus laid out
toward this first warm night all year.

Today at work all afternoon
it was spring in people's heads
till they would talk of nothing else
but a typist who lost touch, quit,
after the boss got her down.

I would never ask
did you tell him about those years,
the others between us
blown off like seeds across the lawn.
I nod. Sure, the kids went to sleep easily.

Alternatives

You would sleep with the moon
if she would listen. Make the move.
You need it that much.

You would fall through grass
that it take on, naked,
the garment of flesh. And fall away.

You would lie with the oak
if it should come down & bear you
nut-brown daughters in spring.

You would ask the river
to take you into her mouth
be she the vessel & current of hope.

You would put it to the mosquito
if you could pin her down
with a line on this white sheet.

Then there's the desire
to throw yourself into valleys, to root
among meadows at night. To climb

ladders of azure, the moist wind
undoing salmon, rabbits, a fly
in fine hair of its kiss. Or even

to lie like a dog on the side
of some hill, raising a whelp
in the bitch, the moon, to go down

among the possibles, spilling yourself
in every seed that lifts its head
to ask *& aren't I Lord the world*

& aren't I & aren't I as long
as I go on laying myself down
longing to burst through my skin

the wild cry of your blossoming?

PHILIP DACEY

The Birthday

Thirty candles and one
to grow on. My husband
and son watch me
think of wishes.

I wish I found it
easier to make wishes
than I do. Wasn't it,
years ago, easy to make wishes?

My husband and son *are* wishes.
It is as if
every day I wait for them
to happen again,

and they do.
But surely there is much
I am without, yet
I stand here, wishless.

Perhaps I want
what I needn't wish for,
my life: it is
coming, everything will happen.

Or perhaps I want
precisely what I don't know,
all that darkness
so tall and handsome before me.

I have seen women age
beautifully, with a

growing, luminous
sexuality:

now I know, each year
they've been slowly
stepping out of their wishes
like their clothes.

I stand here amazed
at what is happening to me,
how I've begun to lighten
of desires, getting down

to my secret skin,
the impossibly thin
membrane this side
of nothing. Husband,

I wish I could tell you.

The Obscene Caller

Years ago,
he began dialing your number.
He is still dialing.
At the precise moment
he finishes dialing,
you will arrive home.
He will not sound
as you might expect.
For a moment
you will think it could be
your father.
Gentle and patient,
he will understand

the great distance
you have had to come.
You ask him who he is.
He tells you his name
is not in the phonebook.
He cannot be called
by the authorities.
So reassuring is he,
that when he asks you
to take off your clothes,
you do so.
He says, Look at yourself.
You do so.
When he begins telling you
the secrets of your life,
you will not be inclined
to hang up.
He will use
the most graphic terms.
Nothing he says
will shock you.
If he is doing anything
with his free hand,
you will know it is only
checking the next name
on the list.
Soon you begin
to breathe heavily.
It will be he
who hangs up first.

Form Rejection Letter

We are sorry we cannot use the enclosed.
We are returning it to you.
We do not mean to imply anything by this.

We would prefer not to be pinned down about this
  matter.
But we are not keeping—cannot, will not keep—
  what you sent us.
We did receive it, though, and our returning it to you
  is a sign of that.
It was not that we minded your sending it to us
  unasked.
That is happening all the time, they
  come when we least expect them,
  when we forget we have needed or might yet need
    them,
  and we send them back.
We send this back.
It is not that we minded.
At another time, there is no telling . . .
But this time, it does not suit our present needs.

We wish to make it clear it was not easy receiving it.
It came so encumbered.
And we are busy here.
We did not feel
  we could take it on.
We know it would not have ended there.
It would have led to this, and that.
We know about these things.
It is why we are here.
We wait for it. We recognize it when it comes.
Regretfully, this form letter does not allow us to
  elaborate why we send it back.
It is not that we minded.

We hope this does not discourage you. But we would
  not want to encourage you falsely.
It requires delicate handling, at this end.
If we had offered it to you,
  perhaps you would understand.
  But, of course, we did not.

You cannot know what your offering it
  meant to us,
And we cannot tell you:
There is a form we must adhere to.
It is better for everyone that we use this form.

As to what you do in future,
we hope we have given you signs,
that you have read them,
that you have not misread them.
We wish we could be more helpful.
But we are busy.
We are busy returning so much.
We cannot keep it.
It all comes so encumbered.
And there is no one here to help.
Our enterprise is a small one.
We are thinking of expanding.
We hope you will send something.

RITA DOVE

Nigger Song: An Odyssey

We six pile in, the engine churning ink:
We ride into the night.
Past factories, past graveyards
And the broken eyes of windows, we ride
Into the gray-green nigger night.

We sweep past excavation sites; the pits
Of gravel gleam like mounds of ice.
Weeds clutch at the wheels;
We laugh and swerve away, veering
Into the black entrails of the earth,
The green smoke sizzling on our tongues . . .

In the nigger night, thick with the smell of cabbages,
Nothing can catch us.
Laughter spills like gin from glasses,
And "yeah" we whisper, "yeah"
We croon, "yeah."

Adolescence—II

Although it is night, I sit in the bathroom, waiting.
Sweat prickles behind my knees; the baby-breasts are
  alert.
Venetian blinds slice up the moon; the tiles quiver in
  pale strips.

Then they come, the three seal-men with eyes as round
As dinner plates and eyelashes like sharpened tines.
They bring the scent of licorice. One sits in the
washbowl,

One on the bathtub edge; one leans against the door.
"Can you feel it yet?" they whisper.
I don't know what to say, again. They chuckle,

Patting their sleek bodies with their hands.
"Well, maybe next time." And they rise,
Glittering like pools of ink under moonlight,

And vanish. I clutch at the ragged holes
They leave behind, here at the edge of darkness.
Night rests like a ball of fur on my tongue.

This Life

The green lamp flares on the table.
You tell me the same thing
as that one,
asleep, upstairs.
Now I see: the possibilities
are like golden dresses in a nutshell.

As a child, I fell in love
with a Japanese woodcut
of a girl gazing at the moon.
I waited with her for her lover.
He came in white breeches and sandals.
He had a goatee—he had

your face, though I didn't know it.
Our lives will be the same—
your lips, swollen from whistling
at danger,
and I a stranger
in this desert,
nursing the tough skin of figs.

PHILIP DOW

The Life

Hunchbacked
by his heart
swollen with dreams
of wings, of girls whose breasts are antelope
trembling beneath the lightning
that seeds his spring: he hears the bones
of their unborn children
growing.
In his heart hut he lives,
a mute
chewing crimson flowers
to make speech, to keep
saying
        what does this do
                        to save my life?

His words stall for time,
slave for the mortgage on his bones:
he knows he is the fool
who cannot solve it—
yet, goes at his heart over and over
repairing: with jellyfish, lame horses,
whistles, white cords of his body, white moths
seeking colors, damp alleys,
odors of knives,
trees, stumped, putting out tiny wings
of translucent new leaves anyway.

Listening to twilight schools of spooky minnows
tuning their scales, he has got the drift

of this night sea of star
-fish that stops all eyes:
he sees the boats go on,
overhead, with cargoes of ocarinas
and red melons—

Swimming to any shore, he finds himself
there, already, with his black horse
and his cart, heaped with salt,
paying back the sea.

The Duck Pond at Mini's Pasture, a Dozen Years Later

Walking out, I flushed some meadowlarks—
Now they're down, and redwings gone into cattails.
A loose strand of barbwire begins softly thrumming.
Out over San Pablo Bay, clouds
Blow up from sunset, fading yellow
Off the Indian Tobacco.

Remembering all those nightfalls
Spent anywhere rain gathered
In corn or barley fields and ducks flew,
I hunch in pickleweed, shooting distance
From the pond, make a raspberry
With my lips and roll a whistle for Greenwing Teal
The old way learned from my brother.

Mosquitos rise out of sedge. White faces
Of Herefords bob dreamily as they graze.
In quirky teal-like flight, bats
Startle. Oil slickens my thumb on the safety
And I rub it into the marred walnut stock

Of the Winchester double, sniffing
Hoppe's lubricant, souring weeds in the flooded pond.
Behind me, darkness comes on.
A shitepoke crosses the Evening Star.

Far off, beyond the eucalyptus groves,
A pair of mallards
Cross the powerlines—
And I call, rough-voiced. They weave, dip,
Then flare. Afraid they'll pass,
I call again and my throat burns. They circle,
But I don't turn. I know to watch over water.

Out of darkness overhead, drake first,
Slowly they drop, rocking gently
On set wings, down
Slowly, into the last light—

Twilight in California

for My Father

Day of hunting done,
you find this downhill climb hardest.
But where the vineyard road begins
you balk. Breathing the good scent of sweat
and gun oil, you sit cross-legged and tense,
your hunting cap brim full of grapes;
the valley cupped below, shadowless—
waiting for the wine to be poured.
First darkness sifts out of trees into your hair.

Beyond the last ridge
your Rockies pile up,
enfolding wings, antlers,

hides of slain game
that rise, now, in twilight,
with spaniels, moving down gametrails
to drink.

At day's end
your blue eyes rust
like buckshot, changing
wine to blood.

NORMAN DUBIE

Pastoral

for H.S.

It all happened so fast. Fenya was in the straight
Chair in the corner, her youngest sucking
On her breast. The screams, and a horseman
Outside the cottage. Then, her father in a blue tunic
Falling through the door onto the boards.
Fenya leaned over him, her blouse
Still at the waist and a single drop of her yellow milk
Falling into the open eye of her father. He dies
Looking up through this screen, what he sees

Is a little lamp-glow,
Like the poet describes less often even than harness bells
Or the icon with pine boughs. He sees snow
Falling into a bland field where a horse is giving
Birth to more snow, dragging its placenta all over
The glaze which is red; all the snow is red, the horse's
Blood is white. He sees tears on Fenya's face and
Milk coming like bone hairpins from her breasts.
The straight force in the twig that makes a great black
Branch. Two of which are crossed over his chest. Terror is

The vigil of astonishment.

Balalaika

Three strings, a neck of almond, and the heart
Is a triangle like the small seed
With its little white feather taking the air

And looking now like the inside
Of the ears of an old peasant, the orange wax
And white hairs.

The great red muscle of a cow sprinkled
With snow. The dogs being attacked
With a pine bough. Old Russia.
In winter the rough daughters stepping
In and out of their clothes, the smoke
From the tubs, the long handled brushes
And soap. The black nipples of the oldest girl,
Now, gooseflesh; surrounds of lilac and butter.
The long legs on the youngest,
Her yellow hair. The buttocks on these girls
Are round, just round.

There are sticks of ammonia being broken
Under the nose of the grandmother,
Faint she returns remembering a barn
From her childhood entering it on winter
Evenings to the odor of manure, so sharp
And incidental.

Upstairs the father sleeps in a chair
With the balalaika in his lap: the head
Of a child, white fat in a net for the birds,
Or just a large bird in the lap being plucked.

Little Peter in the kitchen takes his very first
Swallow from a cup, some cold water
Down his chin, he gurgles and looks up at
His mother. Smiles and flings the wooden
Cup breaking a blue window. She frowns
And turns her back to him, laughing into
Her apron. A mouse scampers out of the cupboard.

There is the sound of the balalaika waking in heaven.

From Alehouse Sonnets
The Killigrew Wood

We've taken our burlap sacks and entered
the Killigrew Wood.
We're gathering winter mushrooms. We have faith
in what grows wild, what might poison us.
Miss Warminister is here exercising
her hounds. We'll start foraging in the south
and walk clear through to Northparks and the road.
(The hunters pass with headless game

bouncing at their belts. Their valuable animal hides.)
Here, these pliers will pull the burrs
from your coat. (What have you
discovered beneath that log,
among the puffballs. Is it a woman or a young orphan.)
William, you mustn't look up. I'm walking backwards
through wet leaves and brush. We sober at these
homicides.

From Alehouse Sonnets
The Dressing Stations

William, the wild round plums are falling
and the last lovely glider is coming in
along the coast; the girls in the bathhouses
are bending over to soap their white ankles.
And you had no idea that there

had been seventeen new wars since Waterloo.
First, you ask of dear Clarissa.
(She'll still resist undress like an arm that

is fractured and swollen. You must rip open
the sleeve of her blouse. Your embrace
will be like a dressing of gauze and plaster
of paris.) And, yes, we have new weapons:
tanks, flamethrowers, bomber squadrons,
choking gas with the odour of horseradish, the H-bomb
and our Pope's most recent encyclical on contraception.

In the Dead of the Night

for Weingarten

There's the story of me sitting in the grass in the dark
With the dark cat; for hours she has been at it,
Stalking fireflies and sometimes falling
On her back, sometimes her jaws working
Very fast. For a moment I thought of
A few friends; only for a moment,
I thought. And then up the stairs to bed,
Thinking then of the old rabbi in Poland, large
And in a forest poking with a stick
In his own black manure for the gold tooth
He swallowed at a feast.
I remembered a photograph of the lights of Dresden
During a blizzard, one old bus making it
Slowly along a warehouse. For a moment
I thought it was a dream, only for a moment I did
Dream: the cat entering by a large window leaping
Onto the bed.
She strains and vomits hundreds of dead bugs,
Some green and black,

Then solid areas of light, yellow, next
To the sad half-lights that miss and strike again.
Not a constellation going out in your lap.
What can't you make out: the great bear
Hobbled with a short ladder, or a plough blade,
Or perhaps just a whole city impoverished but for
Shovels. The story of its light
As the last insect tries the last light.
And a rabbi dancing in the forest, he spins
Twice around and then unwinds, his arms flying,
Laughing and crying; look sharply at the hand that
Is most above him, lovely man, something very
Black, something very bright, from inside him.

STEPHEN DUNN

Looking for a Rest Area

I've been driving for hours,
it seems like all my life.
The wheel has become familiar,
I turn it

every so often to avoid the end
of my life, but I'm never sure
it doesn't turn me
by its roundness, as women have

by the space inside them.
What I'm looking for
is a rest area, some place where
the old valentine inside my shirt

can stop contriving romances,
where I can climb out of the thing
that has taken me this far
and stretch myself.

It is dusk, Nebraska,
the only bright lights in this entire state
put their fists in my eyes
as they pass me

Oh, how easily I can be dazzled—
where is the sign
that will free me, if only for moments,
I keep asking.

On Hearing the Airlines Will Use a Psychological Profile to Catch Potential Skyjackers

They will catch me
as sure as the checkout girls
in every Woolworth's have caught me, the badge
of my imagined theft shining in their eyes.

I will be approaching the ticket counter
and knowing myself, myselves,
will effect the nonchalance of a baron.
That is what they'll be looking for.

I'll say "Certainly is nice that the
airlines are taking these precautions,"
and the man behind the counter
will press a secret button,

there'll be a hand on my shoulder
(this will have happened before in a dream),
and in a back room they'll ask me
"Why were you going to do it?"

I'll say "You wouldn't believe
I just wanted to get to Cleveland?"
"No," they'll say.
So I'll tell them everything,

the plot to get the Pulitzer Prize
in exchange for the airplane,
the bomb in my pencil,
heroin in the heel of my boot.

Inevitably, it'll be downtown for booking,
newsmen pumping me for deprivation

during childhood,
the essential cause.

"There is no one cause for any human act,"
I'll tell them, thinking *finally*,
a chance to let the public in
on the themes of great literature.

And on and on, celebrating myself, offering
no resistance, assuming what they assume,
knowing, in a sense, there is no such thing
as the wrong man.

Day and Night Handball

I think of corner shots, the ball
hitting and dying like a butterfly
on a windshield, shots so fine
and perverse they begin to live

alongside weekends of sex
in your memory. I think of serves
delivered deep to the left-hand,
the ball sliding off the side wall

into the blindnesses of one's body,
and diving returns that are impossible
except on days when your body is all
rubber bands and dreams

unfulfilled since childhood.
I think of a hand slicing the face
of a ball, so much english
that it comes back drunk

to your opponent who doesn't have
enough hands to hit it,
who hits it anyway, who makes you think
of "God!" and "Goddamn!", the pleasure

of falling to your knees
for what is superb, better than you.
But it's position I think of most,
the easy slam and victory

because you have a sense of yourself
and the court, the sense that old men
gone in the knees have,
one step in place of five,

finesse in place of power,
and all the time
the four walls around you
creating the hardship, the infinite variety.

RUSSELL EDSON

Children

When they ask you your name your head knows what to say, it has the brain and the mouth. The rest is all a mobile pedestal.

But when the head replies it is talking only for itself. The mute feet have certain ideas. The left one might want to be called Speedy; perhaps the right one, High Stepper.

But the head says, Henry.

That physical presence that we take to ourselves is like an endless childhood of sibling rivalry.

The right-hand, if you are right-handed, proves early to be the brighter one; the left-hand the less bright, the weaker twin.

And while the right-hand will learn to write with much facility, it never learns to speak.

The head is always quick to say, I am Henry.

The rest of the body, the mute feet, Speedy and High Stepper; the good hands, Squeezer and Pinch; the sleepy penis, who chooses to be Earnest, and who is downgraded and hidden from public view, until the proper moment when he rises, particularly in milady's estimate . . . All know that for all of Henry's eloquence, he is but a field of hair; a rat with its tail down the body's back.

In All the Days of My Childhood

My father by some strange conjunction had mice for sons.

. . . And so it was in all the days of my childhood . . . The winds blew, and then abated, the rains fell, and then climbed slowly back to heaven as vapor.

Day became night as night became day in rhythmic lengthenings and shortenings.

Time of the blossoming, and time of decline.

The sense of permanence broken by sudden change.

The time of change giving way again to a sense of permanence.

In the summer my brothers' tails dragged in the grass. What is more natural than their tails in the grass?

Upon their haunches, front paws feebly paddling air, whiskers twitching, they looked toward father with mindless faith.

In the winter father would pick them up by their tails and put them in cages.

The ping of snow on the windows; bad weather misunderstood . . . Perhaps all things misunderstood?

It was that understanding came to no question.

Without sense of the arbitrary no process of logic was instigated by my brothers. Was this wrong?

Again in the spring we moved out of doors, and again dragged our tails in the grass, looking toward father with mindless faith.

. . . And so it was in all the days of my childhood.

The Childhood of an Equestrian

An equestrian fell from his horse.

A nursemaid moving through the wood espied the equestrian in his corrupted position and cried, what child has fallen from his rockinghorse?

Merely a new technique for dismounting, said the prone equestrian.

The child is wounded more by fear than hurt, said the nursemaid.

The child dismounts and is at rest. But being interfered with grows irritable, cried the equestrian.

The child that falls from his rockinghorse refusing to remount fathers the man with no woman taken in his arms, said the nursemaid, for women are as horses, and it is the rockinghorse that teaches the man the way of love.

I am a man fallen from a horse in the privacy of a wood, save for a strange nursemaid who espied my corruption, taking me for a child, who fallen from a rockinghorse lies down in fear refusing to father the man, who mounts the woman with the rhythm given in the day of his childhood on the imitation horse, when he was in the imitation of the man who incubates in his childhood, said the equestrian.

Let me help you to your manhood, said the nursemaid.

I am already, by the metaphor, the son of the child, if the child father the man, which is involuted nonsense. And take your hands off me, cried the equestrian.

I lift up the child which is wounded more by fear than hurt, said the nursemaid.

You lift up a child which has rotted into its manhood, cried the equestrian.

I lift up as I lift all that fall and are made children by their falling, said the nursemaid.

Go away from me because you are annoying me, screamed the equestrian as he beat the fleeing white shape that seemed like a soft moon entrapped in the branches of the forest.

A Performance at Hog Theater

There was once a hog theater where hogs performed as men, had men been hogs.

One hog said, I will be a hog in a field which has found a mouse which is being eaten by the same hog which is in the field and which has found the mouse, which I am performing as my contribution to the performer's art.

Oh let's just be hogs, cried an old hog.

And so the hogs streamed out of the theater crying, only hogs, only hogs . . .

The Retirement of the Elephant

An elephant of long service to a circus retired to a small cottage on a quiet street, to spend its remaining days in the study of life after death.

It had looked forward to these quiet years, when the mind would be readied for the coming collapse of the biology.

But the elephant found that it was too big to fit through the front door. The elephant pushed through anyway, smashing the front of the cottage. As it started upstairs to the bathroom it fell into the cellar.

The elephant climbed out and went to the back of the cottage and broke in again, pushing down the remaining walls.

Now the elephant realizes that its only course is to run amuck—Yes, just to run amuck!

Goddamn everything!

SUSAN FELDMAN

Sea Legs

for H.

Welcome home from the exhausting voyage
on the savage sea! Welcome home, sweetie,
in your vicuna coat. It wasn't true, I know,
that you were below deck, your hand
on the stray breast of the woman in the geranium
dress. When I heard, my head swam a bit,
but welcome home! Here are the vellum envelopes,
unsteamed, notice my restraint! Here are the vegetables
waiting in an attractive pile on the hardwood floor.
Welcome home! There's juice on my legs,
leftover cassoulet, and your sousaphone's on the bed,
untouched. When I saw you in that coat,
with the salt shakers in the pockets, with salt burns
on your lips, I was the victim of glad and helpless
laughter: I had all the validation I needed
that you spent the night out in the spray!
I don't suppose you can dance yet, because of
your sea legs, but welcome home, welcome home!
A path of hairpins, gentle arrows, leads to my room.

Intruder

Some morning, while you and I are dozing,
Puss, not puling outside like most mornings,
will try the handle, and finding himself
denied entrance, will kick in the door.

His monstrous head will enter first, next
his vacant grin and his body weighing
four stone. Then, my fair
but furless one, he will seize
you by the scruff, and boot you out.

Maybe I should never have started feeding
him those sides of liver, those fresh eggs,
those vast stinking salmon. But what's done
is done. Puss, clumsy still on two feet,
but eager to please me, reaches into the cupboard
to take down the Limoges, that we two
may enjoy our filets of mackerel, our dishes of cream.

Lamentations Of An Au Pair Girl

Some days, I'm sorely tempted to throw out the baby
with his bathwater, or jettison the babe and save
the juice for soup stock: we're thrifty here. But
his little cries are so sweet!
Days are spent with my marrowbones crossed under me,
apron loose, swabbing the floor with my clubfoot: it's
slow work but I'm satisfied when the job's complete.
My room? A little box with bluing
hanging on hooks, and the master wouldn't think
to ask before entering, but what's to be done?
It's le droit de seigneur, and sex
is a vile itching, peroxide on the skin,
but necessary as bread. One does well,
dear Miss, not to put up a fuss,
and take one's tea, as expected, with the rest.

It's a mutual agreement, this True, I have baked
a hundred humble pies, but then cut wedges for myself.

I am the scullion, the hardworking maid-of-all-work,
but patcher and mender too, fixer and soother:
from scraps I have made a whole cloth. I'm voyeur too,
I know it, I can't avert my face from the underbelly
but I have the good sense to make of it a tasty potage.
I am the interpreter of messages on faces,
the crooner of lullabies, the keeper of beasts,
in short: the poet.

How The Invalids Make Love

The room must be warmer than
the root cellar, yet cooler than
the grape arbor in high summer,
the window shade should be raised
to allow the proper amount of hedge
to come between shade and sill.
Of utmost importance are the pressure
and texture of the counterpanes,
the crispness of the square pillows,
the cups of jasmine tea and the cherries
in a bowl lacquered black.

Violets on the writing table,
little brittle saucers, and
portraits on the walls of macrantha
roses, Belle de Crecy roses, dog roses.
The filigree tongs and the double-ended
paintbrush must be nearby, and
the letters of intent. The drink made
of poppies and cold water, the dark
rinds, the thimbles glinting in
the half-light, the wide-meshed gauze,

the blunt ivory tiles, the black bees
in their box.

The invalids, swathed in linen, lie raw
and alive under the white. Bodies
rotate slowly, buttons that fastened
fall off and skitter across parquet,
palm presses palm. Then, the clink of tiles,
pressure of bone on bone, black juice
of cherries. And across the eyelid,
the shadow of the black bee.

CAROLYN FORCHÉ

Taking Off My Clothes

I take off my shirt, I show you
I shaved the hair out under my arms
I roll up my pants, I scraped off the hair
on my legs with a knife, getting white.

My hair is the color of chopped maples
My eyes are dark as beans cooked in the south
(Coal fields in the moon on torn up hills)

Skin as polished as a Ming bowl
showing its blood cracks, its age, I have hundreds
of names for the snow, for this, all of them quiet.

In the night I come to you and it seems a shame
to waste my deepest shudders on a wall of a man.

You recognize strangers,
think you lived through destruction.
You can't explain this night, my face, your memory.

You want to know what I know?
Your own hands are lying.

Kalaloch

Bleached wood massed in bone piles,
we pulled it from dark beach and built
fire in a fenced clearing.

Wood stubs were sunk down,
they circled and were roofed by milled
lumber dragged at one time to the coast.
We slept there.

Each morning the minus tide—
weeds flowed it like hair swimming.
Starfish gripped rock, pastel, rough.
Fish bones lay in sun.

Each noon milk fog sank
from cloud cover, came in
our clothes, held them
tighter on us. Sea stacks
stood and disappeared.
They came back when the sun
scrubbed out the inlet.

We went down to piles to get
mussels. I made my shirt a bowl
of mussel stones and carted them
to our grate where they smoked apart.
I pulled the mussel lip bodies out,
chewed their squeak.
We went up the path for freshwater,
berries. Hardly speaking, thinking.

During low tide we crossed
to the island, climbed
its wet summit. The red foots
and pelicans dropped for fish.
The oclets so silent fell
toward water with linked feet.

Jacynthe said little,
her tuk pulled down her hair, long
since we had spoken *Nova Scotia, Michigan*

and knew beauty in saying nothing.
She told me about her mother who would
come at them with bread knives then stop
herself, her face emptied.

I told her about me,
never lied. At night
at times the moon floated.
We sat with arms tight
watching flames spit and snap.
On stone and sand, picking up
wood shaped like a body, like a gull.

I ran barefoot not only
on beach but harsh gravels
up through the woods.
I shit easy, covered my dropping.
Some nights no fires, we watched
the sea pucker and get stabbed
by the beacon
circling on Tatoosh.

II

I stripped and spread
on the sea lip, stretched
to the slap of the foam
and the vast red dulce.
Jacynthe gripped the earth
in her fists, opened—
the boil of the tide
shuffled into her.

The beach revolved,
headlands behind us
put their pines in the sun.
Gulls turned a strong sky.

Their pained wings held,
they bit water quick, lifted.
Their looping eyes continually
measure the distance from us,
bare women who do not touch.

Rocks drowsed, holes filled
with suds from a distance.
A deep laugh bounced
in my flesh and sprayed her.

III

Flies crawled us,
Jacynthe crawled.
With her palms she
spread my calves, she
moved my heels from each other.
A woman's mouth is
not different, sand moved
wild beneath me, her long
hair wiped my legs, with women
there is sucking, the water
slops our bodies. We come
clean, our clits beat like
twins to the loons rising up.

We are awake.
Snails sprinkle our gulps,
fish die in our grips, there is
sand in the anus of dancing.
Tatoosh island
hardens in the distance.
We see its empty stones
sticking out of the sea again.
Jacynthe holds tinder
under fire to cook the night's wood.

If we had men I would make
milk in me simply. She
is quiet. *I like that you*
cover your teeth.

Burning The Tomato Worms

That from whence these things are born
That by which when born they live
That into which at their deaths they reenter
Try to know that

Now the pines lift
Linking their dark spines
Weak clouds fly the breaks like pelicans
over ploughed land.

During thick fields of american wind
Between apples and the first snow
In the horse breath weather I remember her

II

Before I was born, my body as snowfat
Crept over Wakhan
As grandfathers spat into fires and thawed
Their tarpaulin
Sending crackled paths of blood
Down into my birth

Their few logs were sleeves of fire
Twists of smoke still brush
Out of the ice where they died

III

Anna's hands were like wheat rolls
Shelling snow peas, anna's hands
Are both dead, they were uzbek
Uzbek hands known for weaving fine rugs.

Eat Bread and Salt and Speak the Truth

She was asking me to go with her
To the confrontation of something
That was sacred and eternal
It was a timeless, timeless thing
Nothing of her old age or of my childhood
Came between us

IV

Her footsteps bloodied the snow
Through the louver, bread smoke left
The wood skin whitened

When time come
We go quick
I think
What to take

On her back the ground wheat and straw dolls
In the sack the white cheese and duck blood

Mother of God
I tell you this
Dushenka
You work your life
You have nothing

V

I came down from her in south Michigan
Picture the resemblance

Now I squint out over the same fields scraped in sun
Now I burn the tomato worms and string the useless
  gords

She had drawn apple skin
Tightly bent feet
Pulled babushkas and rosary beads
On which she paid for all of us

She knew how much grease
How deep to seed
That cukes were crawlers

Every morning at five she would market
Or wake me to pick and hoe, the crows
Cacking between us, Slovakia swear words
Whenever I stopped to feed them

This is the way we have it
Light a glass of candles
Heavy sweatered winter woman
Buried the october before I was grown

VI

She would take her gladiolas to the priest
Like sword sprouts they fumed near her bed

After raising my father and nine others
In a foreign country
Find yourself a good man
Get married
There is nothing left

Before we have a village
Across the slovakian border
Now
There is no slovakia

Before we dance like gypsies
Listen
You young yet

VII

And still the china virgin
Plugs in below the mantelpiece, lights up
Pointing at her own heart
Big as a fist and full of daggers

I get down on my knees with every other slavic woman
And we speak the language

VIII

She took up against her hoe stick and watched the moon
She could hear snow touching the chopped wood
Her room smelled of advent candles
Her face was clung with cake flour

IX

Between apples and the first snow
In the horse breath weather
Birds form the wind
Hoarse dogs are chained to the ground
So there is dog dung where once
There were ditches burning

And I wish she were alive
But she is big under the ground
Dead. I walk to the eastern market
A half block, under october suns that move away
Women still there selling summer squash
But always more die

X

Moons fill with blood nights
Crab walking to the northeast
My mother has left the garden cover
With quack, in first frost
We lug tomatoes in worms and all

XI

Stiff air, same color as a child's vein
Rigid against the freezing curls of birch bark
The snow's round thaw at fence post bases
Snow deep across the yard
Ice grunting with boot heels
And a small sun an inch across like blood
On the frost when some trap
Chomps down a rabbit
And his dark eyes seem to wait for dogs

XII

I chew up my gloves on the way to the barn
I wait in the pony stall for a boy
To come and circle his tongue in my mouth
While the stud horse muds floor boards
Beside us

Bales of feed split beneath our bellies
Our jacket zippers flush open, we wait
Like nothing, for tires to grind past
Beside us
Over the new fall in the road

All day landing knives in the backside of the shed
He waits for me
Winter light spreading out in our houses

His own father downing a shot of Four Roses
Playing songs on a comb and Kleenex

When you hear them hoot owls hollerin
It's a sign of rain

XIII

Flakes wind around us and seep out
I want to ask you why I live
And we go back apart across the field
Why I am here and will have to feel the way I die

It was all over my face
Grandma flipped the kolačy rolls
Dunked her hands in bowls of water
Looked at me
Wrung the rags into the stoop
Kept it from me
Whatever she saw

KATHLEEN FRASER

What You Need

What you need is
a compliment to plump you up

tired ass down flat to blue chair
(supposed to be a touch of brightness)
yes
your mind jumped at *that* when she said how are you
and you tried not to tell

but to be a sample and a dimple
and finding the proper response to goodness, to a really
kind question.

And then he handed it to you,
the quick observation that you looked beautiful and oh
your heart let go a spurt,
a little thin skin cracked and loosened,

propelled yourself up the hill and into the ladies & gents
and cookies
tasting of wallpaper paste . . . your ideal in her perfect
suit went by
and glad you'd sewn the button on at the last.

You are alone but don't listen.

All of literature rains down lots of commas.

And even feel fine most evenings, sliding into the
flowered sheets
so relieved to have your spreading to all corners two
could fit in easily.

Bones fall gently towards the floor, you sleep with
regular breathing.

It's the unexplained wakings and where they leave you.

In a clearing
with someone who loved you
alive in the dark.

You are brave. But you need to be touched.

Casa de Pollos

The August wind rides Spain tonight in a fierce saddle,
its maddened spurs of weather jabbing me on
to the chicken lady's house, where the inside roof is pink
and the rafters hang with yellow feet of hens,
the silenced beaks, the glazed eyes of young cocks.

I pass through her door; the chicken lady darts
through the room in a trail of blood and dries
her red hands on a splattered apron front.
Her collar is a ruff of white feathers that fits
tightly around her neck, screws her eyes
to quick yellow jots of chicken feed.
"We celebrate love, tonight," I tell her,
clutching my purse with its coins for sweet chicken.
"We want rooster flesh tonight," I say,
tasting its strut already, and its hot blood.

Her hands are yellow claws. She carries them
to the coop, concealed like weapons,
and curls them around the neck of a shrieking cock.
"The wind is a white chicken wing," she says,
"for death to flap in on. But I carry the knife."

Poem in Which My Legs Are Accepted

Legs!
How we have suffered each other,
never meeting the standards of magazines
or official measurements.

I have hung you from trapezes,
sat you on wooden rollers,
pulled and pushed you
with the anxiety of taffy,
and still, you are yourselves!

Most obvious imperfection, blight on my fantasy life,
strong,
plump,
never to be skinny
or even hinting of the svelte beauties in history books
or Sears catalogues.
Here you are—solid, fleshy and
white as when I first noticed you, sitting on the toilet,
spread softly over the wooden seat,
having been with me only twelve years,
yet
as obvious as the legs of my thirty-year-old gym teacher.

Legs!
Oh that was the year we did acrobatics in the annual
gym show.
How you split for me!
One-handed cartwheels
from this end of the gymnasium to the
other,
ending in double splits,
legs you flashed in blue rayon slacks my mother bought
for the occasion

and though you were confidently swinging along,
the rest of me blushed at the sound of clapping.

Legs!
How I have worried about you, not able to hide you,
embarrassed at beaches, in high school
when the cheerleaders' slim brown legs
spread all over
the sand
with the perfection
of bamboo.
I hated you, and still you have never given out on me.

With you
I have risen to the top of blue waves,
with you
I have carried food home as a loving gift
when my arms began un-
jelling like madrilène.
Legs, you are a pillow,
white and plentiful with feathers for his wild head.
You are the endless scenery
behind the tense sinewy elegance of his two dark legs.
You welcome him joyfully
and dance.
And you will be the locks in a new canal between
continents.
The ship of life will push out of you
and rejoice
in the whiteness,

in the first floating and rising of
water.

TESS GALLAGHER

Kidnaper

He motions me over with a question.
He is lost. I believe him. It seems
he calls my name. I move
closer. He says it again, the name
of someone he loves. I step back pretending

not to hear. I suspect
the street he wants
does not exist, but I am glad to point
away from myself. While he turns
I slip off my wristwatch, already laying a trail
for those who must find me
tumbled like an abandoned car
into the ravine. I lie

without breath for days among ferns.
Pine needles drift
onto my face and breasts
like the tiny hands
of watches. Cars pass.
I imagine it's him
coming back. My death
is not needed. The sun climbs again
for everyone. He lifts me
like a bride

and the leaves fall from my shoulders
in twenty-dollar bills.
"You must have been cold," he says
covering me with his handkerchief.
"You must have given me up."

The Horse In The Drugstore

wants to be admired.
He no longer thinks of what he has given up
to stand here, the milk-white reason
of chickens over his head in the night, the grass
spilling on through the day. No, it is enough
to stand so with his polished chest among the nipples
and bibs, the cotton and multiple sprays, with his
    black lips
parted just slightly and the forehooves doubled back
in the lavender air. He has learned here when maligned
    to snort
dimes and to carry the inscrutable bruise like a bride.

Breasts

The day you came
this world got its hold on me.
Summer grass and the four of us pounding hell
out of each other for god knows what
green murder of the skull.
Swart nubbins, I noticed you then,
my mother shaking a gritty rag from the porch
to get my shirt on this minute. Brothers,
that was the parting of our ways, for then
you got me down by something else than flesh.
By the loose skin of a cotton shirt
you kept me to the ground
until the bloody gout hung in my face like a web.

Little mothers, I can't find your children.
I have looked in a man

who moved through the air like a god.
He brought me clouds
and the loose stars of his goings.
Another kissed me on a pier in Georgia
but there was blood on his hands,
bad whiskey in the wind. The last one,
he made me a liar until I stole
what I could not win. Loves,
what is this mirror you have left me in?

I could have told you at the start
there would be trouble
from other hands, how the sharp mouths
would find you where you slept.
But I have hurt you as certainly
with cold sorrowings as anyone,
have come the long way
over broken ground to this softness.
Good clowns, how could I know, all along
it was your blundering mercies kept me alive
when heaven was a luckless dream.

Stepping Outside

for Akhmatova

Hearing of you, I never lost a brother
though I have, never saw a husband to war,
though I have, never kept with my father
the emptiness of his hands, my mother
the dying of her womb.

Return: husbands, sons, fathers return.
Many with both arms, with dreams

broken in both eyes.
They try, they try
but they cannot tell us
what comes back with them.

One more has planted his hoe
in my heart like an ax, my farmer uncle
slain by thieves
in the night, burned down
with his house, buried, dug up
to prove he was no dog.
He was no dog.

You, who lived in your pain until it grew
its own face, would have left all this
like a monument in a field. Your words
would have made a feast of what ate you.

Sit with me.
No one has left; no one returns.

GARY GILDNER

First Practice

After the doctor checked to see
we weren't ruptured,
the man with the short cigar took us
under the grade school,
where we went in case of attack
or storm, and said
he was Clifford Hill, he was
a man who believed dogs
ate dogs, he had once killed
for his country, and if
there were any girls present
for them to leave now.
                                        No one
left. OK, he said, he said I take
that to mean you are hungry
men who hate to lose as much
as I do. OK. Then
he made two lines of us
facing each other,
and across the way, he said,
is the man you hate most
in the world,
and if we are to win
that title I want to see how.
But I don't want to see
any marks when you're dressed,
he said. He said, *Now.*

Digging for Indians

The first week the soil was clean,
except for a shrew's lobster-
colored jaw, a bull snake caught
in its long final bellow,
and an ocher mouse holding
its head, as if our trowels had given it
a migraine. Then we hit bird-bone
beads, clam shells,

and then we struck a spine.
Digging slowly we followed it
north, toward a stand of cottonwood
overlooking the river and, beyond,
a patch of abandoned pickups and plows
taking the sun.
We stopped
below the shoulder blades for lunch.

Then we resumed, working down
and into the body,
now paring
the dirt like exotic fruit,
now picking between the ribs
as if they were bad teeth
aching with impacted meat.
We were dripping wet,

and slapping at sweat bees
attacking the salt
on our backs—
but he was taking shape,
he was beginning to look,
as his pelvis came through,

like a man. We uncovered
his thighs and brittle, tapering feet,

and then we went for his skull.
Shaving close, slicing off
worms that curlicued
like brains out of place,
we unearthed his hollow expression,
his bony brow,
and finally, in back of his neck,
an arrowhead stuck to the vertebrae.

The ground rumbled under our knees—
Quickly we got the Polaroid
and snapped him from several angles—
except for the scattered fingers
we could not have planned a better specimen . . .
Then we wrapped him up in foil.
Tomorrow we would make a plaster cast,
and hang it in the junior college.

Meeting the Reincarnation Analyst

I guess because it was Key West
and I was a little drunk
I expected some ridiculous facsimile
of Sidney Greenstreet, puffing hard, to slip
through the beaded curtains first—
to set me up with secrets smirking
on his sweaty mug.

But nobody like that came in
to the Immortality Consultation Room

off Whitehead Street that smelled
of incense, salt, and cat shit—
just Patricia Peel, Ph.D.,
the mystic in a flaming beehive
hairdo, teardrop earrings, and a sheet.

She offered me her hand—snakes and snappers,
swordfish, flies and eyeballs
—these were on the rings
her fingers wiggled at me.
On the middle knuckle of her middle
finger, dominating all the fauna,
was a baby's skull, in gold.
I kissed her blue-veined wrist.

She said, "Please sit"—
and pointed to the satin sofa.
At my side she opened up her sheet
to show a copper cross inlaid
with writhing octopuses
hanging down between her breasts.
"You have," she said, "six former lives
and many, many Karmic ties—"

I interrupted: "Have you really got a Ph.D.?"
She continued, "—and in each past life
you loved an evil woman."
The first, reported Dr. Peel, was a Carib maiden
taken by Cortez to entertain him
on the voyage back to Spain . . .
"She succumbed to lust, disease, and worms."

My mystic gripped her cross.
"The second girl, a Salem witch,
accused of lying down with pigs—"
"Hey wait a minute," I said.
But Dr. Peel spoke on, her eyes

as hard and green as early walnuts,
killing off my Salem witch by stuffing
down her throat her lovers' testicles.

An octoroon of Jefferson's
who later slept with Madison,
and a Cajun who was burned
alive with John Wilkes Booth
were my ladies three and four
and I had had it. I dropped
the Consultation fee in Patty's lap, and left.

That night, in my air-conditioned Holiday,
I showered with a smiling bonefish—
then fixed a gin and tonic,
and watched debilitated Ponce de León
arrive in Florida at Eastertide
above my bed. Oh, I'd love to say
she came around without her junk,
and that we had a laugh, and maybe
even said what we were looking for.
But the truth is no one came,
and the next day I moved on.

The Life of the Wolf

Surrounded by tigers,
pandas, and piles
of marked-down sweat-
shirts, by blown-up gnus
chewing their cuds and clerks
huddled like pocket mice,

he presses *The Life
of the Wolf* to his coat

and trembles to own it,
to have hairy feet
and impossibly keen
hearing, and to move

mainly by moonlight.
His cousins, the coyote
and kit fox, would call him
swift, and sheep
dreaming his jaws,
dreaming his rangy legs

would swoon in their fur
at his touch.
A most faithful beast,
if the right female
pricked up the hairs on his neck
he would mate forever.

For her he would tear out
the best meat, give her silver
pups to suckle, and tackle
ranchers if the moose and caribou,
the deer and elk gave out.
On rainy nights in the den

he would treat her to rhythms:
"Delicate little dik-diks
scamper on the savannah"—
and she would roll over,
rubbing his side as if lost
in the ripest flesh.

Or maybe he'd fall for a collie,
and get shot forsaking safety
in the outskirts—
and she too would get shot

going for the killer's, her owner's,
throat in revenge . . .

And they'd all die out,
as in fact they were,
unable to find a place in the country,
a place away from men
riding shotgun in low-
flying planes . . .

With only their ghosts
on the shelves,
reduced and filled
with stuffing,
with fake gray fur
and satin ribbons.

LOUISE GLÜCK

All Hallows

Even now this landscape is assembling.
The hills darken. The oxen
sleep in their blue yoke,
the fields having been
picked clean, the sheaves
bound evenly and piled at the roadside
among cinquefoil, as the toothed moon rises:

This is the barrenness
of harvest or pestilence.
And the wife leaning out the window
with her hand extended, as in payment,
and the seeds
distinct, gold, calling
Come here
Come here, little one

And the soul creeps out of the tree.

Gretel in Darkness

This is the world we wanted.
All who would have seen us dead
are dead. I hear the witch's cry
break in the moonlight through a sheet
of sugar: God rewards.
Her tongue shrivels into gas . . .

Now, far from women's arms
and memory of women, in our father's hut
we sleep, are never hungry.
Why do I not forget?
My father bars the door, bars harm
from this house, and it is years.

No one remembers. Even you, my brother,
summer afternoons you look at me as though
you meant to leave,
as though it never happened.
But I killed for you. I see armed firs,
the spires of that gleaming kiln—

Nights I turn to you to hold me
but you are not there.
Am I alone? Spies
hiss in the stillness, Hansel,
we are there still and it is real, real,
that black forest and the fire in earnest.

The School Children

The children go forward with their little satchels.
And all morning the mothers have labored
to gather the late apples, red and gold,
like words of another language.

And on the other shore
are those who wait behind great desks
to receive these offerings.

How orderly they are—the nails
on which the children hang
their overcoats of blue or yellow wool.

And the teachers shall instruct them in silence
and the mothers shall scour the orchards
for a way out,
drawing to themselves the gray limbs of the fruit trees
bearing so little ammunition.

The Racer's Widow

The elements have merged into solicitude.
Spasms of violets rise above the mud
And weed and soon the birds and ancients
Will be starting to arrive, bereaving points
South. But never mind. It is not painful to discuss
His death. I have been primed for this,
For separation, for so long. But still his face assaults
Me, I can hear that car careen again, the crowd
coagulate on asphalt
In my sleep. And watching him, I feel my legs like snow
That let him finally let him go
As he lies draining there. And see
How even he did not get to keep that lovely body.

Phenomenal Survivals of Death in Nantucket

I

Here in Nantucket does the tiny soul
Confront water. Yet this element is not foreign soil;

I see the water as extension of my mind,
The troubled part, and waves the waves of mind
When in Nantucket they collapsed in epilepsy
On the bare shore. I see
A shawled figure when I am asleep who says, "Our lives
Are strands between the miracles of birth
And death. I am Saint Elizabeth.
In my basket are knives."
Awake I see Nantucket, the familiar earth.

II

Awake I see Nantucket but with this bell
Of voice I can toll you token of regions below visible:
On the third night came
A hurricane; my Saint Elizabeth came
Not and nothing could prevent the rent
Craft from its determined end. Waves dent-
ed with lightning launched my loosed mast
To fly downward, I following. They do not tell
You but bones turned coral still smell
Amid forsaken treasure. I have been past
What you hear in a shell.

III

Past what you hear in a shell, the roar,
Is the true bottom: infamous calm. The doctor
Having shut the door sat me down, took ropes
Out of reach, firearms, and with high hopes
Promised that Saint Elizabeth carried
Only foodstuffs or some flowers for charity, nor was I
  buried
Under the vacation island of Nantucket where
Beach animals dwell in relative compatibility and peace.
Flies, snails. Asleep I saw these
Beings as complacent angels of the land and air.
When dawn comes to the sea's

IV

Acres of shining white body in Nantucket
I shall not remember otherwise but wear a locket
With my lover's hair inside
And walk like a bride, and wear him inside.
From these shallows expands
The mercy of the sea.
My first house shall be built on these sands,
My second in the sea.

The Garden

1 *The Fear of Birth*

One sound. Then the hiss and whir
of houses gliding into their places.
And the wind
leafs through the bodies of animals—

But my body that could not content itself
with health—why should it be sprung back
into the chord of sunlight?

It will be the same again.
This fear, this inwardness,
until I am forced into a field
without immunity
even to the least shrub that walks
stiffly out of the dirt, trailing
the twisted signature of its root,
even to a tulip, a red claw.

And then the losses,
one after another,
all supportable.

2 *The Garden*

The garden admires you.
For your sake it smears itself with green pigment,
the ecstatic reds of the roses,
so that you will come to it with your lovers.

And the willows—
see how it has shaped these green
tents of silence. Yet
there is still something you need,

your body, so soft, so alive, among the stone
  animals.

Admit that it is terrible to be like them,
beyond harm.

3 *The Fear of Love*

That body lying beside me like obedient stone—
once its eyes seemed to be opening,
we could have spoken.

At that time it was winter already.
By day the sun rose in its helmet of fire
and at night also, mirrored in the moon.
Its light passed over us freely,
as though we had lain down
in order to leave no shadows,
only these two shallow dents in the snow.
And the past, as always, stretched before us,
still, complex, impenetrable.

How long did we lie there,
as, arm in arm in their cloaks of feathers,
the gods walked down
from the mountain we built for them.

4 *Origins*

As though a voice were saying
You should be asleep by now—
But there was no one. Nor
had the air darkened,
though the moon was there,
already filled in with marble.

As though, in a garden crowded with flowers,
a voice had said
How dull they are, these golds,
so sonorous, so repetitious
until you closed your eyes,
lying among them, all
stammering flame:

And yet you could not sleep,
poor body, the earth
still clinging to you—

5 *The Fear of Burial*

In the empty field, in the morning,
the body waits to be claimed.
The spirit sits beside it, on a small rock—
nothing comes to give it form again.

Think of the body's loneliness.
At night pacing the sheared field,
its shadow buckled tightly around.
Such a long journey.
And already the remote trembling lights
  of the village
not pausing for it as they scan the rows.
How far away they seem,
the wooden doors, the bread and milk
laid like weights on the table.

LINDA GREGG

The Girl I Call Alma

The girl I call Alma who is so white
is good, isn't she? Even though she does not speak
you can tell by her distress that she is
just like the beach and the sea, isn't she?
And she is disappearing, isn't that good?
And the white curtains and the secret smile
are just her way with lies, aren't they?
And that we are not alone, ever.
And that everything is backward
otherwise.
And that inside the no is the yes. Isn't it?
Isn't it? And that she is the god who perishes:
the food we eat, the body we fuck,
the looseness we throw out that gathers her.
Fish! Fish! White sun! Tell me that we are one
and that it's the others who scar me
not you.

We Manage Most When We Manage Small

What things are steadfast? Not the birds.
Not the bride and groom who hurry
in their brevity to reach one another.
The stars do not blow away as we do.
The heavenly things ignite and freeze.
But not as my hair falls before you.

Fragile and momentary, we continue.
Fearing madness in all things huge
and their requiring. Managing as thin light
on water. Managing only greetings
and farewells. We love a little, as the mice
huddle, as the goat leans against my hand.
As the lovers quickening, riding time.
Making safety in the moment. This touching
home goes far. This fishing in the air.

Sigismundo

The fete confused me. Guests played the part of gods.
There was a woman with white skin who stood
with her pale green robe open all night throwing roses.
A lady caught me in the only quiet room and demanded
I take her to him. I refused even when she begged.
And went down by the sea and thought of something else.
Sun broke that morning on the torches.
Cool air over the tepid sea. Sigismundo the Beautiful.
Out for himself. Killer of cities.
Killer of wife before breakfast. Sigismundo,
who built a church to a woman who was not beautiful,
with roses cut in the stone.
Whose dream was to resurrect the goddesses.
All through my boyhood I was told I'd walk hand in
hand
with death. Chose the good and cried
when I saw how they marred the statues.
But there is nothing, nothing to say about my life.
Unmerciful Sigismundo did many wrongs and his people
loved him
and he will live forever. I who go down like Persephone
with my accomplishments of silence and weeping
unrecorded,

even I if I were a girl would answer Yes, I know how to
swim,
for a chance to drown in that blue water of his.
Sigismundo.

The Beckett Kit

I finally found a way of using the tree.
If the man is lying down with the sheep
while the dog stands, then the wooden tree
can also stand, in the back, next to the dog.

They show their widest parts
(the dog sideways, the tree frontal)
so that being next to each other
they function as a landscape.

I tried for nearly two months to use the tree.
I tried using it by putting the man,
standing of course, very far from the sheep
but in more or less the same plane.
At one point I had the man almost off the table
and still couldn't get the tree to work.
It was only just now I thought of a way.

I dropped the wooden sheep from a few inches
above the table so they wouldn't bounce.
Some are on their backs but they serve
the same as the ones standing.
What I can't get over is their coming right
inadvertently when I'd be content with any solution.

Ah world, I love you with all my heart.
Outside the open window, down the street near the
Hudson,

I can hear a policeman talking to another
through the car radio. It's eleven stories down
so it must be pretty loud.
The sheep, the tree, the dog and the man
are perfectly at peace. And my peace is at peace.
Time and the earth lie down wonderfully together.

The blacks probably do rape the whites in jail
as Bill said in the coffee shop watching the game
between Oakland and Cincinnati. And no doubt
Karl was right that we should have volunteered
as victims under the bombing of Hanoi.

A guy said to Mishkin, "If you've seen all that,
how can you go on saying you're happy?"

MARILYN HACKER

Presentation Piece

About the skull of the beloved, filled
with unlikely innocence, liver pâté,
tidbits in aspic. You were never
anybody's "lover," should live
in staterooms full of temporary homage.
The corridor slants, cradled on the
crest of an
earthquake. Far above, smokestacks
proceed through badlands of snapped bridges.

About the skull of the beloved, filled
with a perilous remedy, sloshing
into the corners of the damp eyes
where you are reflected, twice, upside
down. The last image before
death is recorded photographically
on the retina for half an hour.
Prints can be made. The darkroom
is at the end of the corridor.

"These are worlds that were his thighs." You are
the assistant purser, translating
and filing telegraphic messages. "Arriving
Thursday 2 PM." "Take another little
piece of my heart now baby." "Armed and awaiting
signal before tides change." One of the messages
may be for you. "In an affluent society
cannibalism
is a sexual predilection."

That is not fresh meat. It was kept overnight
in a tub of brine. Hand remembers
the ribs' wet parting, the heavy pulse on the palm.
This is not the door to the engine room
though a pulse whines in the walls.
Green velvet ropes enlace a green
velvet chaise-longue, beneath
the purple jewels of the parvenu
empress. Meet me tonight under your tongue.

There is no easy way up. Bite
on your lip; do you taste what I do?
A gold skewer
pierces and joins his hands; the handle
is a five-leafed rose. Let me live
in your mouth; I know a place
where the earlobe is imperfectly joined to the skull.
At sunrise
we can look across the wasted sea for miles.

Aube Provençale

Absent, this morning
the cock crowed later than the nine o'clock
church bells. Cherry boughs
bronzed outside the casement,
and I woke

sweating, with my hands
between my thighs, from a dream
of archives, wanting you
under me, my breasts hollowed in the arc
below your ribs,

my knees between your knees,
my hands behind your ears, my cheek
furrowed in your chest, tasting
our mingled night-sweat, tasting
your sleep.

I'll make a song
on your neck-cords. Wake up,
bird asleep against my hip-bone,
and crow, it's already
morning.

Villanelle

for D.G.B

Every day our bodies separate,
exploded torn and dazed.
Not understanding what we celebrate

we grope through languages and hesitate
and touch each other, speechless and amazed;
and every day our bodies separate

us farther from our planned, deliberate
ironic lives. I am afraid, disphased,
not understanding what we celebrate

when our fused limbs and lips communicate
the unlettered power we have raised.
Every day our bodies' separate

routines are harder to perpetuate.
In wordless darkness we learn wordless praise,
not understanding what we celebrate;

wake to ourselves, exhausted, in the late
morning as the wind tears off the haze,
not understanding how we celebrate
our bodies. Every day we separate.

Before the War

We are asleep under mirrors. What do I
look like? Your mouth
opens on a dream of altered landscapes.
Hidden in the Iron Mountains,
the adolescent general is in love
with you. Noon light stands in the window,
cloudy and white. They are using mustard gas.
That night child anarchists besieged the corners.
Tin cans exploded in front of us; rhythm
escaped in the blistered rain. Everyone
was hungry. You sound
like that in the morning, someone
told her on the telephone, and all
the bar heard it Friday night.
Culled from a garden in Pacific Heights,
the charred corpse of her last lover, ankles crossed
at a vulnerable and tender angle,
embellishes the service porch
above an architecture of dead boys.
It happens every morning at the gas
station while we are still asleep
around the pillow like a third lover.
Covered in burning Saran Wrap,
the young attendant knocks the telephone
off the hook, crashes through
the plate-glass window
and flames out like a screaming Bunsen burner

under the open hood of a '39
Renault sedan. I wake up with your elbow
under my neck. Come here.
Tell me what that eruption on the sun
is.

After the Revolution

There are different ways of dying without
actually dying. I was nineteen.
So was Milo. Pavel was twenty-two. The square
was hotter than this beach; the no-man's land
between July and October
when anything can happen
                                        and nothing does.
They searched me. Nothing. They left me behind.
Every touch threatened; not the way a boy's
skin tingles to be touched.
                                    If the gift leaves?
Might as well die.
                            I woke up with that line
and a bad temper. We waited
to see them on those balconies
as if they were girls.
                                I hardly know you:
an approximate age, oiled skin,
stones in the sun. We smelled each other.
Fear, yes. And, then, they had touched me.
So we waited. Are you a journalist?
I hope not. Why does it come down to
language? Pressures of bright air
over that other city; incipient autumn
swelled red and yellow skins. An instrument
incises the rough bark (feel it

signalling in the palm's crutch) thick sap
oozes amber marbled cream, the instant's
crystal, for the cabinet, crammed
with history. There are
unchronicled moments, the plane tree
knifed on the air in the square court.
The boys waited.
                                        We waited.
                                                                  Dear friend; I am trying
to organize my expedition towards
the source.
                    Every bedizened traveller
retailing gossip in the Market with
chunks of dark amber, angels enamelled on tin,
makes me believe I can discover, if not
the actual "lake between three purple mountains,"
above the falls, at least some old bachelor
with odd tastes, some witch's brat daughter,
who has been there, or claims it, and will show
(but not sell) a pebble, a dried herb
that smells like copper and quince . . . If I do not
come back, if I disprove your theory
in a large-circulation periodical
or anything equally tasteless, remember
this note, and the token
I enclose.
                    I will not be able
to lunch with you on Saturday.
                                                                  Sincerely,
Dear friend;
                      Perhaps you will understand
when I say, I can no longer tolerate
this city . . . No . . . The two young nuns
whom we once watched strolling in the cloister
through the gap in the wall . . . if I said, their gait
seemed peculiar; if I added
the ostensible boy poet lodged

in what was Mother's room has got a pattern
to his intensities . . . I will not be
drawn into events that I cannot
control or understand. These things concern
soldiers, economists, geographers,
but I will not be made historical
by chance. Good-bye. Perhaps you know
more of this than I do, have considered
the possibility of my . . . retreat.
I must miss you on Saturday.
                                        Yours faithfully,
Read it back. Tell me what I said.
                                        Words.
The body's heavy syllables. Touch me.
Say. Nerves said, You will begin
to finish dying. The children are running away.
They are hiding in the gorse bushes. They
dribble your inner thigh. They are throwing
chocolate wrappers from the balcony.
What are they whispering? Tell me.
                                        Milo remembered
a child on the beach, a fox-faced little girl
carving something from driftwood. It was late August,
early evening. He was nineteen. He gave her
half his cheese and two tomatoes. She was carving
an old woman in a shawl. Cheese brine
on her fingers stained the dry wood. Her hair
was cropped against lice, gold stubble on her neck.
I thought of touching her there. It was not
Milo, it was I. The salt still on her mouth.
Pavel had a stolen rifle. Milo
had an American pistol. You are not
a journalist?
                    I'm almost twelve
she said. I already have breasts.
I can read French. I read *Madame Bovary*.
If they fire into the crowd, I said. I thought

Pavel would be a handsome grandfather.
We are playing stupid games. I will kiss you, I said,
but I'll never speak to you again
if you tell anyone.
                                        It flowered
his sweaty shirt-front. He crumpled, quizzically,
into the dazed heat. "*Pavel!*"
They searched me. Nothing. They left me behind.
A red ball sun plumbed the translucent water.
She lay on top of me, her knees
rubbing my trunks, her cotton shirt
damp and gritty on my bare chest. Licked salt
off my lips.
                        I looked for Milo for three days.
Dear friend;
                        It was once my language; now I can
barely read it. Even this note
may be written in code.
                                        Yours in haste,
Here comes Pavel with lunch. The children
went crabbing with Milo and Douina. Don't
say anything to Milo . . . his job . . .
you understand. Not
as one might have wished.

DANIEL HALPERN

Street Fire

for Chico

It is past midnight in a thick fog when sirens
call us to the terrace.
We look down onto blossoms of bright fire
opening from manholes on Fifth Avenue.
There are men standing and smoking in rubber jackets
outside a garment district café,
the lights fluttering, the fire
offering us its electric smoke.
In bare feet and robes—the cat
and dog at our feet—we hear
the heat pound tubes stuffed with wire.
And somewhere down there, under the softening
  blacktop,
the gas mains wait to take in the whole block.
We bring the two or three small relics of our lives,
the dog and cat, and the elevator to the street.
There is a cold wind and ice in the gutters.
There is the street's midnight population
leaning against the wall of Reverend Peale's Sunday
  Church.
We note the taxis that deliver strangers
to watch with us as the street shrivels and begins
to flow around the manhole covers.
They are all there: men of the brigade, the police,
women from nearby hotels, their furred men,
the strangers from the city.
What we see is the tip of the iceberg,
they tell us—and underneath
the tubes alive with flames.
For an hour we watch from the corner—

in this weather tragedies are distant.
The elevator back up contains the momentary explosion
in the eye where disasters flare—
our section of New York, between the flowers and furs,
is full of bright red petals.
We reach the ninth floor and step into air
powdered with radiator heat.
The tiny, muffled beats of fire below the street
pant through the window an even pulse.
The dog moves into the living room where the fire is dying
on bricks. The cat takes the warm tiles
of the bathroom. We stand silently, listen
a few minutes, then move to each other.
Our own fire is watered by the conviction
that things are right. Later, we listen to the small puffs
of heat spit from the manholes outside, smell
the smoke from live wires
bound with rubber that smolders into morning.

Fish

She is washed by white-water, white if she looked up.
She fingers the pebbles. This fancy of water for her,
touched now only by surf
and the grey temples of kelp.
There is a single boy in a caique,
his drop line and the fish that moves off,
hooked, thinking itself free
with the taste of silver. The fish
is not destined to return with flesh of the hunt.
It moves for the woman on the beach without reason.
Its smooth body takes on the legs of the boy
in shallow water, grows a face

and stands in air, breathing
as if for the first time, and walks
to where the woman waits.
As the boy begins to sink the fish touches the woman
on her hair that spreads upon her shoulders.
The kelp is green in the shallows beyond the breakers.
The fish now tall in the light, the woman's hair, yellow
from the cliffs over her shoulders.
The boy descending. The woman looking up.
The fish bending to touch her.

The Landing

Out here a woman wonders.
And if she has no man
her arms get strong.
—Carolyn Forché

On the prow,
standing on red planks,
the white maiden holds
hand to temple,
faint, keening.
The fog snags the edge
of her gown, dissolves
it at the ankle, begins
for thighs, for breasts
unlike white stone, her
neck, and then her
lips like white stone.
She sees scrub, dabbed
on a mountain, its peak
thrust through the layer of air-cloth.
There are sirens of anger in the air
that call to trees.
Wasps prowl the reef—
the maiden, kneeling now,

watches them,
watches parrot fish bite and snap
for food, lovers
of the vegetable, hanging in kelp beds.
And now, behind her,
behind wasp and siren,
the ship of women prisoners
begins to undo itself.
The fog,
the life's-breath in a cold
climate, lifts.
Their legs are thin and hard
from the voyage, they are wise
progeny of the white maiden
who moves their vessel
past wasps who have given way,
past parrot fish in kelp
with their bright colors
less brilliant than hers,
and onto the wave that rises,
lifts them, lifts them up
level with mountain scrub,
then down
through layers of water,
down to the soft fingers of sand
that are not their fathers
and yet,
and yet take them in.

Summer, 1970

for B.

Now, after a party with the consul and our best friend,
my mother, I walk back to your flat over the Arno
freckled with light, lined by a small wind

or frogs, and hold you in the air of your terrace.
Your black hair a wood scent and dark,
the thickness of pitch or dark amber—
an olfaction of night. We go inside
to comb your hair. You bring brandy, there is glass
on wood, our tongues on fire, the flames licking
the lonely caves of speech by day, together
here, moving quickly in silence. We are
silly in the brillance, the giddy moon
eats your secret, the long upturning of nose
and breast (hydrangeas after water at sunset),
the wedge of light upon the couch
near brandy, and my mouth that calls you, calls you.

The Ethnic Life

I've been after the exotic
For years: champac
And patchouli in air, distant
Root scents, their smoke
Dazing rooms where dark men
Sit on legs
On rugs.

I ride teak trains
Through the Khyber Pass
Into Pakistan, and speak
Tongues I can't write

My wife is young,
She turns to me from the East
After prayer—
Her black hair, her
Eurasian face spreading
Below the long eyes
Like Asian night itself.

On summer evenings before the monsoon
I meet my contortionist
Lover from India
Over Campari.
In her room my eyes roll
To paradise, click
Like a pair of Moroccan dice;
The undoing of her spine
Releases me from mine.

In my life
There is no room
For bikinis or Chanel,
Or the waxed beauty of the West. . .

For years I've lived simply,
Without luxury—
With the soundness of the backward
Where the senses can be heard.

MICHAEL S. HARPER

We Assume: On the Death of Our Son, Reuben Masai Harper

We assume
that in 28 hours,
lived in a collapsible isolette,
you learned to accept pure oxygen
as the natural sky;
the scant shallow breaths
that filled those hours
cannot, did not make you fly—
but dreams were there
like crooked palmprints on
the twin-thick windows of the nursery—
in the glands of your mother.

We assume
the sterile hands
drank chemicals in and out
from lungs opaque with mucus,
pumped your stomach,
eeked the bicarbonate in
crooked, green-winged veins,
out in a plastic mask;

A woman who'd lost her first son
consoled us with an angel gone ahead
to pray for our family—
gone into that sky
seeking oxygen,
gone into autopsy,

a fine brown powdered sugar,
a disposable cremation:

We assume
you did not know we loved you.

Deathwatch

Twitching in the cactus
hospital gown, a loon
on hairpin wings,
she tells me how
her episiotomy
is perfectly sewn
and doesn't hurt
while she sits in a pile
of blood
which once cleaned
the placenta
my third son should be in.
She tells me how early
he is, and how strong,
like his father,
and long, like a black-
stemmed Easter rose
in a white hand.

Just under five pounds
you lie there, a collapsed
balloon doll, burst in your
fifteenth hour, with the face
of your black father,
his fingers, his toes,

and eight voodoo
adrenalin holes in
your pinwheeled hair-lined
chest; you witness
your parents sign the autopsy
and disposal papers
shrunken to duplicate
in black ink
on white paper
like the country
you were born in,
unreal, asleep,
silent, almost alive.

This is a dedication
to our memory
of three sons—
two dead, one alive—
a reminder of a letter
to DuBois
from a student
at Cornell—on behalf
of his whole history class.
The class is confronted
with a question,
and no one—
not even the professor—
is sure of the answer:
"Will you please tell us
whether or not it is true
that negroes
are not able to cry?"

America needs a killing.
America needs a killing.
Survivors will be human.

A Mother Speaks: The Algiers Motel Incident, Detroit

It's too dark to see black
in the windows of Woodward
or Virginia Park.
The undertaker
pushed his body back
into place
with plastic and gum
but it wouldn't
hold water.
When I looked
for marks
or lineament
or fine stitching
I was led away
without seeing
this plastic
face they'd built
that was not my son's.
They tied the eye
torn out
by shotgun
into place
and his shattered
arm cut away
with his buttocks
that remained.
My son's gone
by white hands
though he said
to his last word—
"Oh I'm so sorry,
officer, I broke your gun."

MICHAEL S. HARPER

"Bird Lives": Charles Parker in St. Louis

Last on legs, last on sax,
last in Indian wars, last on *smack*,
Bird is specious, *Bird* is alive,
horn, unplayable, before, after,
right now; it's heroin time:
smack, in the melody a trip;
smack, in the Mississippi;
smack, in the drug merchant trap;
smack, in St. Louis, Missouri.

We knew you were through—
trying to get out of town,
unpaid bills, connections
unmet, unwanted, unasked,
Bird's in the last arc
of his own light: *blow Bird!*
And you did—
screaming, screaming, baby,
for life, after it, around it,
screaming for life, *blow Bird!*

What is the meaning of music?
What is the meaning of war?
What is the meaning of oppression?
Blow Bird! Ripped up and down
into the interior of life, the pain,
Bird, the embraceable you,
how many brothers gone,
smacked out: blues and racism,
the hardest, longest penis
in the Mississippi urinal:
Blow Bird!

Taught more musicians, then forgot,
space loose, fouling the melodies,
the marching songs, the fine white
geese from the plantations,
syrup in this pork barrel,
Kansas City, the even teeth
of the mafia, the big band:
Blow Bird! Inside out Charlie's
guts, *Blow Bird!* get yourself killed.

In the first wave, the musicians,
out there, alone, in the first wave;
everywhere you went, Massey Hall,
Sweden, New Rochelle, *Birdland,*
nameless bird, Blue Note, Carnegie,
tuxedo junction, out of nowhere,
confirmation, confirmation, confirmation:
Bird Lives! Bird Lives! and you do:
Dead—

Dear John, Dear Coltrane

a love supreme, a love supreme
a love supreme, a love supreme

Sex fingers toes
in the marketplace
near your father's church
in Hamlet, North Carolina—
witness to this love
in this calm fallow
of these minds,
there is no substitute for pain:
genitals gone or going,
seed burned out,

you tuck the roots in the earth,
turn back, and move
by river through the swamps,
singing: *a love supreme, a love supreme;*
what does it all mean?
Loss, so great each black
woman expects your failure
in mute change, the seed gone.
You plod up into the electric city—
your song now crystal and
the blues. You pick up the horn
with some will and blow
into the freezing night:
a love supreme, a love supreme—

Dawn comes and you cook
up the thick sin 'tween
impotence and death, fuel
the tenor sex cannibal
heart, genitals and sweat
that makes you clean—
a love supreme, a love supreme—

Why you so black?
cause I am
why you so funky?
cause I am
why you so black?
cause I am
why you so sweet?
cause I am
why you so black?
cause I am
a love supreme, a love supreme:

So sick
you couldn't play *Naima,*

so flat we ached
for song you'd concealed
with your own blood,
your diseased liver gave
out its purity,
the inflated heart
pumps out, the tenor kiss,
tenor love:
a love supreme, a love supreme—
a love supreme, a love supreme—

JIM HARRISON

Sketch for a Job Application Blank

My left eye is blind and jogs like
a milky sparrow in its socket;
my nose is large and never flares
in anger, the front teeth, bucked,
but not in lechery—I sucked
my thumb until the age of twelve.
O my youth was happy and I was never lonely
though my friends called me "pig eye"
and the teachers thought me looney.

> (When I bruised, my psyche kept intact:
> I fell from horses, and once a cow but never
> pigs—A neighbor lost a hand to a sow.)

But I had some fears:
the salesman of eyes
his case was full of fishy baubles,
against black velvet, jeweled gore,
the great cocked hoof of a Belgian mare,
a nest of milk snakes by the water trough,
electric fences
my uncle's hounds,
the pump arm of an oil well,
the chop and whirr of a combine in the sun.

From my ancestors, the Swedes,
I suppose I inherit the love of rainy woods,
kegs of herring and neat whiskey—
I remember long nights of pinochle,
the bulge of Redman in my grandpa's cheek;

the rug smelled of manure and kerosene.
They laughed loudly and didn't speak for days.

(But on the other side, from the German
Mennonites,
their rag smoke prayers and porky daughters
I got intolerance, an aimless diligence.)

In '51 during a revival I was saved:
I prayed on a cold register for hours
and woke up lame. I was baptized
by immersion in the tank at Williamston—
the rusty water stung my eyes.
I left off the old things of the flesh
but not for long—one night beside a pond
she dried my feet with her yellow hair.
O actual event dead quotient
cross become green
I still love Jubal but pity Hagar.

(Now self is the first sacrament
who loves not the misery and taint
of the present tense is lost.
I strain for a lunar arrogance.
Light macerates
the lamp infects
warmth, more warmth, I cry.)

Suite to Fathers

for D.L.

I

I think that night's our balance,
our counterweight—a blind woman
we turn to for nothing but dark.

*

In Val-Mont I see a slab of parchment
a black quill pen in stone.
In a sculptor's garden
there was a head made from stone,
large as a room, the eyes neatly hooded
staring out with a crazed somnolence
fond of walled gardens.

*

The countesses arch like cats in chateaux.
They wake up as countesses and usually sleep with
  counts.
Nevertheless he writes them painful letters,
thinking of Eleanor of Aquitaine, Gaspara Stampa.
With Kappus he calls forth the stone in the rose.

*

In Egypt the dhows sweep the Nile
with ancient sails. I am in Egypt,
he thinks, this Baltic jew—it is hot,
how can I make bricks with no straw?
His own country rich with her food and slaughter,
fit only for sheep and generals.

*

He thinks of the coffin of the East,
of the tiers of dead in Venice,
those countless singulars.
At lunch, the baked apple too sweet with kirsch
becomes the tongues of convent girls at gossip,
under the drum and shadow of pigeons
the girl at promenade has almond in her hair.

*

From Duino, beneath the mist,
the green is so dark and green it cannot bear itself.
In the night, from black paper
I cut the silhouette of this exiled god,
finding him as the bones of a fish in stone.

II

In the cemetery the grass is pale,
fake green as if dumped from Easter baskets,
from overturned clay and the deeper marl
which sits in wet gray heaps by the creek.
There are no frogs, death drains there.
Landscape of glass, perhaps Christ
will quarry you after the worms.
The newspaper says caskets float in leaky vaults.
Above me, I feel paper birds.
The sun is a brass bell.
This is not earth I walk across
but the pages of some giant magazine.

*

Come song,
allow me some eloquence,
good people die.

*

The June after you died
I dove down into a lake,
the water turned to cold, then colder,
and ached against my ears.
I swam under a sunken log then paused,
letting my back rub against it,
like some huge fish with rib cage
and soft belly open to the bottom.
I saw the light shimmering far above
but did not want to rise.

*

It was so far up from the dark—
once it was night three days,
after that four, then six and over again.
The nest was torn from the tree,
the tree from the ground,
the ground itself sinking torn.
I envied the dead their sleep of rot.

I was a fable to myself,
a speech to become meat.

III

Once in Nevada I sat on a boulder at twilight—
I had no ride and wanted to avoid the snakes.
I watched the full moon rise a fleshy red
out of the mountains, out of a distant sandstorm.
I thought then if I might travel deep enough
I might embrace the dead as equals,
not in their separate stillnesses as dead, but in music
one with another's harmonies.
The moon became paler,
rising, floating upwards in her arc
and I with her, intermingled in her whiteness,
until at dawn again she bloodied
herself with earth.

*

In the beginning I trusted in spirits,
slight things, those of the dead in procession,
the household gods in mild delirium
with their sweet round music and modest feasts.
Now I listen only to that hard black core,
a ball harsh as coal, rending for light
far back in my own sour brain.

*

The tongue knots itself
a cramped fist of music,
the oracle a white-walled room of bone
which darkens now with a greater dark;
and the brain a glacier of blood,
inching forward, sliding, the bottom
silt covered but sweet,
becoming a river now

laving the skull with coolness—
the leaves on her surface
dipping against the bone.
*
Voyager, the self the voyage—
dark let me open your lids.
Night stares down with her great bruised eye.

Locations

I want this hardened arm to stop
dragging a cherished image.
—Rimbaud

In the end you are tired of those places,
you're thirty—your only perfect three—
you'll never own another thing.
At night you caress them as if the tongue
turned inward could soothe, head lolling
in its nest of dark, the heart fibrotic,
inedible. Say that on some polar night
an eskimo thinks of his igloo roof, the blocks
of ice sculptured to keep out air, as the roof
of his skull; all that he is, has seen,
is pictured there—thigh with the texture
of the moon, whale's tooth burnished from use
as nothing, fixtures of place some delicate
as a young child's ear, close as snails to earth,
beneath the earth as earthworms, further beneath
as molten rock, into the hollow, vaulted place,
pure heat and pure whiteness,
where earth's center dwells.

You were in Harar but only for a moment,
rifles jostling blue barrels against blue barrels

in the ox cart, a round crater, hot, brown,
a bowl of hell covered with dust.

The angels you sensed in your youth
smelled strongly as a rattlesnake
smells of rotten cucumber, the bear
rising in the glade of ferns of hot fur
and sweat, dry ashes pissed upon.

You squandered your time as a mirror,
you kept airplanes from crashing at your doorstep;
they lifted themselves heavily to avoid your sign,
fizzling like matches in the Atlantic.

You look at Belteguese for the splendor
of her name but she inflames another universe.
Our smallest of suns barely touches earth
in the Gobi, Sahara, Mohavi, Matto Grosso.

Dumb salvages: there is a box made of wood,
cavernous, all good things are kept there,
and if the branches of ice that claw against the window
become hands, that is their business.

Yuma is an unbearable place.
The food has fire in it as
does the brazero's daughter
who serves the food in an orange dress
the color of a mussel's lip.
Outside it is hot as the crevasse
of her buttocks—perfect body temperature.
You have no idea where your body stops
and the heat begins.

On Lake Superior the undertow swallows
a child and no one notices until evening.
They often drown in the green water

of abandoned gravel pits,
or fall into earth where the crust is thin.

I have tried to stop the war.

You wanted to be a sculptor
creating a new shape that would exalt itself
as the shape of a ball or hand
or breast or dog or hoof,
paw print in snow, each cluster of grapes
vaguely different, bat's wing shaped
as half a leaf, a lake working
against its rim of ground.

You wear yellow this year for Christmas,
the color of Christ's wounds after three days,
the color of Nelse's jacket you wear when writing,
Nelse full of Guckenheimer, sloth, herring, tubercules.

There were sweet places to sleep: beds warmed
by women who get up to work or in the brush
beneath Coit Tower, on picnic tables in Fallon, Nevada
and Hastings, Nebraska, surrounded by giant curs,
then dew that falls like fine ice upon your face
in a bean field near Stockton, near a waterfall
in the Huron mountains, memorable sleeps
in the bus stations of San Jose and Toledo, Ohio.

At the roller rink on Chippewa Lake
the skaters move to calliope music.
You watch a motorboat putt by the dock;
they are trolling for bass at night
and for a moment the boat and two men
are caught in the blue light of the rink,
then pass on slowly upon the black water.

Liquor has reduced you to thumbnails,
keratin, the scales of fish
your ancient relatives,
stranded in a rock pool.

O claritas, sweet suppleness
of breath,
love within a cloud that
blinds us
hear, speak, the world without.

Grove St, Gough St, Heber, Utah,
one in despair, two in disgust,
the third beneath the shadow
of a mountain wall, beyond
the roar of a diesel truck,
faintly the screech of lion.

Self immolation,
the heaviest of dreams—
you become a charcoal rick
for Christ, for man himself.
They laugh with you as you disappear
lying as a black log upon the cement,
the fire doused by your own blood.

The thunderstorm moved across the lake
in a sheet of rain, the lightning
struck a strawpile which burned in the night
with hot roars of energy
as in '48 when a jetplane crashed near town,
the pilot parachuting as a leaf through the red sky,
landing miles away, missing the fire.

There was one sun,
one cloud,
two horses running,

a leopard in chase;
only the one sun and a single cloud
a third across her face.
Above, the twelve moons of Jupiter
hissing in cold and darkness.

You worshiped the hindquarters
of beautiful women,
and the beautiful hindquarters of women
who were not beautiful;
the test was the hindquarters
as your father judged cattle.

He is standing behind a plow
in a yellow photograph,
a gangster hat to the back of his head,
in an undershirt with narrow straps,
reins over a shoulder waiting for the photo,
the horses with a foreleg raised,
waiting for the pull with impatience.

The cannon on the courthouse lawn was plugged,
useless against the japs.

In the dark barn
a stillborn calf on the straw,
rope to hoofs, its mother bawling,
pulled nearly to death.

You've never been across the ocean,
you swept the auditorium with a broom
after the travel lectures and dreamed of going
but the maps have become old, the brain
set on the Mackenzie river, even Greenland
where dentists stalk polar bears from Cessnas.

The wrecked train smelled of camphor,
a bird floating softly above the steam,
the door of the refrigerator car cracked open
and food begins to perish in the summer night.

You've become sure that every year
the sky descends a little,
but there is joy in this pressure,
joy bumping against the lid
like a demented fly, a bird breaking
its neck against a picture window
while outside new gods roll over
in the snow in billowy sleep.

The oil workers sit on the curb
in front of the Blue Moon Bar & Cafe,
their necks red from the sun,
pale white beneath the collars
or above the sleeves; in the distance
you hear the clumping of the wells.
And at a friend's house
there are aunts and uncles, supper plates
of red beans and pork, a guitar is taken
from the wall—in the music
the urge of homesickness, a peach not to be held
or a woman so lovely but not to be touched,
some former shabby home far south of here,
in a warmer place.

Cold cement, a little snow upon it.
Where are the small gods who bless cells?
There are only men. Once you were in a room
with a girl of honey-colored hair,
the yellow sun streamed down air of yellow straw.
You owe it to yourself to despise this place,
the walls sift black powder,
you owe yourself a particular cave.

You wait for her, a stone in loamy stillness,
who will arrive with less pitiful secrets
from sidereal reaches, from other planets of the mind,
who beneath the chamber music of gown and incense
will reflect the damp sweetness of a cave.

At that farm there were so many hogs,
in the center of the pen in the chilled air
he straddles the pig and slits its throat,
blood gushes forth too dark to be blood,
gutted, singed, and scraped into pinkness
there are too many bowels, the organs
too large, pale sponges that are lungs,
the pink is too pink to understand.

This is earth I've fallen against,
there was no life before this;
                                        still icon
as if seen through mist,
cold liquid sun, blue falling
from the air,
                                foam of ship's prow
cutting water, a green shore beyond
the rocks,
beyond, a green continent.

ROBERT HASS

In Weather

1

What I wanted
in the pearly repetitions of February
was vision. All winter,
grieved and dull,
I hungered for it.
Sundays I looked for lightning-
stricken trees
in the slow burning of the afternoon
to cut them down, split
the dry centers,
and kindle from their death
an evening's warmth
in the uxorious amber repetitions
of the house. Dusks
weighted me, the fire,
the dim trees. I saw
the bare structure
of their hunger for light
reach to where darkness
joined them. The dark
and the limbs tangled
luxuriant as hair.
I could feel night gather them
but removed my eyes from the tug of it
and watched the fire,
a smaller thing,
contained by the hewn stone
of the dark hearth.

I can't decide
about my garbage and the creatures
who come at night to root
and scatter it. I could lock it
in the shed, but I imagine
wet noses, bodies grown alert
to the smells of warm decay
in the cold air. It seems a small thing
to share what I don't want,
but winter mornings the white yard
blossoms grapefruit peels,
tin cans, plastic bags,
the russet cores of apples.
The refuse of my life
surrounds me and the sense of waste
in the dreary gathering of it
compels me all the more
to labor for the creatures
who quiver and are quick-eyed
and bang the cans at night
and are not grateful. The other morning,
walking early in the new sun,
I was rewarded. A thaw turned up
the lobster shells from Christmas eve.
They rotted in the yard
and standing in the muddy field I caught,
as if across great distances,
a faint rank fragrance of the sea.

3

There are times
I wish my ignorance were
more complete. I remember
clamming inland beaches

on the January tides
along Tomales Bay. A raw world
where green crabs
which have been exposed
graze nervously on intertidal kelp
and sea anemones are clenched and colorless
in eddying pools
near dumb clinging starfish
on the sides and undersides of rock.
Among the cockles and the horseneck clams,
I turned up long, inch-thick
sea worms. Female,
phallic, ruddy brown, each one
takes twenty years to grow.
Beach people call them *innkeepers*
because the tiny male lives inside
and feeds on plankton
in the water that the worm
churns through herself to move.
I watched the brown things
that brightness bruised
writhing in the sun. Then,
carefully, I buried them.
And, eyes drifting, heart-
sick, honed to the wind's edge,
my mind became the male
drowsing in that inland sea
who lives in darkness,
drops seed twice in twenty years,
and dies. I look from my window
to the white fields
and think about the taste of clams.

4

A friend, the other night,
read poems full of rage
against the poor uses of desire

in mere enactment. A cruel music
lingered in my mind.
The poems made me think
I understood
why men cut women up. Hating
the source, nerved,
irreducible, that music hacked
the body till the source was gone.
Then the heavy cock wields,
rises, spits seed
at random and the man
shrieks, homeless
and perfected in the empty dark.
His god is a thrust of infinite desire
beyond the tame musk
of companionable holes.
It descends to women occasionally
with contempt and languid tenderness.
I tried to hate my wife's cunt,
the sweet place where I rooted,
to imagine the satisfied disgust
of cutting her apart,
bloody and exultant
in the bad lighting and scratchy track
of butcher shops
in short experimental films.
It was easier than I might have supposed.
o spider cunt, o raw devourer.
I wondered what to make
of myself. There had been a thaw.
I looked for green shoots
in the garden, wild flowers in the woods.
I found none.

5

In March the owls
began to mate. Moon

on windy snow. Mournful,
liquid, the dark hummed
their cries, a soft
confusion. Hard frost
feathered the windows.
I could not sleep.
I imagined the panic
of the meadow mouse,
the star-nosed mole.
Slowly at first, I
made a solemn face
and tried the almost human wail
of owls, ecstatic
in the winter trees, *twoo, twoo.*
I drew long breaths.
My wife stirred in our bed.
Joy seized me.

6

Days return
day to me, the brittle light.
My alertness has no
issue. Deep in the woods
starburst needles of the white pine
are roof to the vacancies
in standing still. Wind
from the lake stings me.
Hemlocks grow cerebral
and firm in the dim attenuation
of the afternoon. The longer
dusks are a silence
born in pale redundancies
of silence. Walking home
I follow the pawprints of the fox.
I know that I know myself
no more than a seed

curled in the dark of a winged pod
knows flourishing.

Song

Afternoon cooking in the fall sun—
who is more naked
                                        than the man
yelling, "Hey, I'm home!"
                        to an empty house?
thinking because the bay is clear,
the hills in yellow heat,
& scrub oak red in gullies
            that great crowds of family
should tumble from the rooms
                        to throw their bodies on the Papa-body,
                                        I-am-loved.

Cat sleeps in the windowgleam,
                    dust motes.
        On the oak table
    filets of sole
stewing in the juice of tangerines,
    slices of green pepper
            on a bone-white dish.

Fall

Amateurs, we gathered mushrooms
near shaggy eucalyptus groves
which smelled of camphor and the fog-soaked earth.

Chanterelles, puffballs, chicken-of-the-woods,
we cooked in wine or butter,
beaten eggs or sour cream,
half expecting to be
killed by a mistake. "Intense perspiration,"
you said late at night,
quoting the terrifying field guide
while we lay tangled in our sheets and heavy limbs,
"is the first symptom of attack."

Friends called our aromatic fungi
"liebestoads" and only ate the ones
that we most certainly survived.
Death shook us more than once
those days and floating back
it felt like life. Earth-wet, slithery,
we drifted toward the names of things.
Spore prints littered our table
like nervous stars. Rotting caps
gave off a musky smell of loam.

The Return of Robinson Jeffers

1

He shuddered briefly and stared down the long valley
  where the headland rose
And the lean gum trees rattled in the wind above Point
  Sur;
Alive, he had littered the mind's coast
With ghosts of Indians and granite and the dead fleshed
Bodies of desire. That work was done
And, whether done well or not, it had occupied him
As the hawks and the sea were occupied.

Now he could not say what brought him back.
He had imagined resurrection once: the lover of a
  woman
Who lived lonely in a little ranch house up the ridge
Came back, dragged from the grave by her body's need
To feel under ashen cloud-skies and in the astonishments
Of sunrise some truth beyond the daily lie
Of feeding absolute hunger the way a young girl might
  trap meadow mice
To feed a red-tailed hawk she kept encaged. She
  wanted to die once
As the sun dies in pure fire on the farthest sea-swells.
She had had enough and more of nights when the brain
Flickered and dissolved its little constellations and
  the nerves
Performed their dumb show in the dark among the
  used human smells of bedsheets.
So she burned and he came, a ghost in khaki and
  stunned skin,
And she fled with him. He had imagined, though he
  had not written,
The later moment in the pasture, in moonlight like pale
  stone,
When she lay beside him with an after-tenderness in all
  her bones,
Having become entirely what she was, though aware
  that the thing
Beside her was, again, just so much cheese-soft flesh
And jellied eye rotting in the pools of bone.
Anguish afterwards perhaps, but he had not thought
  afterwards.
Human anguish made him cold.
He told himself the cries of men in war were no more
  conscious
Nor less savage than the shrill repetitions of the Steller's
  jay
Flashing through live oaks up Mal Paso Canyon

And that the oaks, rooted and growing toward their
grace,
Were—as species go—
More beautiful.

2

He had given himself to stone gods.
I imagine him thinking of that woman
While a live cloud of gulls
Plumes the wind behind a trawler
Throbbing toward the last cannery at Monterey.
The pelicans are gone which had, wheeling,
Written Chinese poems on the sea. The grebes are gone
That feasted on the endless hunger of the flashing runs
Of salmon. And I imagine that he saw, finally,
That though rock stands, it does not breed.
He feels specific rage. Feels, obscurely, that his sex
Is his, not god-force only, but his own soft flesh grown
thick
With inconsolable desire. The grebes are gone.
He feels a plain man's elegiac tenderness,
An awkward brotherhood with the world's numb poor
His poems had despised. Rage and tenderness are pain.
He feels pain as rounding at the hips, as breasts.
Pain blossoms in his belly like the first dark
Stirrings of a child, a surfeit of the love that he had
bled to rock
And twisted into cypress haunts above the cliffs.
He knows he has come back to mourn,
To grieve, womanish, a hundred patient years
Along this fragile coast. I imagine the sky's arch,
Cloud-swift, lifts him then, all ache in sex and breasts,
Beyond the leached ashes of dead fire,
The small jeweled hunger in the seabird's eye.

Against Botticelli

I

In the life we live together every paradise is lost.
Nothing could be easier: summer gathers new leaves
to casual darkness. So few things we need to know.
And the old wisdoms shudder in us and grow slack.
Like renunciation. Like the melancholy beauty
of giving it all up. Like walking steadfast
in the rhythms, winter light and summer dark.
And the time for cutting furrows and the dance.
Mad seed. Death waits them out. It waits us out,
the sleek incandescent saints, earthly and prayerful.
In our modesty. In our shamefast and steady attention
to the ceremony, its preparation, the formal hovering
of pleasure which falls like the rain we pray not to get
and are glad for and drown in. Or spray of that sea,
irised: otters in the tide-lash, in the kelp-drench,
mammal warmth and the inhuman element. Ah, that is
the secret.
That she is an otter, that Botticelli saw her so.
That we are not otters and are not in the painting
by Botticelli. We are not even in the painting by Bosch
where the people are standing around looking at the
frame
of the Botticelli painting and when love arrives, they
throw up.
Or the Goya painting of the sad ones, angular and
shriven,
who watch the Bosch and feel very compassionate
but hurt each other often and inefficiently. We are not
in any painting.
If we do it at all, we will be like the old Russians.
We'll walk down through scrub oak to the sea
and where the seals lay preening on the beach

we will look at each other steadily
and butcher them and skin them.

II

The myth they chose was the constant lovers.
The theme was richness over time.
It is a difficult story and the wise never choose it
because it requires a long performance
and because there is nothing, by definition, between the
acts.
It is different in kind from a man and the pale woman
he fucks in the ass underneath the stars
because it is summer and they are full of longing
and sick of birth. They burn cooly
like phosphorus, and the thing need be done
only once. Like the sacking of Troy
it survives in imagination,
in the longing brought perfectly to closing,
the woman's white hand opening, opening,
and the man churning inside her, thrashing there.
And light travels as if all the stars they were under
exploded centuries ago and they are resting now,
glowing.
The woman thinks what she is feeling is like the dark
and utterly complete. The man is past sadness,
though his eyes are wet. He is learning about gratitude,
how final it is, as if the grace in Botticelli's *Primavera,*
the one with sad eyes who represents pleasure,
had a canvas to herself, entirely to herself.

Songs to Survive the Summer

These are the dog days,
unvaried
except by accident,

mist rising from soaked lawns,
gone world, everything
rises and dissolves in air,

whatever it is would
clear the air
dissolves in air and the knot

of days unties
invisibly like a shoelace.
The grey-eyed child

who said to my child: "Let's play
in my yard. It's OK,
my mother's dead."

*

Under the loquat tree.
It is almost a song,
the echo of a song:

on the bat's back I fly
merrily toward summer
or at high noon

in the outfield clover
guzzling orange crush,
time endless, examining

a wooden coin I'd carried
all through summer
without knowing it.

The coin was grandpa's joke,
carved from live oak,
Indian side and buffalo side.

His eyes lustered with a mirth
so deep and rich he never
laughed, as if it were a cosmic

secret that we shared.
I never understood; it married
in my mind with summer. Don't

take any wooden nickels,
kid, and gave me one
under the loquat tree.

*

The squalor of mind
is formlessness,
unforma,

the romans said of ugliness,
it has no form,
a man's misery, bleached skies,

the war between desire
and dailiness. I thought
this morning of Wallace Stevens

walking equably to work
and of a morning two Julys ago
on Chestnut Ridge, wandering

down the hill when one
rusty elm leaf, earth-
skin peeling, wafted

by me on the wind.
My body groaned toward fall
and preternaturally

a heron lifted from the pond.
I even thought I heard
the ruffle of the wings

three hundred yards below me
rising from the reeds.
Death is the mother of beauty

and that clean-shaven man
smelling of lotion,
lint-free, walking

toward his work, a
pure exclusive music
in his mind.

*

The mother of the neighbor
child was thirty-one,
died, at Sunday breakfast,

of a swelling in the throat.
On a toy loom
she taught my daughter

how to weave. My daughter
was her friend
and now she cannot sleep

for nighttime sirens,
sure that every wail
is someone dead.

Should I whisper in her ear,
death is the mother
of beauty? Wooden

nickels, kid? It's all in
shapeliness, give your
fears a shape?

*

In fact, we hide together
in her books.
Prairie farms, the heron

knows the way, old
country songs, herbal magic,
recipes for soup,

tales of spindly orphan
girls who find
the golden key, the

darkness at the center
of the leafy wood.
And when she finally sleeps

I try out Chekhov's
tenderness to see
what it can save.

*

Maryushka the beekeeper's
widow,
though three years mad,

writes daily letters
to her son. Semyon tran-
scribes them. The pages

are smudged by his hands,
stained with
the dregs of tea:

"My dearest Vanushka,
Sofia Aggrapina's ill
again. The master

asks for you. Wood
is dear. The cold
is early. Poor

Sofia Aggrapina!
The foreign doctor
gave her salts

but Semyon says her icon
candle guttered
St. John's eve. I am afraid,

Vanya. When she's ill,
the master likes to have
your sister flogged.

She means no harm.
The rye is grey
this time of year.

When it is bad, Vanushka,
I go into the night
and the night eats me."

*

The haiku comes
in threes
with the virtues of brevity:

> *What a strange thing!*
> *To be alive*
> *beneath plum blossoms.*

The black-headed
Steller's jay is squawking
in our plum.

Thief! Thief!
A hard, indifferent bird,
he'd snatch your life.

*

The love of books
is for children
who glimpse in them

a life to come, but
I have come
to that life and

feel uneasy
with the love of books.
This is my life,

time islanded
in poems of dwindled time.
There is no other world.

*

But I have seen it twice.
In the Palo Alto marsh
sea birds rose in early light

and took me with them.
Another time, dreaming,
river birds lifted me,

swans, small angelic terns,
and an old woman in a shawl
dying by a dying lake

whose life raised men
from the dead
in another country.

*

Thick nights, and nothing
lets us rest. In the heat
of mid-July our lust

is nothing. We swell
and thicken. Slippery,
purgatorial, our sexes

will not give us up.
Exhausted after hours
and not undone,

we crave cold marrow
from the tiny bones that
moonlight scatters

on our skin. Always
morning arrives,
the stunned days,

faceless, droning
in the juice of rotten quince,
the flies, the heat.

*

Tears, silence.
The edified generations
eat me, Maryushka.

I tell them
pain is form and
almost persuade

myself. They are not
listening. Why
should they? Who

cannot save me any more
than I, weeping
over *Great Russian Short*

Stories in summer,
under the fattened figs,
saved you. Besides

it is winter there.
They are trying out
a new recipe for onion soup.

*

Use a heavy-bottomed
three- or four-quart pan.
Thinly slice six large

yellow onions and sauté
in olive oil and butter
until limp. Pour in

beef broth. Simmer
thirty minutes,
add red port and bake

for half an hour. Then
sprinkle half a cup
of diced Gruyère and cover

with an even layer
of toasted bread and
shredded Samsoe. Dribble

melted butter on the top
and bake until the cheese
has bubbled gold.

Surround yourself with friends.
Huddle in a warm place.
Ladle. Eat.

*

Weave and cry.
Child, every other siren
is a death;

the rest are for speeding.
Look how comically the jay's
black head emerges

from a swath of copper leaves.
Half the terror
is the fact that,

in our time, speed saves us,
a whine we've traded
for the hopeless patience

of the village bell
which tolled in threes:
weave and cry and weave.

*

Wilhelm Steller, form's
hero, made
a healing broth.

He sailed with Bering
and the crew despised him,
a mean impatient man

born low enough
to hate the lower class.
For two years

he'd connived to join
the expedition and put
his name to all the beasts

and flowers of the north.
Now Bering sick,
the crew half-mad with scurvy,

no one would let him
go ashore. Panic,
the maps were useless,

the summer weather almost gone.
He said, there are herbs
that can cure you,

I can save you all. He didn't
give a damn about them
and they knew it. For two years

he'd prepared. Bering listened.
Asleep in his bunk, he'd
seen death writing in the log.

On the island while
the sailors searched for water
Steller gathered herbs

and looking up
he saw the blue, black-crested
bird, shrilling in a pine.

His mind flipped
to Berlin, the library, a glimpse
he'd had at Audubon,

a blue-grey crested bird
exactly like the one
that squawked at him, a

Carolina jay, unlike
any European bird; he knew
then where they were:

America, we're saved.
No one believed him or,
sick for home, they didn't care

what wilderness
it was. They set sail
west. Bering died.

Steller's jay, by which
I found Alaska.
He wrote it in his book.

*

Saved no one. Still,
walking in the redwoods
I hear the cry

thief, thief and
think of Wilhelm Steller;
in my dream we

are all saved. Camping
on a clement shore
in early fall, a strange land.

We feasted most delicately.
The swans are stuffed with grapes,
the turkey with walnut

and chestnut and wild plum.
The river is our music: *unalaska*
(to make bread from acorns

we leach the tannic acid out—
this music, child,
and more, much more!)

*

When I was just
your age, the war was over
and we moved.

An Okie family lived
next door to our new
country house. That summer

Quincy Phipps was saved.
The next his house became
an unofficial Pentecostal church.

Summer nights: hidden
in the garden I ate figs,
watched where the knobby limbs

rose up and flicked
against the windows where
they were. *O Je-sus.*

Kissed and put to bed,
I slipped from the window
to the eaves and nestled

by the loquat tree.
The fruit was yellow-brown
in daylight; under the moon

pale clusters hung
like other moons, *O*
Je-sus, and I picked them;

the fat juices
dribbling down my chin,
I sucked and listened.

Men groaned. The women
sobbed and moaned, a
long unsteady belly-deep

bewildering sound, half
pleasure and half pain
that ended sometimes

in a croon, a broken song:
O Je-sus,
Je-sus.

*

That is what I have
to give you, child, stories,
songs, loquat seeds,

curiously shaped; they
are the frailest stay against
our fears. Death

in the sweetness, in the bitter
and the sour, death
in the salt, your tears,

this summer ripe and overripe.
It is a taste in the mouth,
child. We are the song

death takes its own time
singing. It calls us
as I call you *child*

to calm myself. It is every
thing touched casually,
lovers, the images

of saviours, books, the coin
I carried in my pocket
till it shone, it is

all things lustered
by the steady thoughtlessness
of human use.

WILLIAM HEYEN

Dog Sacrifice at Lake Ronkonkoma

Now spears lift them by their ribs
over the black water to heaven.
Now they are almost dead.
Their eyes blaze in the moonlight,

as, all dark long,
the sacred lake laps shore
with syllables of approaching spring.
Men listen, the dogs stare and die, until,

Ronkonkoma, its curves a skull,
dreaming in its own bottomless bed,
fills with the first light of morning,
and the sun rises, clothed in the dogs' blood.

The Spirit of Wrath

I

Off Crane's Neck the sun
  reaches a few feet down
    into the dark water,
      but what it is you're after

feeds at the bottom
  below the reach of your anchor.
    Your heavy-test line
      plummets with its lead sinkers

down deeper than Twain ever
  marked the depth of his river,
    and strikes sand
      with a slight thud and shudder

you feel in your fingers.
  The line bows out. The sinkers must
    touch, lift, and touch again,
      raising swirls of sand,

trailing smells of the squid
  hooked higher on the line. You drift
    in swells, as though the Sound
      drew breath beneath you.

II

As you wait for shark, remember:
  from here, crossing to Connecticut,
    Walt Whitman saw poems,
      watched the small boats troll

for striped bass, for blues
  that bent rods double,
    for porgies that shimmered
      in the sun like coral.

But you've reached deeper,
  down to where the sandshark cruises,
    glides among the dunes like a shadow,
      slashes anything that moves.

Its flesh, cut in strips,
  will quiver, like a turtle's, or snake's.
    Its eyes will stare through you, focus
      beyond you. Its teeth

can snap off the neck of a bottle.
  You'll feel it strike,
    hook itself, sweep your line
      back and forth under the boat.

III

Hold the line taut.
  Reel the shark to surface.
    Gaff its white abdomen.
      Raise it to an oarlock.

Batter its head with a hammer.
  Taste the blood that runs
    from its gills, hack off its tail.
      Draw your knife across its eyes.

You've done what can be done
  to the snarling shark that still
    moves like a dead snake until
      the sun dies beyond the horizon.

Rip your hook from its gullet.
  With both hands, hold the shark
    above your head. Pray:
      never again to fear the dark

sea's depths. Pray: *never to fear*
  yourself. Pray: *never to fear love.*
    When you lift it back to water
      the shark will swim away.

I Move to Random Consolations

Walking the small oval of Gibbs Pond,
scaring the leopard frogs to jump

and the snappers to swim out to darkness,
watching the emerald and ruby needles trail
their frail legs and copulate hovering in air,

noticing the black spiders stride their shadows,
I came across within some razor weeds
some sort of crane that came to die.

And I, kneeling beside its quick rising
and falling body, seeing the ants
had begun crawling its stilt legs
to its moulted sternum and sad, lidded eyes,
took up a death-watch with the rising gnats.

I was at first no mourner, but a scientist:
soon the bird folded its right leg to body;
in one hour it lay down, in two, closed its eyes.

By last light the frogs had again begun
and a snake had wriggled to the shore
and flicked something to its pink tongue.
A turtle gnawed the belly of a fish.
But, being less objective than I'd wish,

I rose to rock the crane's death; and, needing something
to affirm, held to the knowledge that a bird's beak,
born of cells of bone, discourages the worm.

The Snapper

He is the pond's old father, its brain
and dark, permanent presence.

He is the snapper, and smells
rich and sick as a mat of weeds; and wears

a beard of leeches that suck frog, fish,
and snake blood from his neck; and drags

a tail ridged as though hacked out
with an ax. He rises: mud swirls

and blooms, lilies bob, water washes
his moss-humped back where, buried

deep in his sweet flesh, the pond ebbs
and flows its sure, slow heart.

LAWSON FUSAO INADA

Plucking Out a Rhythm

Start with a simple room—
a dullish color—
and draw the one shade down.
Hot plate. Bed.
Little phonograph in a corner.

Put in a single figure—
medium weight and height—
but oversize, as a child might.

The features must be Japanese.

Then stack a black pompadour on,
and let the eyes
slide behind a night of glass.

The figure is in disquise:

slim green suit
for posturing on a bandstand,
the turned-up shoes of Harlem . . .

Then start the music playing—
thick jazz, strong jazz—

and notice that the figure
comes to life:
sweating, growling
over an imaginary bass—

plucking out a rhythm—
as the music rises and the room is full,
exuding with that rhythm . . .

Then have the shade flap up
and daylight catch him
frozen in that pose

as it starts to snow—
thick snow, strong snow—

blowing in the window
while the music quiets,
the room is slowly covered,

and the figure is completely
out of sight.

From Our Album

I "Before the War"

"Before the war"
means Fresno, a hedged-in house,
two dogs in the family.

Blackie, the small one, mine,
lapped at his insides
on the floorboard, on the way to the doctor.

Jimmy, my father's shepherd,
wouldn't eat after the evacuation.
He wouldn't live with another master

and pined away, skin and bone.

With feelings more than pride,
we call him our one-man dog.

II Mud

Mud in the barracks—
a muddy room, a chamber pot.

Mud in the moats
around each barracks group.

Mud on the shoes
trudging to the mess hall.

Mud in the swamp
where the men chopped wood.

Mud on the guts
under a loaded wagon—

crushed in the mud by the wheel.

III Desert Songs

1 ALL THAT WE GATHERED

Because there was little else to do,
they led us to the artillery range
for shells, all that we gathered,
and let us dig among dunes
for slugs, when they were through.

Because there was little else to do,
one of them chased a stray

with his tail between his legs
and shot him through the head.

2 SHELLS

A desert tortoise—
something mute and hard—

something to decorate
a desert Japanese garden:

gnarled wood, smooth
artillery shells for a border.

When a guard
smashes one, the shell

cracks open and the muscles ooze.

3 IT IS ONLY NATURAL

The pheasant is an Oriental creature,
so it is only natural
that one should fly into camp

and, famished by rations and cans,
break out in secret, native dance
over a fire, on a black coal stove.

4 SONG OF THE 44ND

Caged creatures
have curious moods.

Some of them choose
to be turned

loose in a group,
to take their chances

in the open.

5 STEERS

Because a dentist
logically drives a butcher truck,

I rode with my father
to the slaughterhouse on an afternoon.

Not hammers, not bullets,
could make him close his eyes.

6 HE TEACHES

He jerks the eyes
from birds, feet
from lizards,

and punishes
ants with the gaze
of a glass.

And with his sly
gaze, his child's face,
he teaches

what has its place,
and must be
passed on to others.

IV Song of Chicago

When the threat lessened,
when we became tame,

my father and friends
took a train to Chicago

for factory work,
for packaging bolts.
One grew a mustache
and called himself Carlos.

And they all made a home
with those of their own—

rats, bedbugs, blacks.

THOMAS JAMES

Mummy of a Lady Named Jemutesonekh XXI Dynasty

My body holds its shape. The genius is intact.
Will I return to Thebes? In that lost country
The eucalyptus trees have turned to stone.
Once, branches nudged me, dropping swollen blossoms,
And passionflowers lit my father's garden.
Is it still there, that place of mottled shadow,
The scarlet flowers breathing in the darkness?

I remember how I died. It was so simple!
One morning the garden faded. My face blacked out.
On my left side they made the first incision.
They washed my heart and liver in palm wine—
My lungs were two dark fruit they stuffed with spices.
They smeared my innards with a sticky unguent
And sealed them in a crock of alabaster.

My brain was next. A pointed instrument
Hooked it through my nostrils, strand by strand.
A voice swayed over me. I paid no notice.
For weeks my body swam in sweet perfume.
I came out scoured. I was skin and bone.
They lifted me into the sun again
And packed my empty skull with cinnamon.

They slit my toes; a razor gashed my fingertips.
Stitched shut at last, my limbs were chaste and valuable,
Stuffed with a paste of cloves and wild honey.

My eyes were empty, so they filled them up,
Inserting little nuggets of obsidian.
A basalt scarab wedged between my breasts
Replaced the tinny music of my heart.

Hands touched my sutures. I was so important!
They oiled my pores, rubbing a fragrance in.
An amber gum oozed down to soothe my temples.
I wanted to sit up. My skin was luminous,
Frail as the shadow of an emerald.
Before I learned to love myself too much,
My body wound itself in spools of linen.

Shut in my painted box, I am a precious object.
I wear a wooden mask. These are my eyelids,
Two flakes of bronze, and here is my new mouth,
Chiseled with care, guarding its ruby facets.
I will last forever. I am not impatient—
My skin will wait to greet its old complexions.
I'll lie here till the world swims back again.

When I come home the garden will be budding,
White petals breaking open, clusters of night flowers,
The far-off music of a tambourine.
A boy will pace among the passionflowers,
His eyes no longer two bruised surfaces.
I'll know the mouth of my young groom, I'll touch
His hands. Why do people lie to one another?

Hunting for Blueberries

Like two somnambulists we entered the dawn sun,
Its plumskin flashing. I squinted at its brightness.

The sky was colorless, merely a picked bone.
A few frayed clouds dissipated downfield.
You, my little cousin, eight years blind,

Guarded the lunch basket. Down at the horse pond,
  frogs
Regarded us below a layer of scum.
You cried and cried because I hugged you close
And would not let you go. In your shadow-peopled head
I must have been unwieldy as a python.

The mayflies had been three months dead,
But I could see them flickering in your eyes,
Those two gooseberries. I loved to lick them clean,
My tongue grazing the broken winter field
That was your only landscape, eight years old.

My hands were two large spiders that reached your bed
Each night; all day they picked blueberries
Out of the hidden thickets by the horse pond.
In that hard morning light, moonglow to you,
We might have been two trails of marsh vapor

Imperfectly matched, dissolving in the thickets.
You found blueberries in the oddest byways—
In a vein of the hill where harebells broke and faded,
Behind a clump of oaks that held the clouds up—
Plump globes the color of the evening sky,

Frosted with dust. What colors would leap
Out of the hedges! Your mother's arms,
Riddled with tiny punctures, needled blue,
Held nothing solid as these. Their blueblack juices
Stained your small mouth like watercolor.

We found a thicket dripping its liquors down.
Drunk on the fruit, a hornet threaded among them.

They plunked like raindrops in our coffee tin,
Each rain tap punctuated with a vibrant silence.
Sunflowers cluttered the grass with burnt-out tongues.

You knelt down in the leaves. And then I saw it—
I held you close again. Confused,
You pulled away from me and went on picking,
Unaware of the blacksnake coiled in the berries,
Its eyes clouded with sun, its face a death mask.

Letter to a Mute

If I could reach you now, in any way
At all, I would say this to you:
This afternoon I walked into a thicket

Of gold flowers that had no idea
What they were after. They couldn't hear a thing.
I walked among a million small, deaf ears

Breaking their gold into the afternoon.
I think they were like you, golden, golden,
Unable to express a single thing.

I walked among them, thinking of you,
Thinking of what it would be like
To be completely solitary. Once I was alone like that.

All the field was humming, brimming
With some brazen kind of song, and I
Thought that somehow I could disappear

Into the empty hall of your right ear,
Wandering through the slender bones of you.
But I knew that I could never let you know

That it is late summer here, that I
Can hear the crickets every evening
Hollowing out the darkness at my window,

That you have vanished into a dark tunnel
Where I have tried to reach you with my mouth
Till my mouth ran gold, spilling over everything.

Tonight I looked into your face, tenderly,
Tenderly, but I can never find you there.
I can only touch your quiet lips.

If I could stick my pen into your tongue,
Making it run with gold, making
It speak entirely to me, letting the truth

Slide out of it, I could not be alone.
I wouldn't even touch you, for I know
How you are locked away from me forever.

Tonight I go out looking for you everywhere
As the moon slips out, a slender petal
Offering all its gold to me for nothing.

Letters to a Stranger

I

In April we will pierce his body.
It is March. Snow is dust over the branches.
A pony hunches in the orchard.
I stand at the frozen mouth of the river,
Thinking of you.

In the house where you live
Frost glitters on the windows
Like uncounted pieces of silver.
Already they are preparing the wine and the bread.

II

The field is banked with purple asters
And a spill of mustard flowers.
The earth has taken on terrible proportions.
Out in an unused meadow
The wildflowers have already covered
The delicate bones of an Indian.
Bees are flying across the meadow
To a hive under the rafters of the barn.
Someone is leading a horse with crippled bones
Into the spikes of clover.

III

Alexander died this morning,
Leaving his worldly possessions
To the strongest.
I watched an empire fade across his lips.
They propped him in the sun a while,
And then three women came to scour his body
Like a continent.
I am afraid of what the world will do.
Only this afternoon
I heard two worms conversing
In the shadow of his breastbone.
I slipped out of the palace
And entered a vein of gillyflowers
On the edge of potter's field.
I will not be missed.
No one even noticed.

IV

I have been thinking of the son
I would like to have.
The leaves have all gone yellow
Overnight, wrinkling like hands
In the updraught.
I drove my car by the creek
Because I had nowhere else to go.
The milkweed's delicate closet had been fractured,
Filling the air with rumors.
Despite all I could do, the sumac
Had taken on the color of a mouth
Tonight, I perceive the young girls
In my mother's blood
Letting their seed pass by unnoticed,
A red nativity.

V

Last night they dragged the canal
For an old man's body.
Now he is singing for a hook
Just below water level.
A branch of ice is splitting open
Across each window,
And snow is dismantling the weeds
Like the breakable furniture of a boudoir.
I have been rereading your letters.
It is too cold for a virgin birth to occur
Even in the frosty suburbs
Of a wildflower.

VI

I have learned to camouflage myself in church,
Masking my body

With the body of a saint.
Last night frost glazed the face of Mary Magdalene,
And snow rode up to the altar windows.
Before morning, the sparrows came down
To the body of Saint Francis.
Now he is upholstered in oak leaves
Like a living room chair.
This morning we are preparing a crucifixion.
I am thinking of you now.
With the velvet at my knees
And the silverware shining on the altar
And the stained glass moving out of focus
And the cross veiled in black,
I am present for the news of an enormous death.
I take the bread on my tongue
Like one of Christ's fingers,
And the wine rides through my breast
Like a dark hearse.
All the while I am thinking of you.
An avalanche of white carnations
Is drifting across your voice
As it drifts across the voices of confession.
But the snow keeps whispering of you over and over.

LAURA JENSEN

After I Have Voted

I move the curtain back,
and something has gone wrong.
I am in a smoky place,

an Algerian cafe.
They turn the spotlight toward me;
the band begins to play.

The audience stares back at me.
They polish off their glasses.
They ask the waiter, "Who is she?"

He holds his pen
against his heart.
He speaks behind his hand.

There are tea bags swinging
from their mouths.
Their teeth are made of brass.

The jello sighs into the candlelight.
My eyes turn into stars.
Ah—the colored spangles on my clothes,

the violet flashlights and guitars!

Indian

I

In lungs fresh like honeycomb
my fiery bright breath has trundled

victorious, a forest full of fire,
plunging as one with the bear.

And I am the cover girl,
the vestibule neck above the satin,
chiffon hands that dine and dance
under scented awnings.

For my heart is like an orange,
my teeth are white again like painted gates,
my nest of hair entirely feathers,
black hair adorned with petals.

I am swan flower, winged rose,
I bring my language rightly to my tongue,
(where sweet genetics veer like dragonflies)
its battles distant and clear.

II

I watch whim, with narrow eyes,
fly true into darkness like an arrow;
buried in the sand, lit by a fire, past
becomes crime, branded by haste.

Dogs growl in their dark leather,
and ducks ask, loosening over water;
with the Navajo blood and turquoise rings
I look out soon as moonset,

a fluorescent skeleton,
steps down the cliff of this lighted building,
the burning and brick-red and desert rose,
to the dark, certain people

under a room of banners
which are a coarse black flag few people name.
I am entrusted to the ignorant prejudice—
loose my braid to fly my hair.

Talking to the Mule

In the evening there is a snail
passing through life across your lawn,
his trail official, a government seal.
The lawn is delicious, dry and cool,
the color of pepper.

Someone took a gun and shot that cone
off the pine tree.
He might have stopped to think
you heard for weeks the way the wind
blew through its sculptured sections.
It had skin soft as your ears.

The stars have started out the night.
They are something of importance
that clouds cover. They are too much
to be seen, but still they belong to us.

Rub your nose along the fence.
Tip back your head and bray,
for night is yours. It is never
against you. You are not its enemy.

Sleep in the Heat

I switch on the light. Crickets tick,
and the clock hands grow together, no record
of their own nocturnal repetitions.
Some things, for instance, branches,
can recall their circle
in the wind's big silent whistle,
their circle and returning touch.

The dark is dizzy. Within the shade
of heat, this stubborn demand for sleep
is slender. I try to please, I think
of hearts, their shape like lilac leaves;
I try to balance—one sheep fills me,
one is a shapeless chance,
one disobedience, one regard.
They feel I do not deserve them;
they are sleepy and kept up all night.

The sheep have hunger. Slowly they fade
into my eyes. My breath is their noon
whistle. Waking, they are in me,
grazing in the pastures of my tongue.
It is morning and I brush them out.

When the tricks have all worn out
it will be winter.
The rain will replace the rage
of the sizzling crickets.
I know this—I am looking back.
Heat does not decieve me; when the rains come,
they will not blame me for anything.

In the Hospital

Night breaths, short ones
from the garden, soft gasps
of snapdragon. Winter
reminds me of flowers.
Breath, where are you traveling?
You are not a caretaker,
but an illegible flower.
Winter reminds me of flowers.
Breath, the follower of air.

Night. Snow.

You forgot geriatrics,
anaesthetic pillows,
taking back the seagull,
the spiritual moments of air.
Breath was what you lost
of her, that last moment.

Her love returns to you,
moment by moment, in the oval
messages of snow, in the oval
lips of cups. The curtains
are a message of her veil,
the glass the thin wall
of her clothes, the drawers
like the lives who used her cradle.

I look out my window
at the bent man and his
frosty plumes of breath
which explain a wealth of sight
within his dark coat, within
his cold shoes and questionable
books. I look at your tears,
the white cinders of snow
that the earth is carrying.

At this moment the reason
for your breath is given, the reason being
truce between bones
and the skin of your hands,
the truce of these dark trees
on the clean sheets of snow.

A thought at a time, a world
at a time, like the sky

without another meaning, no matter
how you look, no matter how
you lower your eyes
from its opening heart of color,
an answer to an answer to a prayer.

Mother, I speak softly,
and father does not hear.
The times he has cupped his hand
and shaken his paper
are a welcome from your mother,
who now sends me running and grasping
through the invisible cells, into mysteries
of shapes and existence, our lives
tumbled into us like a cord of firewood
burning, the pain forgetfulness,
the message a puzzle like one of the cups—
Made in Occupied Japan.

I have been embarrassed by the testimony
of the tongues, changed roads, habits,
of the moment of prayer
for the opening of my heart,
the pain and swelling.
Didn't I always understand
the snow and the laughter, the bay leaves
of the cupboards resting in the snow?

ERICA JONG

Alcestis on the Poetry Circuit

in Memoriam MARINA TSVETAYEVA,
ANNA WICKHAM, SYLVIA PLATH, SHAKESPEARE'S
SISTER, ETC., ETC.

The best slave
does not need to be beaten.
She beats herself.

Not with a leather whip,
or with sticks or twigs,
not with a blackjack
or a billyclub,
but with the fine whip
of her own tongue
& the subtle beating
of her mind
against her mind.

For who can hate her half so well
as she hates herself?
& who can match the finesse
of her self-abuse?

Years of training
are required for this.
Twenty years
of subtle self-indulgence,
self-denial;
until the subject
thinks herself a queen
& yet a beggar—

both at the same time.
She must doubt herself
in everything but love.

She must choose passionately
& badly.
She must feel lost as a dog
without her master.
She must refer all moral questions
to her mirror.
She must fall in love with a cossack
or a poet.

She must never go out of the house
unless veiled in paint.
She must wear tight shoes
so she always remembers her bondage.
She must never forget
she is rooted in the ground.

Though she is quick to learn
& admittedly clever,
her natural doubt of herself
should make her so weak
that she dabbles brilliantly
in half a dozen talents
& thus embellishes
but does not change
our life.

If she's an artist
& comes close to genius,
the very fact of her gift
should cause her such pain
that she will take her own life
rather than best us.

& after she dies, we will cry
& make her a saint.

The Man Under the Bed

The man under the bed
The man who has been there for years waiting
The man who waits for my floating bare foot
The man who is silent as dustballs riding the darkness
The man whose breath is the breathing of small white
  butterflies
The man whose breathing I hear when I pick up the
  phone
The man in the mirror whose breath blackens silver
The boneman in closets who rattles the mothballs
The man at the end of the end of the line

I met him tonight I always meet him
He stands in the amber air of a bar
When the shrimp curl like beckoning fingers
& ride through the air on their toothpick skewers
When the ice cracks & I am about to fall through
he arranges his face around its hollows
he opens his pupilless eyes at me
For years he has waited to drag me down
& now he tells me
he has only waited to take me home
We waltz through the street like death & the maiden
We float through the wall of the wall of my room

If he's my dream he will fold back into my body
His breath writes letters of mist on the glass of my
  cheeks

I wrap myself around him like the darkness
I breathe into his mouth
& make him real

The Wives of Mafiosi

Thinking to take on the power
    of a dark suit lined with lead
    of a man with a platinum mouth & knuckles of
        brass
    of a bullet the color of a Ferrari

the wives of Mafiosi stay home
decanting the Chianti
like transparent blood.

They crochet spiders for the furniture.
They go to Confession.
They fill the ears of the priests
with mozzarella & nougat candy.

We too stay home
& dream of power.
    We sacrifice the steakblood to the dishwasher.
    We bring clear offerings of water to the plants.
    We pray before the baby pictures.

We dream of swallowing bullets
& coupling with money.
    We dream of transparent armor.
    We imagine we want peace.
    We imagine we are different
    from the wives of Mafiosi.

Seventeen Warnings in Search of a Feminist Poem

for Aaron Asher

1 Beware of the man who denounces ambition;
his fingers itch under his gloves.

2 Beware of the man who denounces war
through clenched teeth.

3 Beware of the man who denounces women writers;
his penis is tiny & cannot spell.

4 Beware of the man who wants to protect you;
he will protect you from everything but
himself.

5 Beware of the man who loves to cook;
he will fill your kitchen with greasy pots.

6 Beware of the man who loves your soul;
he is a bullshitter.

7 Beware of the man who denounces his mother;
he is a son of a bitch.

8 Beware of the man who spells son of a bitch as one
word;
he is a hack.

9 Beware of the man who loves death too well;
he is taking out insurance.

10 Beware of the man who loves life too well;
he is a fool.

11 Beware of the man who denounces psychiatrists;
he is afraid.

12 Beware of the man who trusts psychiatrists;
he is in hock.

13 Beware of the man who picks your dresses;
he wants to wear them.

14 Beware of the man you think is harmless;
he will surprise you.

15 Beware of the man who cares for nothing but books;
he will run like a trickle of ink.

16 Beware of the man who writes flowery love letters;
he is preparing for years of silence.

17 Beware of the man who praises liberated women;
he is planning to quit his job.

PETER KLAPPERT

The Lord's Chameleons

[*The true or African chameleon, family* Chamaeleontidae *(distinguished from* Anolis carolinensis, *found in Florida and pet stores): true chameleons have prehensile tails and opposed digits; eyes mounted in scaled turrets which can swivel independently of each other; and large heads with various knobs or horns—three horns in the case of* Chamaeleo jacksoni, *sometimes called the "rhinoceros chameleon."*

When exercising territorial behavior, chameleons inflate themselves so that they are thin from side to side but deep from top to bottom, and they advance broadside. When retreating they adopt the same pose but quiver as they back away. Despite these precautions, the boomslang (or tree snake) occasionally eats a chameleon.]

The chameleons saw an arc of color
disperse among the kaffir boom leaves
(more self-effacing than the upper-air)
and began a cult of imitation
coiling and uncoiling their tongues
about the meaning hidden in this vision.
An educated parrot said

That was a vision
of the true chameleon, whose color,
mimicked by the quiet flowers and leaves
in their devotions, saturates the air
with precious light.

So then they, in imitation,
grew a skin of leaves and held their tongues.
But observing the long silence of God's tongue
the family fell into division.
Some argued *He's the promise of all color,*

some *No, He's dark green (like the leaves*
where now He's brooding).

Suddenly the air
turned mutinous with insects, an intimation
of the coming of the Lord of Imitation.
The sun went dark as coffee, tongues
of yellow lightning stunned their vision,
and a three-horned sullen head in thunder color
loomed broadside on the sky.
Quivering like leaves
the chameleons tried to hide themselves in air.

When the rhinoceros chameleon of the air
had passed, there was new intimidation
on the contradictory muscles of their tongues.
Painfully, they trained their vision
to look both ways at once, but saw no color
now in the monotony of leaves.

The true chameleon, smirked the boomslang, *leaves*
no traces when it imitates the air.
A potto yawned *He is all imitation.*
The poor chameleons, stuck in all these tongues,
started to forget their splendid vision
of themselves, grown mythical with color.
And so their vision turned a darker color
and their tongues grew tired of imitation
and they were left to hug what was, and ate the air.

Poem for L. C.

I

I have only the sound of your steps
to guide me in this wilderness.
—Tagore, "The Cycle of Spring"

Honeysuckle, nightshade,
the burdock tree; the hawthorn,
the spiney hawthorn with hand branches
and rock bound roots. Mud.

Protect your face. Know how to
recognize flowers, even in gardens,
know the medicinal herbs,
sweet and rude, though they be tame.
Tread paths with dry feet, leave
careful footprints. Lead me, and follow.

I have seen these thickets before,
though the meadow escapes me;
don't let them tear at your eyes,
don't look back at me now, no more
than a glance. I am lost
as you are, I am tired,
I am making a home of this wood.

Buttercup, columbine, borage,
ash green thyme of the mint family.
Remember them. The weather has not been mild
and will not be mild tonight;
tomorrow, or over that hill,
look back if you can. Frail flowers
tenacious as weeds, have mystical powers.

Love me. Show by the path you tread
you love me now. Tomorrow,
or over that hill, look back if you can.

II *Nothing is competent nothing is*
all there is.
—Creeley, "The Immoral Proposition"

I have brought you the wrong way, and I'm sorry.
The path you wanted is back, out of the thickets

of rhetoric; follow the trampled plants.
Metaphor began with words, and metaphor

misleads: 'buttercup' and 'columbine' are weeds,
they have no healing powers. Shallows of color,
texture and euphony make no flowers last.
The inscriptions of hawthorns cling.

And there is no truth beyond logic—surely
you have walked in circles looking.
Meadows grow into forests, and wilderness
clearings erode or strangle in neglect.

Perhaps there was a valley, and a path,
though this path ended. 'Love' is a conceit
earned in commitment; we are unintentional
liars. My figure has led you to briars.

The Invention of the Telephone

The time it took he could have
crawled—on the hairs of his knuckles,
on his eyelids, on his teeth.

He could have chewed his way.
In a place without friction
he could have re-invented the wheel.

But he wanted you to be
proud of him, so he invented
the telephone before he called.

JUDITH KROLL

Not Thinking of America

Floating across the lake,
lotus-pads upturned with the blank look of clover,

the sun, an unseen presence behind a curtain of heat,
intensifies every tree and flower,
urging them forward like talented children;

the sharp charcoal smoke of the boatman's hookah
floats back in waves, enters the dream,

romance and violence. On the other side of the lake
Shalimar Garden waits;
water-channels, marble pavilions.

Down on the plains, in the winter palace,
a courtier might have been flung from a tower,
the hands of a child cut off to teach a small lesson,

one among many in a realmful of bodies—
playthings, a scattering of coins;
and the wall of blood forever waiting to burst,
an unseen presence, wherever the eyes are turned.

At Shalimar things could seem different,
the pastel valley a landscape of rest
for minds too tired to rest by themselves.

She never existed, one woman the cause of it all;
there might have been someone exquisite who almost
 deserved it,
but she would have been a point of departure,
the small occasion for a larger dream,
who could not really be trusted, though she took on

a luminous presence when set like a pearl in the
    garden,
the garden set in a valley,
the valley an emerald
set in a ring of mountains, a hard cold ring.

Dick & Jane

Dick is the one with the weenie
who gets to be doctor
and never cries,
in love with mechanics and motion.

Jane is the one with nothing under her skirt,
so soft and weepy,
in love with the rulers of earth.

Dick gulps his soup and burns his tongue.
Jane blows and blows to cool hers,
it takes so long
she has ages to see

that Dick is just a boy
with a rubber jiggler.
She can take his tongue on hers and cool it off.
She can cut off his thing at the root.
She can tuck him in bed and sing him to sleep.
She can leave him alone.

Sestina

Is this the object:
not to let things pass

without noticing,
without being in control,
at least of a clear sight?
There are so many things worth nothing.

I sit hour after hour, doing nothing—
dreaming of India, a far green object,
a blinding sun hung on the edge of my sight.
One moment I think I am writing, the next I pass
into infinite fields, and a sky whose control
rains absolute, unnoticing.

I try to think—but find myself noticing
each word sealed off from its thought by a round
    nothing.
Something is out of control;
I do not even object,
unaware that the hours pass,
that the present moment is buried from sight

by this vision of me in India, allowing my sight
to filter off in the distance, noticing
my feet pass over the lawn, my eyes pass
over and over the garden, settling on nothing.
Such a relief, sight without object.
Such a relief, to let control

be a process like breathing; to let control
lie in the targets of sight,
lie, if anywhere, lost in the heart of the object,
and to let the effort of noticing
soak like rain in that tree, that flower, that nothing.
Every moment something is coming to pass.

I remember a high brown mountain: a pass
cut through it, jagged, holding in control
the animals, trees, underbrush, and sky—nothing

escaped, not even my sight;
and the pass extinguished itself at a temple on top,
      without noticing
it had used itself up, it had reached its object.

Is this the object: to pass,
without noticing, beyond control,
beyond fixed sight, beyond nothing?

GREG KUZMA

Journal of the Storm

The Market

There, in the market, with Mrs. Peters
and her young vegetables, I left my blue coat.
What do I tell my wife?
How the young girls and men waltz under the trees
of the market, how the dogs jolt me as I pass,
rupturing my loneliness with their pleas.
Or how with Mrs. Peters above the market in
  the amber rooms
I journey through her into the rare night of my soul.
Her breasts, how I climbed them, naked as a child,
her thighs, my kisses on them like blotches,
and all through us a watery stillness.
My clothes lay on the floor like a man weeping.
And then the bells rising from the wagons
and the swift sifting of the young men and women
and the heavy echoes of the bullocks carrying away
the carts of celery. Where does one begin
to answer the question of what went on at the market.

The House

It is still night. And winter.
The moon through the curtains is orange
and is like the moon of last night. My child
is about to leave to take his exam at the University.
My cat is about to have kittens. I hear her below
in the kitchen running wildly, waiting for them to
overtake her in a thrash of blankets. And now she
is clawing the box I left for her. My wife sleeps.
And I lie here fencing in the toy pastures

and tending the toy cows. She has forgotten
their names,
and has gone back to the house I built with
my own hands
and saved from the storm in the first summer of our
marriage. Even now she is doing the dishes silky with
gravy
again and again in the sunlight. It is blood upon them.
The blood of our first and second children
killed in the year the hawk landed on her hand
and the earth blackened and spurt black blood.
In the year of the big kill.

Rock

A man's life is not his own. He buys it slowly
and fences it off, and names it. Some of it thrives
and he calls these Paul and Mary. Mary is disappointing.
She screws for the local plowboys. Paul will be a doctor
and heal all the sick in the world while his mother dies
of a strange fever. I will scare the birds from the corn
and learn the names of the stars. There I sometimes
see my own name, spelled backwards and in strange
symbols,
and I wonder how it will come out. Here on this rock
I watch below me Mary going off into the field. I watch
her remove her dress, her nipples tilting up like thumbs
in the pale pink light. And it is Paul who mounts her
with a curse and cures her deep wound. I do not own
these things. I watch them, and forget.

The Young Man Who Loved the Girl Who Took Care of Her Aging Father

One night he dreamed he was a
kerosene lamp left over from the

old days. And she had come into
the room where the old man was
dying, where he had been dying,
and in whose presence no electric
light was permitted, and the old
man had died and was there in the
bed like a clothespole fallen under
the sheets off the line, and
she reached across to the night stand
and blew softly into the turned
down wick of his mouth, and the
room went dark.

The Pelican

I don't know if he is rare on these northern lakes
where the wind blows in unbroken by a tree
and sweeps the water dry in any but the most tenacious
  lakes,
but there he is, in the picture in the water of Oak Lake
in the evening paper on the very first page.

The Pelican, with his bill like a boat, with his hidden
habits and scary flight, comes to rest in the middle
of Nebraska ten blocks from my house.
He must be far either way from where he was
and where he is going.

I thought once I was a native creature, full of
habitat and little loves, unable to advance our evolution
by adapting, but stuck in the mud where I found myself
the very first time I ever "found" myself. The Pelican,
with his rather accidental occurrence in my life,
makes me suspect I am like him, confused at least
in appearance, and apt to fly to anywhere out of dim
instinct, and who will let the winds blow as they will,

and be glad to be flying at all, and say so to
everyone watching by setting down in a neighborhood
like this one.

Tomorrow he will be gone from the lake and the news,
the way I suspect I'm likely to leave
this place and that, pushing my gift of a face,
the only one like it in these parts, before me,
glad to be flying.

The Monster

The monster they caught
Out behind Flannery's barn
And carried back to town by torchlight
In a huge metal net
And bleeding from a hundred holes
They shot in him or poked in him
With pitchforks or with the
Special spears some of them had made
In secrecy, looked a lot like
Jim MacDorty, who, rumor said,
When he lost his wife to fever
Three years before, went away
Into the woods and went mad,
Jim MacDorty with a beard, that is,
But when the barber shaved the thing
Whatever it was,
Was nobody they'd ever seen.

Mrs. Morrison, who'd lost a dog
And two daughters, said that there
Must be some connection between
This latest finding and the burning

Of Doctor Snow's house and laboratory
A few days before, when
Paula and Bill Thompson were kept
Up all night at their window
Watching the lights in Snow's cellar
Flickering as shadows moved
Across them.
How the sounds alone were terrible
Enough, and Jones' cat had her first
Miscarriage in four years, some said
From the fright of seeing what left
The burning house just at dawn,
And how the stench from the fire
Was the worst since half
The County Hospital, the cancer ward,
Burned back in '59, and how
The bones they found so many of
That afternoon after the fire died
Had had to belong to somebody.

Those older folks who had been around
The time of the big scare, the time when
Dorothy Dalton disappeared,
And Molly and Freda, returning
From Jason's bar and grill
Were grabbed up,
And how after killing the tramp
By his fire under the full moon
And burying him in Rockton cemetery
Only to find that the murders
Didn't stop, and that the tramp's
Grave was dug up by something
That got in, or out,
Were all for making sure
This time. So it took
All of Dr. Wallace's formaldehyde
And most of Mother Ripton's

Prize vinegar to pickle him
After they'd drawn out
Ten quarts of blood
(Enough for an Angus bull)
Which Edna Elmonds
Said they had better
Put in a barrel
And sink in the deepest part
Of Lake Charles, with a buoy
Over it,
And how some, still not sure,
Asked Bishop Bitely
Who had been called in
To represent the faith
To OK the dismembering
Of the corpse, and how
They cut the tendons
At the joints and removed
And burned most of the
Strange organs, and even bored
Two holes in the giant skull
To pour in hydrochloric acid
And then, how Coroner Aldridge
Swears he saw a yellow eye turn
Up, although it must have been
Just reflex.

And when it came to burying
Although there were many for
Cremation, how the oldsters
Who remembered the other time,
Asked that Waldron and Smith
Be called in to lay forty cubic
Yards of concrete
Over the steel box they put him
In up on Old Low's Hill,
And Farrow's Electric said

They'd have a 500-watt lamp
Installed to burn constantly.

So they took all the precautions
Although it seemed silly to the thousands
Of readers who followed the proceedings
All the weeks it took to get the job done,
And Melbourne surely had the most
Publicity ever, and until the reporters
Left, enjoyed a rich tourist trade—
All those who came miles to see
The body—and every night for weeks
The streets filled with lovers
And drunks, fat-waisted women and
Golf-capped husbands
Cruising the town in big cars,
Although there were still some
Farmers on the outskirts near
Flannery's barn who hadn't slept
For five years, and wouldn't sleep
Much even with the newly installed
Street lights all the way to Buck Mountain.

And how gradually water skiers
Returned to Melbourne Pond,
And some hardy campers stayed
All night,
And no one was disturbed
Again
For a long while.

Although just last week
Mrs. Smith, a woman not easily
Given to hallucination, and rather
Modest besides, said she'd passed
A huge human stool
Black as bears' shit

Out on Old Indian Trail,
And how when half the town
Got there a pack of dogs
Had all but finished
Whatever it had been,

And all the nights afterwards
To hear them howling
In the hills.

AL LEE

Among Sharks

for Antonia Strand and John A. Williams

Cold-blooded in warm waters, my Nurse
Shark basks along the bottom under
My underbelly. She slithers unconcerned
Through corridors of coral.
My snout is glass. I do not thrash
To get attention or away. Bulbous-
Looking in her depth, boneless,
She muscles the fear of death
Into our territorial waters.

Come dive with me. The Nurse has scared away
The Triggerfish, Grunts, and Sergeant Majors—
But we are bigger swimmers, who have so long
Glided coolly among man-eaters
That we do not panic. You and I and it
Will skim the living reef in a froth.
Great bouffant mounds of coral grow
Gardens of spines and swaying stalks
And in grottoes we shall glide to
With a swirl of fins, ruddy
Contours like faces and bodies flower
In the plankton-yellow sunlit sea.

Here are the violet fans of summer.
Here are domes of green brain coral.
This is the jawbone of a politician:
Scrape to his memory, big
And fractured as your ambition.
And these are jawbones of ministers.
This thigh-bone of a foreigner,

Chrome-plated for its greater glory,
Was partway melted in the tropics.
The President's brain breaks up like coral
And floats in slow motion beyond
An umbrella open in the sunlight
Of a chilly windy day.
The assassin James Earl Ray,
Flashing another twenty, flourishing
In the splendor of speculation, dances
With sleepy eyes around the world.
His chin and shoulders low, his elbows
Back, Robert Kennedy swirled
Out of the crowd in the ballroom
Toward a grieving mystic Boom! Boom!

You glide in the air with the ocean
Stroking your belly. You slide
As an airplane over the feeding villages,
And swoop across the lowlands where they grow
And die; they lose their iridescences
In the dangerous night. Behind you swims
The body politic sidewinding
Sluggishly but with a feeling
For too much movement anywhere.
She has been known lazily to circle,
Then smack a man with her bulk
And the teeth of her sandpaper hide.
You will be raw and panicky,
No matter what your courage, when your Nurse
Shark
Opens her prehistoric jaw and lunges.

Weathering the Depths

Dear fellow castaway, the cruise ships
Are going down with spouting belches

All over the Atlantic. Someone's years
Are sinking over there, another's sense
Of self is splintering like a wooden boat.
And we have gone down too
To where even the phosphorous eels
Can't light the way, nor the Gulf Stream
Warm and soothe the choppy bottom.

We alone have buoyed up yet,
This rubber raft is bouncing
Like a trampoline. Oh shipmate,
Let us hold together under pressure
And hide in the deeps as a bathysphere—
Provisioned with Dramamine and code books,
Thick-skinned with stabilizers—private,
My shipmate, among the great big Uglyfish.

Surely by the end of summer
The sea will be all tuckered out
And we can rise again whale-wise and spout
Out our balms. Shall our dreamboat
Become a lunging nuclear *Enterprise*
Launching us like high-flying admirals
To parachute on the capitals of gaiety?

Karl Marx

"The stingier your suppers
And the less you live it up,
The more money you save.
You can work overtime
If that's all you've got to do.
The less you are,
The more you have.

"You can't help it,
Either—
There are two of you.

"One likes to doze all morning
While his wife strokes his balls.
He wants to grow tomatoes
Lazily in his back yard.
The other
Drags him off to work.

"Sure you would kick
The boss's ass
If it weren't yours too.
You would help the boss
Forget the working class
If you didn't need the money.

"You can't be both forever.
Help them have it out.
When they are dead,
You will be whole at last."

The Lie

Think of it little, a fib
We used to giggle ourselves into,
Kids after grade school wanting
The yoyo salesman to dazzle us.
He could rock the baby and walk the dog.
He could contrive celebrity,
He gave cash prizes!
You were a fourth grade tournament master
Of the glass-studded yoyo. Believe

In the ornamental bush of sparkle
Criss-crossing its branches with a whirr
Of string and sunshine. Believe!
If you disbelieve, your eyes
Looking for the truth
Will roll like a damaged boxer's.
Burn the tall grass that conceals.

The fib is an exquisite antique bush.
Its leaves are bells tinkling
A bit too far away for seeing,
Its grandeur is said to be
Almost at hand. Believe
It is there and wade into the woods
Toward it, and like it
Be bright with the dreams my parents
Have deferred to me. I see the green
Of a forested New World in summer,
Not the magic tree eyes water for.
Burn the obstructive shagbark trees.

Presidents on color television say
We must sacrifice for the belief.
An honored professor writes
It is most hard to find but its leaves
Were used by the Kwakiutl Indians.
The men whose wives most wives admire
Commit their cities to the quest.
And heroes with fruity names parade
As if already they had seen it.
Burn the Douglas firs.

The gongs of the lumbercamps
Summon the nation as an army.
Burn the redwoods if you would see
The continent flat and the story
Standing there

Spangled with crystal.
Will it be? Cinders
Spin as the wind whirlpools
Over a people trying to believe.

Around the corner from the school,
The man peddling yoyos keeps up
His banter with the children. Their nerves
Everyday now are as unreliable
As their eyes.

Poem for the Year Twenty Twenty

Had I lived till now,
I would have thumbed your soil
Into my palm and felt the plain soot
And sandiness of your life.
We leached it for you, Twenty Twenty.
Is it scorched?

Honor your grandparents and the riches
They quit accumulating and consumed.
They are out of your reach,
You are under our butt.

The past storms dingily
Through tracts that curl like wet veneer.
Your cities buckle, seas fail.
Fish older than the Bering Strait
Rise from the oceans' valleys—
Armored with denticles, they beach
Where the spangled tide comes in.
In my time we never saw

A shore of mouths so gnarled,
Or smelled a breeze like this.
You sail in steerage
In passage to the great famines.

We offered you the Moon,
That big chalky ball of a suburb
For thousands of your extra billions
To grow orchids under Astrodomes,
To mine the lodes we left to you.

We saw it up close on television:
The sky was colorless, the dust all over,
It could have been Sonora
If you were bleary with marijuana.
You ought to read Scott's log
Of dying in the polar snows.

I think of Nineteen Twenty and of my father,
A dazzled country boy,
Waiting for the future with his crystal set.
When I think of Twenty Twenty,
I rejoice that my soul and I
Are mortal and will not last.

FRED LEVINSON

no more than five

the woman I want
cuts hyacinths
she uses gloves
for this

somewhere she has a lover
whom she watches sleep

her sorrows
running one finger
up and down
between her breasts

from my window
most people
are unconscious
of their own beauty
they have something
rough and capable
to do with reality
their palms are never wet

I see her
briefly
on wednesday
among three
good friends
who console her
by growing old
simultaneously

poem

why should we rise because 'tis light?
did we lie downe because twas night?
—Donne

the country
was back in the hands of the patriots
the cruel tendency
to undergovern
had been relieved

someone wrote
a widely published paper
establishing
the enemy
were getting shorter

it was
clearly
a good year

considering the magnitude
of our problems
things were going very well
the president wore white shoes
and the children
had all become agents

sharks in shallow water

it is reported
in an old book
that a certain chamberlain

tested many new swords
against the bodies
of condemned criminals

this chamberlain insisted
on examining each blade
before wiping
to observe how the fat stuck
how the bones severed

some of his followers declared this
a filthy business

the chamberlain quietly replied
nothing can be changed
unless
there are hundreds and thousands
of advantages

a translation from . . .

the japanese realize
the absence of effort
is a characteristic
of great vigor
—David Stacton

I was sleeping
near a grove of hinoki
ghost foxes loped
behind ruined samurai
three worlds
two of which I inhabit
the third
providing forms
to die in

my wife writes waka
while I guard the frontiers
of yamashiro province
I practice calligraphy
in the dust
with the foot of my spear

one day
we will put out
the last watch fires
and go home
my wife and I
will talk for hours
I will tell her
that the reason
haniwa figures
were placed
on burial mounds
was so they could
speak freely

later
while she rubs my feet
I will softly
rebuke her

no bow is strung forever

a poem against rats

I don't know
it was the smell of mock orange
or pttosporum
but I opened the door

while I worked
I tell it differently now

later the air changed
I closed the door
he was locked inside
and must have watched me
for an hour or more
before he made a move
to test the door

I saw him
no longer than a foot
a brown rat bloated on garbage

I threw a book at him
he ran under a chair
I opened the door
he sat watching me
out of sober rat eyes
poking him with a music stand
I thought of bruises sinking
and shuddered
gritting my teeth
tough little bastard
somewhere such scenes
never subside

I'm not the type to stay with friends
and call the authorities in the morning
but I can't kill
the way I could as a boy
things have other dimensions
but don't think I'm blind to the danger
they died in the dump
doing a ballet
somehow unconnected to my rifle

25c a carcass
dressed the whole thing up

then again
rats have nowhere to go
viscera moves them
it is a matter of calming down
I have a pistol in the next room
loaded against my own avatars
the room is too small
ricochet concussion
so I took a walking stick
out of the closet

for half an hour
we watched each other
he was already a moulage
and I would soon be prostrate with grief
feeding extra honey into the hummingbird feeder

he didn't die easily
bit the shaft of the spear
squealed mournfully
his rage was all defensive
he made his error
when he veered
into the corner
at the angle of two walls and the floor
he reared and reeled
I caught him
and pushed until the stick hit wood

he never would have waxed in my care

LARRY LEVIS

The Poem You Asked For

My poem would eat nothing.
I tried giving it water
but it said no,

worrying me.
Day after day,
I held it up to the light,

turning it over,
but it only pressed its lips
more tightly together.

It grew sullen, like a toad
through with being teased.
I offered it all my money,

my clothes, my car with a full tank.
But the poem stared at the floor.
Finally I cupped it in

my hands, and carried it gently
out into the soft air, into the
evening traffic, wondering how

to end things between us.
For now it had begun breathing,
putting on more and

more hard rings of flesh.
And the poem demanded the food,
it drank up all the water,

beat me and took my money,
tore the faded clothes
off my back,

said Shit,
and walked slowly away,
slicking its hair down.

Said it was going
over to your place.

Bat Angels

Sometimes they smear the evening on the air
with wings that
slap like pistons, just noticed.

In the loose fur,
their armpits fold like rags,
they leave nosebleeds on snow, and fall
like hands dropped on shoulders.
    I saw one lift straight up turning to light.

    Sometimes, out for itself,
an angel like this
comes twisting with its deadpan face
and skitters its blind jaws for meat
over the wind and weeds.

It can't be caught, it's mad,
all night it wants
to chew its own blood and whimper and forget
    the flesh it drags—

while the bare rafters tick under the moon.

Fish

for Philip Levine

The cop holds me up like a fish;
he feels the huge bones
surrounding my eyes,
and he runs a thumb under them,

lifting my eyelids
as if they were
envelopes filled with the night.
Now he turns

my head back and forth, gently,
until I'm so tame and still
I could be a tiny, plastic
skull left on the

dashboard of a junked car.
By now he's so sure of me
he chews gum,
and drops his flashlight to his side;

he could be cleaning a trout
while the pines rise into the darkness,
though tonight trout
are freezing into bits of stars

under the ice. When he lets me go
I feel numb. I feel like
a fish burned by his touch, and turn
and slip into the cold

night rippling with neons,
and the razor blades

of the poor,
and the torn mouths on posters.

Once, I thought even through this
I could go quietly as a star
turning over and over
in the deep truce of its light.

Now, I must
go on repeating the last, filthy
words on the lips
of this shrunken head,

shining out of its death in the moon—
until trout surface
with their petrified, round eyes,
and the stars begin moving.

ELIZABETH LIBBEY

Marceline, to Her Husband

for Linda Orr

> "Yet I realized . . . how much she needed my love, and I enveloped her within it, pretending the need was mine."
>
> —André Gide
> *The Immoralist*

I'm yours, dearest, as are the winter towns,
their heady wines and soups.
My lungs fill.
You do well in this air's thinness, the snow spattering
against your mouth. You love
a sudden crack of ice or larches rushing at us:
landmarks.
Like history, you need them.
Then, now, next month—always
the return to rooms in the evening,
hearing far off the harness bells and noticing how fast
shadows race up the wooded slope.

Tender vigil . . . how kind you are!
And god how your eyes go through me
as if I were the infection itself—unbearable
unless viewed as winter landscape.

This evening, I'll drink your wild face.
That sad wine will slide from my mouth. Let me
offer you my handkerchief, and toss
this dark red luxury in your lap.
The harness bells, hear them now? Harsh,
perfect, consummate.
In this odd transparency of snow
my furs grow stiff around my shoulders.

To Her Dead Mate: Montana, 1966

Hanged man, please grow wild and luminous
like these lanterns I hang from the aspens
to light your way. The moon
won't fall here because of you, but moves
off in the dark like horses.
My body feels empty as reed pipes at the river.
When they speak, they whistle. Can something
this empty break a dead man's fall?

We should have been your mother's couple:
at the seashore, not touching. Admiring the fog.
So, they took their last horse back. How your feet
must have wanted to rest on his back!
I want to wrap you in my long skirt, carry you
until you are tall grass.

Husband, the dance of this hushed wind
is openness, is the gray mouth of your brain.
The long twitch of my arms caught
in your legs—ah, never let go.
Once under, you must
call yourself to yourself for keeps.
The dirt fills us with its taste. And isn't it worth it?
Listen: the river, like riders, approaches from nowhere.

Concerning the Dead Women: The Munitions Plant Explosion: June, 1918

What was most striking about them:
the absence of the expected long hair.

We sorted out blond brunet red gray black,
and matched them as best we could
to the swelling complexions darkening in the heat, yet
not unpleasant to touch.

On the pleasant (though dusty) return to Milan,
we agreed we'd been saved
from the horror of the disaster
by that hair, floating
out from the barbed fence.
Bright as scarves, I remember.

As for those five or six who live on
after metal has entered the brain: though the lieutenant
told us, Leave them alone, I and the corporal
cut off their heads. I won't soon forget my friend
poised above a girl with no face.

We agreed it was best
not to leave them breathing among the dead
in the wide soft trenches we made for them, saving
only the ribbons.

Before the Mountain

Father, I expect your eyes
to regard me as lost. It is my own eyes
that surprise me, gone so far out of me.
They watch the mountain dusk
where you are—so approachable in your disappearance.
The arc of your red flare
patiently erases itself.

Evening being sentimental, how nice
the photographs are in their metal frames:

Father and son on the rock wall, tied
waist to waist. And this one
of the candles we placed below zero
at the heads and feet of the dead ones
so the dead wouldn't freeze.

It's clear now: land seems to stay,
to support us. The mountain, like your hand,
seems to wave at someone beside me, frozen
like the darkening orange helicopters.
Did you, nearly rescued, exchange gifts
briefly with the dark? A celebration of respect.
You never named the gift I am.
In your photograph of no survivors, I'm smiling.

THOMAS LUX

If You See This Man

Notify someone of authority
if you see this man:

He has a fish hook
in his upper lip.
He usually carries a bleeding starfish
in a dixie cup.
He is an excellent fork-lift
operator and is known
to play dice with nuns.
He is big.
He claims to detest miniature golf.

We want him for the robbery
of the first kiss ever given
to a bus driver's sickly daughter.

And remember, he is ruthless.
If he knew you had read this
he would murder you.

History and Abstraction

The dates on bridges
and public buildings—1932, 1951,
19——, and so on: bland

abstractions, bland history.
I like to face history
and abstraction with a positive

condescension. Here's the facts:
technology reached its peak
with the electric chair, nature

poets can't enter the forest
without weapons—this is the truth.
The inexorable boredom of history,

the flat kiss of abstraction . . .
But why do I insist it's too late
to refuse permission

to operate? It's not, it's not
irrevocable, my flesh
is not weightless!

—And, I can be glad
for the small plane of skin
beneath this woman's chin,

and glad for the dead
glassblower's breath still caught
in the red vase behind you.

The Midnight Tennis Match

Note: *In midnight tennis each player gets three serves rather than the usual two.*

You are tired
of this maudlin country club
and you are tired of his insults.
You'd like to pummel his forehead
with a Schweppes bottle
in the sauna, but instead
you agree, this time,

to meet him at midnight
on the tennis court.

When you get there
you can't see him
but you know he is waiting
on the other side of the net.
You consider briefly
his reputation.

You have first serve
so you run toward the net
and dive over it.
You land hard on your face.
It's not a good serve: looking up
you can barely see his white shorts
gleam in the darkness.

You get up, go back
to your side of the net
and dive over again.
This time you slide
to within a few feet of him.
Now you can make out his ankles,
the glint of the moon
on his white socks.

Your last serve is the best:
your chin stops one inch
from the tip of his sneakers.
Pinheads of blood
bloom across your chest.
You feel good crawling
back to your side again.

Now it is his turn
and as he runs toward the net
you know he's the fastest man
you've ever seen.

THOMAS LUX

His dive is of course flawless.
He soars by you,
goes completely off the court
and onto the lawn,
demolishing a few lounge chairs.
To finish, he slides
brilliantly onto the veranda.

You go up and sit beside him
and somehow
you don't feel too humiliated:
he is still unconscious.
At least now you know why
he is undefeated. It's
his sensitive, yet brutal, contempt.
With a similar contempt
you pour a gallon of water on his face.
He still has two more serves—

Lament City

Welcome home, driving downhill
one good eye on the fence, a scar
along the exquisite thigh
of this valley—I don't like it.

Population innumerable, ah Lament
City: where a wagon's
been rotting in a field so long
the earth has grown up
to its axles,
where firing squads go to retire,

where cows lie down all day
and won't eat grass

unless you first lift
their enormous heads and brush
the grayness of it across their lips,

and where obviously, we must *always*
be at one business: contradiction.

So, understand this: it's Friday night
in Lament City and I feel
wonderful. It's Sunday afternoon
in Lament City, and you and I,
Mushroom, spend the entire day
lounging on the porch.

We are alive. Our fingertips
are alive and we love something
even if it is only a spirit
with cloth wings. We don't care
we love it so much!

This is a Poem for the Fathers and for Michael Ryan

Pal, in the Pals of Death Club
we always ask each other: Do we die
like this or do we live

like this? Even novitiates
can answer: No!
We answer before we glance

at our deathwatches, gifts
from particular graduations,
without noticing our wrists,

like the necks of buzzards,
poking from our sleeves.
It's an easy question,

for us. It's easier than choosing
between whiplash and caress: No!:
we *live* like this: blue lights,

black marks that start low
on the fingernail then grow
away. Excellent!

The main idea is to keep our flesh
over our bones and to listen
occasionally to our bodies: when

the blood in our hands lies
down, we should lie down also.
Maybe an example will make it

clear: our fathers who are dead
and our fathers who are alive, are embracing.
Yours reaching out of the grave,

mine reaching . . . Look
at it this way: Nobody's happy. Nobody.
But, that's not the point.

This is: the teasing haunt
of affirmation, the thermometers burning
in the mouths of the gone.

WILLIAM MATTHEWS

Oh Yes

My hands, my fists, my small bells
of exact joy,
clappers cut out
because they have lied.

And your tongue:
like a burnt string
it holds its shape until
you try to lift it.

We're sewn into each other
like money in a miser's coat.
Don't cry. Your wounds are
beautiful if you'll love mine.

The Cat

While you read
the sleepmoth begins
to circle your eyes
and then—
a hail of claws
lands the cat
in your lap.
The little motor
in his throat
is how a cat says
Me. He rasps the soft

file of his tongue
along the inside
of your wrist.
He licks himself.
He's building
a pebble of fur
in his stomach.
And now he pulls
his body in a circle
around the fire of sleep.

This is the wet
sweater with legs
that shakes in
from the rain,
split-ear the sex burglar,
Fish-breath, Wind-
minion, paw-poker
of dust
tumbleweeds,
the cat that kisses
with the wet
flame of his tongue
each of your eyelids
as if sealing
a letter.

One afternoon
napping under the light-
ladder
let down by the window,
there are two of them:
cat and cat-
shadow, sleep.

One night you lay your book
down like the clothes

your mother wanted
you to wear tomorrow.
You yawn.
The cat exhales a moon.
Opening a moon,
you dream of cats.
One of them strokes you
the wrong way. Still,
you sleep well.

This is the same cat
Plunder.
This is the old cat
Milk-whiskers.
This is the cat
eating one of its lives.
This is the first cat
Fire-fur.
This is the next cat
St. Sorrow.
This is the cat with its claws
furled, like sleep's flag.
This is the lust cat
trying to sleep with its shadow.
This is the only cat
I have ever loved.
This cat has written
in tongue-ink
the poem you are reading now,
the poem scratching
at the gate of silence,
the poem
that forgives
itself
for its used-up lives,
the poem
of the cat waking,

running a long shudder
through his body,
stretching again,
following the moist bell
of his nose
into the world
again.

Directions

The new road runs into
the old road, turn
west when your ankles hurt.
The wind will be thinning itself
in the grass. Listen, those thuds
are bees drunk with plunder
falling from the minarets of flowers
like ripe prayers.
Follow the path
their bodies make. Faster.
The dirt in that wineglass
came from Chateau d'Yquem.
You're getting closer.
That pile of clothes
is where some women
enter the river. Hurry up.
The last hill is called
Sleep's Kneecap, nobody
remembers why.
This is where the wind turns
back. From the ridge
you can see the light.
It's more like a bright soot,
really, or the dust

a moth's wing leaves
on the thumb and forefinger.
This is where I turn
back—you go the rest of the way
by eating the light until
there is none and the next one
eats along the glow
of your extinguished hunger and turns
to the living.

The Penalty for Bigamy Is Two Wives

I don't understand how Janis Joplin did it, how she made her voice break out like that in hives of feeling. I have a friend who writes poems who says he really wants to be a rock star—the high-heeled boots, the hand-held mike, the glare of underpants in the front row, the whole package. He says he likes the way music throws you back into your body, like organic food or heroin. But when he sings it is sleek and abstract except for the pain, like the silhouette of a dog baying at the moon, almost liver-shaped, a bell hung from a rope of its own pure yearning. Naturally his life is exciting, but I sometimes think he can't tell the difference between salvation and death. When I listen to my Janis Joplin records I think of him. Once I got drunk & sloppy and told him I feared artists always had more fun and more death, too, and how I had these strong feelings but nothing to do with them and he said *Don't worry I'd trade my onion collection for a good cry, wouldn't you?* I didn't really understand, but poetry is how you feel so I lie back and listen to Janis's dead voice run up and down my body like a fire that has learned to live on itself and I think *Here it comes, Grief's beautiful blow job.* I think about the painter who was said to paint with his penis and I imagine one of his portraits letting down a local rain of hair around his penis now too stiff to paint with, as if her diligent silence meant to say *You loved me enough to make me, when will I see you next?* Janis, I don't care what anybody thinks or writes, I don't care if my friend who writes poems is a beautiful fake, like a planetarium ceiling, I want to hold my life in my arms as easily as my body will hold forever the silence for which the mouth slowly opens.

Praise

First, to the feet, as they bear what you have grown to live
in, your pod of a body, slow to explode.

And to the toes, as they were roots once, and so you go by
me like a bush of bells searching for music, and I sing
in my bad voice *hello* and we turn to each other.

And to the calves, as their long canoe-shaped muscles glide
in the same place always over the sunken bone, the
body's future.

And to the knees, as they are loud echoes of the knuckles
and the backs of them grow pink and painful if you fall
asleep face-down in the sun.

When the thighs are drunk on duty and I creep by, I tell
them a strange dream and they have it and are re-
freshed. Praise to the thighs, stolid and lovely.

And to the buttocks, as they bob like pans of a scale when
you walk away and take my true weight when I lie
down on you.

And to the hips, as every cup should have a handle, as they are the ears and ankles of the body's delta, as they are your calcium outriggers covered by flesh.

And to the navel, as it is the first crater. Its seal is all that's left of your mother's letter explaining happiness and pain. Praise to the navel.

And to the *linea alba*, as it is bellrope for the pubic hair and the tongue's path to music lessons.

And to the clitoris, as it is a loaf of tiny bread, a pearl of blood, because it does nothing but drum and trouble the inner waters.

And to the cunt, as it is the glove that is mother to the finger, mouth that gives speech to the tongue, home that gives restlessness to the cock.

And to the stomach, as it contains the speech your body makes to itself, boring as can be, every day of hunger: *Fill me, I am empty with the knowledge of my need.*

And to the back, as the dunes of muscles shift across it, and that underground river of bones, your spine, flows through it.

And to the shoulders, as they were wings once. Your shoulders gather like dense clouds that are moored by rain to the rest of your body, and I praise the way they float there.

And to the breasts, as they doze waiting for babies, as the nipples sting in cold wind, as a hand or tongue, like a shadow with the right weight, passes over them.

And to the throat, as it is the stalk of your face and the place where your breath breaks into the right syllables: I place my tongue on your throat's bluest vein, in praise.

And to the tongue, as it lolls and darts on its tether—domestic, secret, blunt.

And to the lips, as my name or anything you say blooms on them to die away. When I kiss you I leave my name again for your breath to pass through.

And to the nose, as it remembers and uses fumes from the fire of the arriving future.

And to the ears, as their delicate bones shiver precisely; they are shells listening to themselves, and they can hear the roar of the blood always.

When I stare into your eyes, a little knot of light in mine breaks. Undressing the light, we see that darkness is its birthmark. Praise to the eyes.

And to the hair, as when I sift it with my fingers it remembers its first life as grass on the early earth and springs back to its own shape.

And to the arms, as they hold in order to let go. We rock in the boats of our bodies. The wind rises, the final lust. When you raise your arms, the space between them is a sail I helped to sew.

And to the hands, as their cargo of scars and air can never be given away. You may rest them on my body if you like.

And to the fingers, as they are failed tunnels into nothingness. They went a little way and came home to the body.

And to the bones, the body's ore and its memory of itself
when the rest of it is the breath of something else—to
the bones, praise.

And to the face, as light flares and calms between the skin
and skull. And those blind cows, my fingers, graze
there in any weather.

And to the blood, tireless needle pulling its thread of tides,
tireless praise. Say it again and again, the names are
lying down to sleep together.

ANGELA McCABE

Inside History

History she (Zelda) said stops here. The efforts of history don't belong here, that is true, but there are tangibles.

Last night after they turned the lights out (we are forty women, laid side by side on our backs on white enamelled cot beds like tomb effigies who breathe only in darkness together) I saw history on black velvet: the fires of our flat Autumns tore down the farm house in my eyes, a bicycle child swerved in terrific wind, blinded I suppose by the heat, into the belly of our kitchen stove, instinctively looking for some kind of ashen warmth away from the heat. She heard bellows from her father's room: Don't go there (where? She was standing quite fine in a white nightdress on a silent burnt landscape, bicycle dead like a dog at her feet but unburnt.) Her mother's hand combed her tangled hair. She was all caring.

"You must look your very very best," she said. "And now we will go and see what happened to your father."

Back

Of course when someone leaves you forever you see his back. I could have hit it with a cannonball but, still, there it would have remained: his bristly jacket pinched around the shoulders, the bladed tweed grimace of a retreat, a back with a face, I imagined, that forced off it "I cannot."

Had I left him, and lost the game, would he have longed after my mourning back? No, he would have preferred to think how nonchalant I am, and turned away, maybe even smiling. Later, taking off his jacket, and rubbing his shoulder, he would tell a friend, "How much easier it is for women. Water off a goddamned duck's back."

From Lois in London

Angela Honey (she wrote) I would it were not so but baby I'm broke and there's nothing worse than that unless it's being bankrupt I don't know about the latter but let me tell you what happened. There's nothing worse than being broke in London on a lukewarm day, dig? So I walked out into the smogshine and felt like I was the spirit of food rationing itself, pale after a war, no color in the margerine, and I kept forgetting and walking off the kurb? And these things, these micro minis that they've got around here, whip past and toot the juice through you, something I'm in no shape to handle, and so I went into St. James park which is the park where Billy Graham caught a couple going at it and where on any lukewarm day the grass heaves with sex, which I don't harbour any prejudices against, only wishing I could have a hand in the old moil, when Mr. Jack-the-Ripper himself comes along. Sits down. Raincoat and no jockeys syndrome the whole bit. So we're sitting there, side by side, and nothing happens. I mean nothing. A real Antonioni. I guess he knows I'm broke. Finally, out of utter boredom, I turned and said, "Well aren't you going to say something, do anything, touch and feel?" Angela, dig this: He said, luv, I'm off duty, so I thought I'd try to give you a bit of cheer, you look so glum. Thanks, that's nice, I said. And then he reached into the trench coat, and I thought okay honey here goes, and you know what? He pulled out a *Sock*! he said, it was a real old flesh-colored knitted golf sock, I'll have to present you with this because it's all I've got, but it'll get you a meal somewhere. I was all set to say feh! take that vile thing away, when he told me in the gentlest voice, "This was the sock Wellington had on when he won the battle at Waterloo." I just wanted to tell you that in case the world was too much with you. regards, Lois.

Bloom Street

I will remember you on Bloom Street as you stood in front of the Pontiac showcase, in the brown suit you wore for weddings and all rites of passage, did they bury you in brown? Did they pack your strong white legs together and wind them in burlap brown? Did they press your hard knees and iron down the blisters on your crooked toes and gentle your neck with dull copper flocking? Brown. This is the odor of transience. I cannot remember the color of gold on fire; I will not remember the sound of your voice in my hand.

Blind Adolphus

I remember Longwood. I remember driving there to see Clara and mother's blind cousin, Adolphus, in the Spring, at Longwood, in the Dynaflow. I recall how we stayed at a Tudor Style Inn, near Grand Rapids, and the way the walls there were stained. They looked like Champ Levee, though somewhat irregular, patterns of the fleur-de-lys, in the mellow early evening light before the sun goes down when I was put to bed before I could settle down to sleep, and the next day, Longwood. I recall the avenue to Longwood, and how it seemed never to end, and the muffler dragged on the ground, and when we got to Longwood it was all like a negative, everybody dressed in wheat clothes with white faces and Clara, bleached out, came onto the terrace and seemed to have about her a flock of white doves, though, when she came closer, I could see they were just tissues, for she had a cold or so it seemed to me, and Daddy said why, Emmaline she looks all got up for a *Wedding* and Momma, did she have a cold, too? she laughed and didn't sound exactly happy. We went inside. It smelled of cellar, old damp books crying in a cellar. All the furniture was put in rows alongside the wall. Echo of Auntie Clara's voice: Adolphus is in here, it's cooler in the pantry. In the pantry he was lying on the old zinc table. Uncle Adolphus. And Momma holding me back. And Clara puts her finger to her lips. I remember Uncle Adolphus, his hair flowing over the end of the table, and his eyes wide open and they stare at his feet, not seeing any body, and of course they wouldn't because he's blind. And I recall how I thought oh at last, at last now I know what a blind man is, and thinking how fine a thing to be blind, you can just lie on the pantry table and stare at your feet if you want and no one can talk or disturb you. Mother said, "Well, he had thirty-four *good* years . . ."

DAVID McELROY

Dragging in Winter

Sometimes the sea lays
back nasty white like a girl
(get it?) when draggers anchor
down in weather. And let's say
the sky moved in furniture.
To pass the time, this swirl
of fog is a blanket thrown
over the seabed. What we want
swims in limbo by the tons
under the covers. We're bored
with the diesel's throb, nonchalant
with our handsome hard-ons.

We roll smokes and act
like men of the sea who fit
their own rugged beauty, acting
natural rolling smokes.
Ham it up. We're ugly, get it?
Money is looks when you're broke
in the hole with Friday beat
by next week. Even women break
down like jobs or weather,
cry and skunk you on the beach.
Our skipper jokes about winter
fogs when he-men fuck skate.

"What the hell with time to kill—
and the hole's a dead ringer."
Ugly for love, we imagine fishermen
who get it. The skate's wings, not fins,
smacking on the deck. The tail stinger
you chop off. Stuff a plaid shirt

in that shark-mouth or you'll get hurt
again. Lug your lover to a fo'c'sle
bunk, hook your fingers in gill
slits. Make the most of it, wish
on a star, jab your aching eggs
up the cold ancient fish flesh.

On land we'd act natural, pure
dirt from so much sea—the sea, dirt
cheap and flophouse mean. Who coiled
the kelp like bedsprings? Furniture
broken in a dirty mind? We've all called
that mermaid up, the prettiest flirt
in town who forgot her tail was a fin,
who just wanted someone human, weak
like Robert Young, the American father,
for staying lovely with, loving less
and less, bound in marriage back to back
like purebred dogs stuck together.

Love is ugly, and the child, born wet.

Report from the Correspondent They Fired

Juan, the moron next door,
dreams in green feelings.
The parrot perched on his head is real
friendly, and the avocado right
in his hand is a handful of green.
The brown hand molds its package
around the meat, and the meat molds
around the pit dead center
in the palm. When he is hungry
the avocado is good to eat.

The river standing by is not
a snake, neck bulged out
with bottled news of guerrillas
coming alive in the Guatemala
gloom upstream. The gun butt,
the splintered cheek piece bobbing by,
is only pine, a campesino's table leg.
Water can't talk. The river
and the parrot know their place.
Barges stuck in mud are chunks
of chocolate good to eat.

Crazy with the heat, waiting for mail,
I try to read the river where it curves.
Even boatmen miss the point.
My neighbor and I swing out together
over the bank on a log swing hung
from a ceiba. The dumb bird clings
in Juan's hair turning off and on to green.

Today the butcher killed a sow
then hung a red flag out
to signal flies and mothers in.
Consuelo, another widow dressed up
in black, empty basket on her head,
comes down the road for jowls
and pork brains. The afternoon glows
caramel on her arm, beer-bottle smooth.
In her snappy black cat eyes, slivers
of light damn me, the company I keep,
and my mox-nix vegetarian politics.

Ah vaya!
Two strange ones swinging by the river,
we could be friends, we could be hams
curing in the shade, good to eat.

Spawning in Northern Minnesota

Under cracking pieces of the moon, eelpout
slap their milky bellies home. Water
breaking north turns granite at the mouth.
But here they batter, twist, and squirm over
and over each other, whipping dorsal fins
in a spinning roll, knocking flanks in the wake
of rocks—the splintered river dizzy with oxygen.

Birch explodes at thirty below, and spit
will scrape and clatter on the bank. Liquid fish
don't play games on a shallow bar.
In the bed and mix of the riffle, gills rake
water for air. Females plant gravel
with clouds. Flocks of males boil in a kiss
and make a hundred million chances work.

Cousin to codfish, an eelpout's liver
can't shrink goiters, but crossing moose
are sometimes whales, and any random otter
is a shark. Spawn floats the tinkling moon
downhill to a glacier's melted thumb
where limestone fossils crawl. Granite is ice.
The Mesabi is young, my county an ocean.

Ode to a Dead Dodge

Now corn pushes past the foam
rubber front seat where it sprouted,
pale and aiming like a drunk for the light
up front where glass and guessing

became concrete. One ear taps
code on a dud horn.

The corn drives on, gunning 'til fall
the engine, which, as it now stands,
is a sumac, V crotch in the stem,
four-barrelled leaves doing the job
while all around hang those red fuzzy
berries. Very good, I've heard, for tea.

Making It Simple
December 8, 1969

Married for one year
plus a week and a half,
I watch my black wife, Colleen,
lean from the big chair
toward Vanessa who is puzzled
in soft lamplight.

They are looking for answers
the abacus can give them.

The round wood beads
in ten rows of ten
are red
orange
yellow
green
and blue
repeated twice
counting down.

In the kitchen Kevin is ten,
but she is nine.

Adding is easy,
take-away is hard.

Mamma says
you can subtract by adding.
With pencil and paper
she draws eight pudgy birds,
"How many more birds
do you need
to make twenty-five?"

The many fingers of my wife are lovely,
slender, like the eyes of her daughter
who now has arched her supple arms
back over her head
like the horns of the American gazelle.
She says, "I don't get it."

They are looking for answers
the abacus can give them.

They are looking for the pudgy birds
that won't come home.
The soft Oriental partridges
fluffed up against the cold,
stuffed with buds, roosting in the tops
of birch trees at twilight
when I was fifteen and counted
with a long brown gun.

The wood beads click softly
like jellybeans,
all flavors.
In buttery light
they look full and spongy
as enemy babies
stacked on a path

in ten rows of ten.
The red so real
it's phony blood.
The last rows,
by accident,
green and blue as produce.

Adding is easy,
take-away is hard.

We are hungry for numbers:
correct, no or yes, but definite
like getting pregnant.
My wife bends down with answers
mean as wine that she can't give
Vanessa, for whom my love is legalized.
In some states the papers come soon.

Mother and daughter,
the yellow space between
defines exactly a gold goblet
or two faces in relief,
the profiles classic and blended
from Ife
Chinese
and Seminole.
A handsome hodge-podge, American
even.

When my wife steps out to me from the bath
her wicked limbs are lavish
and our secret, royal.
Our girl climbs from the tub,
eyes closed, feeling for a towel.
Her pussy is perfect without hair,
like the sweet blue clefted plums
waiting for us on the trees

at our first home this fall.
I hand her a towel and feel the power
of all our lost fathers.
I have tasted my sperm from my own hand
to answer their burning.

We are looking for answers
the abacus can give us.

Suddenly it all adds up:
beads
babies
jellybeans
and birds.
With her trigger finger
Vanessa clicks off
the seventeen days till Christmas.

HEATHER McHUGH

Night Catch

The wise fish digs his silver in
to the sludge, at the late
fisherman's bait of lantern.
No light nudges him upward; tail and fin
refuse to flicker and an old old yearning

blackens in the place of burning.
Mud becomes him, who drops
out of the school of luminaries.
You, my brightest educator, must forgive my cool
learning to live in dives. I have made up the whitest

things about me, they are lies. The grace you see
is absence and invention is the blue
space I replace my heart with. Recognize
the artifice of hate, its deep
black glass, the surface that the face
refuses to shine through.

Corps d'Esprit

Just when you're able to admit
you always wanted to whack
her one with your backhand
hard, then some outrageous stroke
of bad luck—backstroke—does
it for you. Just

when you know what to do
with your life, the mother

of it and the wife you fixed
it up with, then it jilts
you all and crawls off
on your belly. Forty-two

is the number of years that fits
like concrete shoes. Just when you regret
your careless walking on the stream
of consciousness, the shoes remember and they haul
you in. What of your dry amusement?

What of your nonchalance? Just when you know
people best and have learned at last by heart
the logic of loving them least, just now

fisheyed and heavyfooted in its wonder,
still fat in the fists of its intelligence,
the body of your life goes under.

Note Delivered by Female Impersonator

Perversion interests me,
a three-legged dog in the driveway,
Coquilles Saint-Jacques on plastic dishes,
anything up the ass.
All I ask is a little retardation.
Let me be more imperative. Walk
your irregularly rhythmic walk
more slowly. Swallow more slowly. Shove
and retract, dump and lap, drill
and withdraw—but slowly. Slowly.
Let me be more specific.
You interest me.

JAMES McMICHAEL

The Cabin North of It All

You build it where you will be heard only by chance
And at a great distance. The hammer is moss

And the saw moves like the wolf's shoulder,
Smoothly, and with no sound. It is a good start.

The seasons themselves come singly, and you are still
North of it all, north of brooding on that later time

When it will be quieter, when the door will not hold,
When the raccoons, on their first night inside,

Will not trouble to be afraid, their heads
Bent in the squares of moonlight, dreaming of the north.

Lutra, The Fisher

The otter is known
for the way his face turns up
anywhere.

On silver coins
or from behind mahogany bureaus

he wears the aspect of a suckling,
innocent
and helplessly

shocked that he should be caught so,

napkin under chin,
his dinner folded
head to tail between his jaws
like a limp bow.

When he goes to work

the surprise is
that he is there at all.

His long neck of a body
streams like sunken
weed-strands,

rises and trails the quiet wake
of any log or stone.

Even in the shallows
he is the thought of his own
absence
and can be found at home

as water would be found there,

filling the den
or strewing over the kitchen floor

bones and vermillion gills.

The Inland Lighthouse

Into the night,
out from him,

out into the air
he throws his frames
and fixes them,
holds them out there.

These are his shores.
The waters never
rush at him, never
follow the beams
back along the watch
to his lean shiver.

Around him, as he
turns, he hears
a dull tick of grains.
He stares into the day.
Sand fills the sky
with its falling

and he turns and turns.
"Nowhere. Nowhere."
It is his oath.
He is the light,
the keeper.
He is not to leave.

The Great Garret, Or 100 Wheels

The curricle and hansom
pretend to such size as would send them

shaking along the lanes
and past the gates to closes,

their separate pedigrees lettered
neatly on each undercarriage: "H. R.

Waiting" and "Thos. 1775 Beeton."
They huddle among the rafters with

models of sedans, wains, herring carts,
cabriolets and a barouche,

all kept at rest in some autistic
pageant of transport, or by the staid

example of the wind toy, its soldiers
frozen forever in mid-stride.

Only the cycles have a muscular past.
From the treadles of the *Draisienne*

it is as far to any point on the whole
vast chase of the manor

as to the next of the measured
interstices between the spokes.

Turning is what would change this.
Because they never turn,

the niceties of the garden are clearly
here, nearer the pediments than those

outlying, lesser strips of arable.
Clearly the forecourts are not behind.

Predictably, and with perfect rigor,
they front for the house in its fixed

severance from the village and the fields.
Because they never turn,

landmarks of this and that are where they are.
Wooded hollows and the Windrush.

Stray brakes of hawthorn on the dark slopes.
Sheepwalks. Trails. Uncertain rights of drift.

The Village of the Presents

The repose they know in storefronts
weighs upon the tree.
Axes and flints, tin pots, some blankets, dolls,

all telling on the limbs,
the ribbons stretched and twisting.

The clubs that hang there
carry in their heads the tapir's puzzled
amble down its ruts,

its fall,
the neck laid open to the white

heart-bundle.
And there are whistles,
hollow wing-bones light enough to strike

beyond the huts the corridors
of saplings,

broader trunks,
lianas plaited through with vines,
all conduits of sound

disturbed and doubling back and knotted.
Pools of it are overgrown,

their leaves
transfixed or like the hidden dead
indifferent,

easy in that place where listening is to eat.
Again and again

the same few shuffles,
the ring of the long blades quitting
just beyond their cuts.

The swath has found the water.
From this side only,

from as far away as some lost bell
the call
across to him in the clearing where he waits

first to throw his set-lines,
turns with the river's leisure to the trees.

SANDRA McPHERSON

His Body

He doesn't like it, of course—
Others, who don't wear it but see it, do.
He's pale, like a big desert, but you can find flowers.
No, not entirely pale:
Between shin and ankle the twin sun marks;
And where his shirt (now draped from a chair back)
Was, he contrasts with dark hands
And neck/face
Like a rained-on street where a car has just been driven
Away.
Don't picture a beer paunch.
And he is a smooth animal, or soft where he isn't
  smooth,
Down to his toadskin testicles.
He lies prone on clean bedsheets.
There is a single light in the room.
Now run your hand down his back, its small, and up
The hips and over. Their sheen's like that
On blue metal music boxes made to hold powder.
But the rest of him is sprouted with black down-going
  hair,
His whiskers in so many foxholes,
Eager to out.
Are they in any order?
Age has so far
Remained locked inside.
I'm not a doctor
And glad not to have a doctor's viewpoint.
I'm glad I haven't the petite,

Overwhelmed sight of an antibody.
And yet I'm not just anybody perusing his body—
I have a reason to like it better than I like other bodies.
Someone else can praise those,
Each lonely and earthly, wanting to be celestial.

Wanting a Mummy

I've always wanted one,
A connection,

Leaning against the bureau, an in
To atrocious kingships,

To stone passages,
Those nights carrying the planets of the dead.

I'd like being able to ask it,
How do you like the rain?

Are you 3000 years old or still 25?
And to hear it replying,

Voluble with symbols
And medallions.

There we would debate, faced off
Across the room,

My room-temperature friend and I,
I with my hands like peaches

And my friend all
Shortbread and roots.

Elegies for the Hot Season

1 *The Killing of the Snails*

Half the year has hot nights, like this,
When gnats fly thick as stars, when the temperature is
taken
On the tongues of flowers and lovers,
When the just-dead is buried in warm sod.
The snail-pebbled lawns glimmer with slime trails,
and the unworried,
Unhurried snail tucks into his dark knuckle, stockaded
With spears of grass, safe. When I first heard
The sound of his dying, it was like knuckles cracking.

The lightest foot can slay snails. Their shells break
More easily than mirrors. And like bad luck, like
A face in a mirror, they always come back.

Good hunting nights were stuffy as a closed room.
No moon shone but my father's flashlight.
As if it were Jericho, he circled the house,
And I'd hear all evening the thick crunch
Of his marching, the sound of death due
To his size 13 shoe.

In the morning I'd find them, little clots on the grass,
pretend
They'd been singed by geranium fire-bursts, asphyxiated
by blue
Iris flame, burnt to shadows under the strawberry
blossom.
The fuchsias bled for them. White-throated calla lilies
Maintained appearances above the snail slum.

But the slow-brained pests forgave and fragilely claimed
the garden
The next hot season, like old friends, or avengers.

2 *The Killing of the Caterpillars*

Today I watch our neighbor celebrating May,
Ringing round the besieged cherry-tree,
His haunted maypole, brandishing his arson's torch
Through the tents of caterpillars. He plays conductor,
Striking his baton for the May music.
And the soft, fingery caterpillars perform,
Snap, crackle, pop.

They plummet through a holiday of leaves like fireworks
or shooting stars or votive candles
Or buttercups, under the hex of the neighbor's wand,
first fruits of euthanasia,
Ripe and red before the cherries. And it is over,
Grown cold as a sunset. They lie on the grass
Still and black as those who lie under it.

It is night. Lights burn in the city
Like lamps of a search-party, like the search-beam
Of my father's flashlight, at every swing discovering
Death.

Marlow and Nancy

I am wondering how I could have changed her blood,
Physician phasing a baby's blue to red,
When I have no skill. My knife I thought
Was just rain's shine on stone. I killed her
Because she was alone, and in the night

The rain, its swallowing sounds, became cold people
Running me down into the softened earth.

I heard a cat
Bite bones in a shrew and couldn't eat.
When my hunger left I still needed food.
So I moved as a cat, with my balls swinging.
She was bottomless in a way. She had antlers
In her from a fighting lover who died.
They hit my edge with a ring echoing their wilderness.

She was bottomless as a cloud
Because she could float
And put her arms around me. That is how
I might move my hands in her like dulled blades
And feel the sharpness in myself that she knew.
I thought she would drown me, then I could sleep.

After, it was as if I'd simply given her change—
In silver, paid her by giving her nothing.
Because I am returning to the earth,
I must stake my life with shrews, antlers, rain and stone.
I feel I am the river bottom between debris
And depths that will never know I balanced here
At this light point in a body
Pushing me away but blue, so blue.

Seaweeds

I know a little what it is like, once here at high tide
Stranded, for them to be so attached to the bottom's
Sarcophagus lids, up to their brown green gold wine
Bottle necks in the prevailing booze, riding, as far
As we can see, like a picnic on a blanket.

Whatever plucks them from below the red horizon
Like snapped pulleys and ropes for the pyramidal effort
Of the moon, they come in, they come through the
  breakers,
Heaps of hair, writing across the beach a collapsed
Script, signers of a huge independence.

Melville thought them pure, bitter, seeing the fog-sized
Flies dancing stiff and renaissance above. But I
Have eaten nori and dulse, and to have gone deep
Before being cast out leaves hardly a taste of loneliness.
And I take in their iodine.

Sisters

She suffers like a red stone, small as a carat.
Her edges show cut to the women crying "Birthstone"
Beside her bed. She needs no mind for you
To see her this way, in a stainless setting,
White meticulous craftsmen turning her. She's been
Years in this Smithsonian and you want to steal her,
Your fine sister, and hang her on your neck . . .

Pearl,

I want no one to find you so! With all
Your appearance of a rich woman, dressing in silk
I cover only my head with, the unraveled *Bombyx mori*
At the other end of the hole dug through to the orient,
Dug through; hard as you are, as the oyster is soft;
Black-pearl, natural-silk-dun, gray-matter vision;
Charity and investments; your skin now
Hangs loose as layers of beads around your throat.

We walked through dimestores and Penney's: you were
Younger. You bought me underwear and taffeta

For dresses with an erotic rustle, so I could stand
On the diningroom table while you hemmed—
Pins and scraps, scissors and punishment. She never
Favored me, an aunt, in the small house behind your
large.
I lost a peridot ring in her garden.
You would find it, wouldn't you? And when I caught
you
Clean as a cake tester in your slip, you blushed
And bawled me out.

No, her heart didn't break you,
Nor your forgotten name, nor the mine made for her.
You can still give the gifts I knew you for,
In dizziness, in high blood pressure. Still, you fail
A bit. While she sleeps you count her, figure
Of a sisterhood in which you are not quite yourself,
Count and put in place like hand-sewn jewels
On your sweater from Hong Kong.

ROBERT MEZEY

In the Soul Hour

Tonight I could die as easily as the grass
and I can't help thinking
whenever the light flickers along the finished blood red
   boards
how just the other side
of the fiery grain
the skull of the house is clapped in darkness

The joys of our lives tonight
the dance sweat the shining sidelong eyes
the faint sweet cuntsmells hiding in perfume

music from another planet

voices at night
carried across the blowing water

Night on Clinton

The bar is closed and I come
to myself outside the door,
drunk and shivering. The talking
champions, the bedroom
killers, the barroom Catholics
have all drifted away and I
am standing in a yellowish
wound of light. Above the blot
my breathing makes on the glass,

I look down the darkened bar
where the bottles are out of breath,
the stale tumblers bunched, and white
glistening webs in the pitchers
dry up and shrivel.
The plastic stools turn
in the hot light that bubbles
from the big Sea Bird, silent now,
and a shape vaguely human
moves with a rag and a limp
among the tables
piled high with surrendered chairs.
Nailed on the back wall, a great
Canadian elk fixes me
with his glazed liquid eyes and
the last lights go out. What I see
is important now, but I see
only the dim half-moon
of my own face in the black
mirror of space, and I lay
my cheek against the cold glass.
Snow is beginning to fall,
huge wet flakes that burst from
the darkness like parachutes
and plunge past the streaming light
and melt into the street.
Freeze, die, says the veteran wind
from the north but he goes on
with his work, the night and the snow,
and was not speaking to me.

Back

Tonight I looked at the pale northern sky
Above the city lights, and both the stars

And the lamps of men faded and burned by turns,
Breathed in and out. You would have liked it here,
The emptiness, the wind across the fields,
And the spring coming on—especially
The strange white almond blossoms, their unfolding
When a car swings down the lane towards the orchard
And turns its headlights on them. Hard as it was,
I forced myself to think of everything
You liked best, the years before you died
In a locked room in an Army hospital.
Or was it after that, in a Southern city,
Watching the traffic lights go on and off
And the big-finned cars swim past in a blur of rain?
I know your heart stopped once when, slightly drunk,
Holding your daughter's hand, you stood before
The cage of a small, shuddering European bear.
That spring in Half Moon Bay, where the sad surf
Felt up and down the beach with endless sighs,
And in the morning the brown seaweed lay
Like old surgical tubing. It could have been
Any one of a hundred times and places.
But last night, opening my eyes from sleep
To the steady courtyard light, I heard your breath
Coming and going like a wounded thing
That would not die. It could have been
Nothing but mine, persisting one more night.

A Confession

If someone was walking across
your lawn last night, it was me.
While you dreamt of prowlers, I was
prowling down empty lanes, to breathe
the conifer coolness of just

before dawn. Your flowers were closed,
your windows black and withdrawn.

Sometimes I see a square of
yellow light shining through the trees,
and I cross the grass and look in.
Your great body on the bed
is nude and white, and though I'm starved
for love like everyone, the sight
of your black sex leaves me cold.

What would I say to a squad car
if it came on its noiseless tires
and picked me out with its lights, like
a cat or a rabbit? That I
only wanted to see how people
live, not knowing how? That I
haven't had a woman in months?

Therefore I stay out of sight
and do not speak. Or if I speak,
I make small animal sounds
to myself, so as not to wake you.
And I touch myself. What
I wanted to do was enter
and bend and touch you on the cheek.

PAUL MONETTE

Degas

There are so many lies in nature,
a painter talking to painters starts
to lie about the plum and yellow tree
he forks for effect on a storm in purple
paint. The fact is, nothing sticks to
particular colors. A pear in old
grass, shy of the sun's bluff, is
ripe and rotting at once. You mix
a mud green and, green being one
of the lies, a pink and summer grey
appear on the pear, its jaded flesh
as futile to do as smoke.

                                        If the boy
with the wagon is empty to Marseilles,
take the ride. They sometimes favor
fancy detours in view of the secret
sea. The horses at a halt dozed
in a vineyard, I remember, and the boy
fell to his mug of chicory coffee
and milk. Baskets piled in the arbors.
And the perfect blue to break the world on
heaves in sudden sight. You couldn't
actually paint it. Lying, massive,
banked by an African sky and an angry
grapeskin red, a sea like that
will queer your heart. The workers wringing
their kerchiefs love to be sketched, but
they are not mad like the sea to be taken
down.

        I could fuck like a sailor in Cannes.
Madame pumps her baton in a seaside

studio. "Move, little girls," she says,
"like cats. Dance like animals drunk
on their dinners. Simone, what are you?"
"A panther, Madame." "No, today you are
heavy as cows, all of you. Tomorrow
I send you home to your pigs and husbands.
Go to your rooms and practice cats."
Simone, when she models at night, will say:
"You, with your mug of brushes, are
as sour as Madame. You think I am such
a dancer, look at the men who clap at
my recital." I could take her, she's
a beggar for a painter, but I don't. I am
terrible in August.

                                        See the sweat on
the jockey's thighs, streaked to his fitted
trousers? Manic from practice. He buffs
his boots, and his manager (Here, in the cream
cravat) berates him. See? The chestnut
horse in the middle ground has torn
a muscle. You are not meant to figure
from the picture who has cheated whom.
All the same, it avoids a poster's
thoroughbreds and dark grooms. In my
races, the people bet like the rich,
because money alarms them. About horses
I have no opinion.

                                  I did a mayor's
wife who posed at a fire from four
to six in a rose salon. Prompt and
uncommonly pale, she took her place
as though for proof if the night came.
Her dilettante hands, a ghost's, I had
to change. Why are we all accused
of motifs? "Another ballerina," my students
write in their Paris journals. "The buyers
buy picnics at the sea. You can always

count on flowers. Degas is stubborn."
When in fact, Degas is probably crazy.
He hates praise. The mayor's lady
is thrilled with the eyes: "I am as pretty
as this," she asks. When she leaves I blot
the hands and do them dead.

Art is
an artist's father-in-law. They drink
a bit the day the daughter is promised,
at pains to indicate nothing amiss.
They make each other sick. Take it
out on their wives. I don't care what
the Greeks mastered. I am quite sure
of just this, that pent up in jockeys
and dancers the moon tortures the sea.
They pass the delirious night, an addict
couple bloated on green liquor,
relieved of the grief of detail. Apparently
for now, I am the first to know.

Bathing the Aged

to my godson.

Their attendant nuns spare the tourists well:
it's not done at midday. Be there at eight
to see them come like brave survivors down
the scrub slope to the public beach. Nude

in their issue blankets, wheeled and held up,
they gather at the early shore, putting off
their day, needlework rolled on the nightstand,
paperbound thrillers in the counterpane's folds.

No one is squeamish. The young nuns water them
down, soap the sores in their shriveling laps.

Thrilled in the dawn water they hold their own,
making no exceptions of themselves. Getting

rinsed in a row, they bellow on the scum line
of the morning sand. They duel like teenage
lovers met again for drinks in their forties,
they shrug off the bobbed hair, the snapshots,

the creases of the time between. Chuckling there
across a cocktail table, they are for a time
their other selves. What have we come to name
wisdom, then? The selves we own to when we can

conceal no private love are not lovely. By now,
of course, the lake flashes in midmorning sun,
they are toweled, packed off uphill, forgetting
already the drum and tingle of the washwater,

but this is to be expected. Last week, leafing
pictures of the Second War dead, I saw their
yearbook poses, old world looks, outdated like
an old magazine. I followed them in the sour

vineyards west of Stuttgart, traced the steps
of their outsize gunner boots, wrote letters
home and hid my fear. There are some splendid
connections I'd trade my life to make, I think.

The tourists lie abed till noon here, and only
one man, white-stomached, churns in the roped
off public water. He trills a familiar lyric
whose name I mean to ask to the wild islands.

Who does live, I suppose, is the obvious
question. Thus, after all, our fictions come
clean. Who would not, given leave, clear up
this halt and blasted gang? Yes, you would.

Into the Dark

to J D McC

I would have run to him, only I was a coward
in the presence of such a mob—would have
embraced him, but that I did not know how he would
receive me. So I did what moral cowardice
and false pride suggested was the best thing—
walked deliberately up to him, took off my hat,
and said, 'Dr. Livingstone, I presume?' 'Yes,'
he said, with a kind smile, lifting his cap
slightly.

—Henry Morton Stanley
How I Found Livingstone

A spider bite the size of a dinner plate
means, when the thing erupts, that I am strapped
to a tree to scream until I black out. Thus,
God is not my favorite reason why
my shadow knocks and curdles in this damned
chaos. The third day I leave for fever
after two on the trail. The quinine's out—
I think the bearers salt the jungle, since
they prefer to ferment for pain what lies
at hand, the gray grass, bananas, a bark
that tastes like bread. In none of these diseases
do I detect a falling off of the main
madness, covering miles. I double up
with cramps, infected, atilt with vertigo,
and still I manage the next stretch and the next,
annexing nowhere bit by bit to the known
contours. My body's ruined balance buoys me.
I am that sick of the well-controlled.

The hills
assert their ups and downs, the violet earth
its pulses and its price. In Zanzibar
the Sultan said: "The gonads grow as fat
as cantaloupes under the sun. A man
has limits. Do consider, along the moon

you mean to map, what can be taken to bed."
As well ask why where the river leads is
worth the losses. I rise above my needs.
The Nile curls a question into Africa
that loosed in the Delta the pharoah's grip on the sun
and stars, their single aberration. "I
am the world," he dreamed in his gold cloaks, "I
must be the Nile in flood, but what"—as the dream
turns—"what is the gate in the dark which spills
the first water that is my blood."

A woman
has limits too in an hour that sees the Nile
narrowed to a source. Actually, I am
saving myself for a finer bed. A crowd
of girls in New York Harbor sighs at the sight
of my ship. In my head they do. They line the piers
and laugh. I hear them above the mosquitoes
who needle the nets, who eat all night. Who else
but the wanderer can own them, marrying
his inland mysteries at last with hers,
at sea? Is pleasure best following pain
because it comes untroubled by the fright
that leads us *here?* I am of those who hurry,
who would be first or nothing.

We're two days
East of Ujiji. Sidh, my scout, ruptured
a column of ants on Monday (careless man.)
and must be carried, regularly bathed
in soda, and induced to vomit. War,
I think, forces the jaws on the same schedule,
next to the jungle the test with a victim's
rictus, mere survival. Here, Livingstone
disagrees. He says there is violence
and violence, some of it suffered and some,
the rarer kind, consumed like a weird meat,
a snake's, a crested crane's, once in the desert
a centipede's, oily and sour.

The spice
for sponging off the spider's kiss freezes
my swollen ribs—they go for the heart—and I
order the march resumed. Livingstone shakes
his head. "Sleep the venom out. I will speak
between your dreams, and you will separate
the one from the other on the coast." I nod,
and the night opens.

And yet how queer. At first
a quiet as fierce as the lost light. Through narrows
awash in ink and pitch, and then a cave
where I neglect to drop a string behind
because I am only going one way. The dark
in certain lights has faces I can see.
Surfacing, I know it has been getting loud
all along. Queerer still, it is purer
than words, taken in change, raw as the dawn
to which it rises up to sing, in which
it dies of exposure. And amnesia is
the shelter at the cave's deserted mouth,
from which I see mirages fume in the dead
distance and, for all of their combustion,
feel the cool of mountain shade. Overnight
the promise of staying lost is broken, much
as you would say the weather broke.

Livingstone
argues that memory serves to announce
what we can do without. His kit contains
a bar of British soap, a tin of crystal
ginger, shillings, port, tobacco, the end
number of *Great Expectations*, and tea—
kept against surrender, should the desire
arise to fly. "These?" He fingers them. "These
are the other side. There is—" His eyes burn
briefly. "—another side. The chain of events,
the river's ruthless indirection don't
demand tribute except from men—" The fire

gutters. "—whom order, the house in the lane, cannot
seduce. Come, disabuse yourself of life
as chosen, as a way of getting better,
it is too fast for such distinctions. See
this ivory ring? A moment ago it was
an elephant."

Livingstone puts the Nile
further West, sprung from a mountain spine. The streams
tributary to the Congo finger some
of the same terrain from the East. He dreams a final
fountain playing its two rivers—a lake,
perhaps a falls, unless, for such issue,
a geyser gives the water up. He is
half dead of bites and welts and venom, skin
pied and chipped in places, as if they have
roasted it. With a habit, when he sits
at a map, of shutting his eyes before he looks.

"And so see it afresh. The map projects
the mind's tunnel and gulf. Well, you go down
deep enough, you draw enough approaches
to the map's blank center, do it long enough,
and, Stanley, you can *will* the last of the Nile.
The way to go is by amazement. Cling
to the line of least reason. Let the river
flow uphill, if that will bring you nearer.
The map has the canyons and cracks in the forest.
When *they* disappear, go home."

I will be back,
but Livingstone needs supplies. I will repair
to Dar-es-Salaam, and he continue South
to Bangweolo, there to rest in a jewelled
city lost on its shores. I will surely
try to come back myself. As a journalist,
of course, I have a certain duty to
a story. Livingstone Alive. In the end,
words are to me what rivers are to him.

Curious, after broken bones, hunger, the stings
and savages, to sweat with horror *now*,
but in my sleep the Nile has drained. We are,
in Livingstone's view, about to finish up
the planet. Then there is just the living
within its fists to do. Where do I start?
I want to get well, I want a woman
and a house in Manhattan, and horses and Irish hounds
on a farm on the Hudson. Livingstone won't attend
to his own future. As a child, I was warned
to turn to stone when a wasp or rattlesnake
was baiting me—then they would go away.
Then they did, now they don't.

Of course I can't
come back, but I will make us kings and get
places for us. "I have swum with crocodiles,"
he says, "in parts of the Nile where nothing kills.
Think of it, Stanley. They come out to bathe."
He goes too far. The world is where we live,
never what we think. They swim, yes, and then
they eat. What does Livingstone mean to imply?
I don't follow it. He can *have* the Nile
because I will have *him*. Our names will link,
like lovers. Or brothers. Brothers, if you like.

CAROL MUSKE

Rice

Their calendars are based on rice.
During drought, the days repeat—
the hours huddle like crows,
wait in lines
for dusk to grow light again.
The people walk in their sleep
to the New Year, an identical dawn
when fish move in threes. A sign of rain.

The monsoon is near.
When the rains come,
knives hang in trees.
They glitter.
A sail passes on the river.

When it pours, the rice is cut free.
It swims east to the river.

What is eaten by fish endures,
turns to weed and sleeps.
What escapes flies in threes to another weather.
What is washed up becomes a ghost,
haunts the paddies at dawn
wearing the masks of the starving.

In spring
The children draw in dust
and tell riddles:
What day comes twice?
Day without rice.

Found

There was an ancient Spring inside the glacier
explorers tapped it
took tin dippers and drank

It melted and goats came out
children thin with cold
blue-eyed

Roses of sage pressed against the underlip of ice
birds turned on wires

The children gathered in twos and threes
followed the long weeping
to the edge of the floe
and stood calling back
across the water

Hyena

She finds grief, her meat,
on a plateau
full of the moon's ammunition.
Her cousins follow, lift eyes
wide as torches
in the storm rock.
Dream birds lengthen
like wounds in the sky.

The shadow's task is primitive:
to sense doom and follow it.

She comes each distance to death
and eats what light is left.

It is her laughter on the slopes
at night.

Child with Six Fingers

I felt no pain when they cut it off
Only a coldness like rain
On the edge of the hand
Where it was
The ache came later

It grew crooked
Its sense was different—sixth
A feel for passing shapes
Edges, lips of bells or bark

Sometimes I tied it with string
It sang to the thumb

Now I lean on trees
Feel the roughness with my shoulders
They gave me a ball
Instead I watch birds fly
Thinking of wings

Swansong

The late Miss H. came to us Wednesdays at four
direct from the steno pool.

We waited, twenty of us in toe shoes,
slumped against her basement barre.

She was big,
her white hair bobbed,
the blue fox insurance against
ladies who called her declassé.

Sometimes she told us how it was
when she danced "Les Sylphides"—
she, the ingenue with natural turnout,
withers drawn in the white light of favored nations,
the Bolshoi sent its guns for her—
the heavy breathers from Minsk.
Miss H. leaped through their lines unruffled,
the season at her feet.
(Her lover Hans, a simple huntsman,
was at her side
the night in Dubrovnik
when a cab crushed her great toe.)

The swan died officially in St. Louis in '53
on a makeshift stage strewn with roses.
She gave her all,
then came to Minneapolis
where she taught us toe-dance.

She often wept, sipping brandy,
nodding when the needle stuck
on a crack in *Romeo and Juliet.*
Those days we stood on ceremony:
mute sisters of the dance, we froze,
holding second position
till six when the mothers came.

JACK MYERS

Mirror for the Barnyard

Nancy, the hogs don't know us.
We roar up in 100 yards of dust
impressing an old hog that jams
his snout against an ass
which squeals a 300-pound pink noise
and doesn't realize we mate without a sound.

I have a horn and you own a purse.
But the chickens don't understand this.
They're snotty and uptight about strutting
perfectly over their food
just waiting for the first weird move
to uncover the homosexual in their midst.
Our neighbors sweat over the same things.

But the boredom of the cows
when the land at last opened up
its heart to us enlightened me.
I knew that leisure, loss of the hands
and lack of any definite commitment to serve
or conquer others was the only difference between us.

So Long Solon

You live here because there's no other place
like it. The post office opens your mail and you
admire the tool they tap your phone with.

You hire the voyeur to wash your windows
from the inside and the kids who cut your tires
mow the lawn. It's cheaper to invite them in,

say, Look we are normal people like you, we are
expecting more cash, another child, and when they feel
every inch of your life is like theirs, you move out.

When I Held You to My Chest, You Fit

At first I was worried about you
liking me. Doesn't every father
think of zoos and long rides
into the interior of his child?

So I took you to the elephant
that held a telephone pole
above his head and swam toward us
with his human eye that said
this is what I do, and you?

You studied the 200-year-old
specks of rust around his cage
and ate a few. Then you wept
for the small snail stuck under his foot.
I too have crawled the underside

of bars watching the sad faces
of gum harden into one drab color.
I know how we belong together:
When I see the big view, you see
how it hides its thousand hearts.

The Apprentice Painter

I stand there slapping a house
in the face as the young girls
slide by on cool bicycles saying
oh, it's only the painters.
No one lets us in. We have to pee
behind trees and eat our one-foot
grinders on the ground.

My Italian boss yells up to me
let go of the house! It won't
fall. I wish the wings of birds
would turn into $8 brushes,
for the hot sun to drop
into the mouth of this house
that screams for more yellow.

Under the table I get good money
to buy more tables with.
I try to think of a better job
but the boss can feel me
dreaming on the other side
of the house and yells
don't die on me!

Each night I lay the new color
of my body down too early,
feeling the dog paws my hands
have become. I dream I'm glad
I'm strong as the boss rides me
from the last job on earth
to the moon's jumbled houses.

GREGORY ORR

Two Lines from the Brothers Grimm

for Larry and Judy

Now we must get up quickly,
dress ourselves, and run away.
Because it surrounds us, because
they are coming with wolves on leashes,
because I stood just now at the window
and saw the wall of hills on fire.
They have taken our parents away.
Downstairs in the half dark, two strangers
move about, lighting the stove.

Poem

This life like no other.
The bread rising in the ditches.
The bellies of women swelling
with air.
Walking alone under the dark pines,
a blue leather bridle in my hand.

The Doll

I carry you in a glass jar.
Your face is porcelain
except for the bullet hole
like a black mole on your cheek.

I want to make you whole again,
but you are growing smaller.
It is almost too late.
When I touch you my fingers
leave dark smudges on your skin.
Each day you are growing
smaller and more intense,
like a drop of acid on my palm;
mothball, snowflake,
dead child.

Gathering the Bones Together

I *A Night in the Barn*

The deer carcass hangs from a rafter.
Wrapped in blankets, a boy keeps watch
from a pile of loose hay. Then he sleeps

and dreams about a death that is coming:
Inside him, there are small bones
scattered in a field
among burdocks and dead grass.
He will spend his life walking there,
gathering the bones together.

Pigeons rustle in the eaves.
At his feet, the German shepherd
snaps its jaws in its sleep.

II

A father and his four sons
run down a slope toward
a deer they just killed.
The father and two sons carry

rifles. They laugh, jostle,
and chatter together.
A gun goes off,
and the youngest brother
falls to the ground.
A boy with a rifle
stands beside him, screaming.

III

I crouch in the corner of my room,
staring into the glass well
of my hands; far down
I see him drowning in air.

Outside, leaves shaped like mouths
make a black pool
under a tree. Snails glide
there, little death-swans.

IV *Smoke*

Something has covered the chimney
and the whole house fills with smoke.
I go outside and look up at the roof,
but I can't see anything.
I go back inside. Everyone weeps,
walking from room to room.
Their eyes ache. This smoke
turns people into shadows.
Even after it is gone, and the tears are gone,
we will smell it in pillows
when we lie down to sleep.

V

He lives in a house of black glass.
Sometimes I visit him, and we talk.

My father says he is dead,
but what does that mean?
Last night I found a child
sleeping on a nest of bones.
He had a red, leaf-shaped
scar on his cheek. I lifted him up
and carried him with me, even though
I didn't know where I was going.

VI *The Journey*

Each night, I knelt on a marble slab
and scrubbed at the blood.
I scrubbed for years and still it was there.
But tonight the bones in my feet
began to burn. I stood up
and started walking, and the slab
appeared under my feet with each step,
a white road only as long as your body.

VII *The Distance*

The winter I was eight, a horse
slipped on the ice, breaking its leg.
Father took a rifle, a can of gasoline.
I stood by the road at dusk and watched
the carcass burning in the far pasture.

I was twelve when I killed him;
I felt my own bones wrench from my body.
Now I am twenty-seven and walk
beside this river, looking for them.
They have become a bridge
that arches toward the other shore.

GREG PAPE

La Llorona

La pena y la que no es pena; ay llorona,
Todo es pena para mí;
Ayer lloraba por verte, ay llorona,
Y hoy lloro porque te ví.
—Mexican folksong

Down a blackened alley
or near a bridge hung
with rivermist and moonlight
she cries,
and if there's wind
her voice is part of it,
and part of you
when it's still.

A child-murderer, some say,
and frighten their children
with stories of little bodies
bumping over stones
on the riverbottom.

Llorona,
unable to die, unable to sleep,
wanders the night, and the children
see fingers drumming on the windowpane,
the white dress waving
in the white mist beyond the fence,
and hear her long slow moan
calling them, each one, by name—
Are you mine? Are you mine?

Men too have known her
disguised as a gleaming fish,

a mermaid, a waitress,
a big-breasted red-haired dancer
in a slick kimono—
One followed her up the stairs
of a dim hotel, one lay with her
in an old chevy
watching the morning star
fade in her ratted hair, or
trailed her at some distance
along a mountain path
until the legs gave out,
and the names were forgotten.

But there are other stories:
the pale, quiet-faced old woman
who stops you on the street
saying "Oh my son   my son"

Mercado

Watch out for the bus
fattened with workers going home.
Watch out for the truck
with the silver horse on the hood.
The driver is drunk and a crow
sleeps in his chest
that a little blood might waken.
Watch out for the cop who is anyone,
and watch out for your own thick tongue
and the thick green of your money,
for the poor surround you.

                    Late afternoon,
a pink sky glows above the town,
a pigeon drops from the roof

and banks over the loud street,
a man with one leg, with blank
white pearls for eyes,
holds a tin can
to the darkening sky
and mutters like the surf.

You push through the crowds
and you are walking in another life
past the holy pyramids of oranges,
apples glowing in their bins, pineapples
hung like trophies, the pink ice
where the fish were sold, and the boy
carving ripe meat from the bones.
Watch out for the wet red face
of the cow that clings to the dull
shine of its eyes. They are your eyes
shining. Watch out for your heart
that beats like the clipped wings
of the parrot.

A girl tugs at your sleeve
and you turn.
Smooth brown skin of her face
asking, baby slung in a scarf
over her shoulder asking,
clear eyes full lips
asking and you are lost
in the dense weather of her hair . . .

Yes, I will go away with you
into the mountains,
I will be father to your child,
yes, I will be all you need.
We will walk the mud path
through the fields all day
and watch the white egret
riding a slow cow into the afternoon . . .

Watch out for your hands
that are dying,
watch out for your blunt life
your heart and your money.
You put a coin in the worn palm
and turn away—
the moon
coming out of Isla Piedra,
one bright horn
that lifts the sky.

October

Two murders this month,
a dozen fist-fights
on the front lawn
and the city has a new siren
that makes the children
gnash their teeth. At night
the flash-lights of the police
violate our shrubs, while the big sycamores
go on dropping their leaves,
rocking slowly
in the new dark of October.

        Morning comes with its workmen
who fire up the bulldozers
and coax those big gaping mouths
into the walls of the *Latin Quarters.*
Tubes in the jukebox
still warm when they haul it away
still glowing with Mexican soul tunes:
Piel Canela, Tenemos Que Sufrir,
Pecadora, El Mal Querido—
Cinnamon Skin, We Have To Suffer,

Sinner, The Unloved Man—
The jukebox rolls off in a pickup
jammed in with the beer-stained pool table,
the slashed stools,
its royal fluorescence dimmed
in the full sun of October.

Afternoons my neighbors and I
kick through the wreckage; bricks, splintered boards
that smell of drunks and dancers.
Night after night
the sudden flash of eyes,
the bets laid down, a match
held too long—
Night after night
the drunks and the dancers
hold still
in the ruined walls.

For Rosa Yen, Who Lived Here

I

Mice in the garbage
mockingbirds in the attic
your iron
gasping over pockets and collars
you dream back into
the hollows of the night . . .

An ocean rocks
under the shadow of a gull

your father stands in the cold water
at dawn

his face and dark hair
tossing in a cloud
his bare feet sucked down
by sand

II

Those mornings
you never saw him leave
you'd slip down from the bed
while your mother slept,
move quietly across the room
and open the tall door
to your own world . . .

Light in the cat's eye
started you singing;
you followed your breath
around the house
and no one saw the schools
of bright fish swim through your fingers
no one saw you walking in and out
of yourself while the sun built a bridge of light
over Culiacán and Kowloon.

III

All night trucks droned
under the bridge at Highway City
dragging their dirty skirts of wind,
blackening the oleanders,
bruising the sleep of workers;
men like your father
who came to this valley and were robbed
and hidden like seeds,
men with too many border crossings
stamped in their faces

whose palms were worn smooth
on the slow fruits of their lives.

All night I sat still
and dreamed you; little girl,
woman, sister to the walls.
I spoke your name
as a charm against nothing
and waited . . .

IV

At the first touch of sun
mist rushes from the grass
and darkness goes back
to its nest of hair
swirling in a toilet
to its bottle of rainwater and dead laughter
lying in the weeds outside.

In this room filling with light
I'm alone as you were
with your beautiful man
nailed to the wall.

I would scream peacocks, break a window,
go back to sleep if I could

but this is California
where no one sleeps
California where your father
pointed a long finger
at the lizard and the fig
and this is the white shack
leaning into the orchard
where you lived Rosa.

JOHN PECK

Cider and Vesalius

Like a fruit wine with earth
  Clouding its sweetness, color
    Of day's end, this cider
Collects light from the window
  Of October—I scan
    Vesalius the surgeon's
Woodcut anatomies
  Sliced and prepared for the eye's
    Terminal erudition:
This solvent ruddy earth,
  Chilled, is best commentary,
    It tilts the wings of bees
Into refraction, wings
  Already numb about
    The body of the queen
Who dies: long live the queen,
  Bright milkweed drifts about
    Her dozing combs, the eye
Burs, rinsing her blind hives.
  We want no other gloss
    On this vivisection,
Yet want the litany
  Of fear transmuted, need
    The slow insinuation
Of spirits through our glance
  At knowledge.
                Look again:
    It did not move, it stands
At ease, it rises well
  Above the horizon, dressed
    In half its muscles. These

Dangle loose here and there,
  Rags in the white air left
    Motionless by the blast
It heard with ears it wears
  No longer. Now it waits
    Attentive toward the bright
Still landscape at its feet,
  The streets and houses empty—
    Its arm crooks in the quick
Arrest of intuition,
  Its finger lightly bent
    Toward a zone haloing
The smooth cope of the skull
  Whose back is all we see,
    White, blooming suddenly
Out of the sinuous stem
  Sheathing the spine. Now, soon,
    That silver sound again—

These streets are some real city,
  No Hieronymus Bosch
    Weaving his figures here,
Arguing brutal and
  Sophisticated joy
    Behind the passionless
And naked faces, through
  Steel wires penetrating
    The body pinioned by
The harp in hell. Threads tensile,
  Demons reaching to pluck
    And stroke them into music,
For we sing without joy
  Or knowledge, bone against
    Muscle, muscle against
Nerve and vessel.
                The young
  Student went from Louvain

Out to the roadside gibbet
Late at night, and he pulled
The femur off the hip—
The bones were bare, still joined
By ligaments—and then
Each night thereafter, piece
By piece, till finally
Only the thorax hung
From its chain. His desire
Was great: he clambered up
And yanked it off, and made
His first articulated
Skeleton. Then he said
Discreetly that he'd bought
The thing in Paris.
But
The first plates that he made
Were thumbed so avidly
That they disintegrated.
And all his woodcut blocks
Were lugged across the Alps,
Over half Germany,
Outliving half a dozen
Publishers. Now it rests
With us to speak the sequel
As if to his portrait, where
He holds the malefactor's
Dissected hand, each tendon
Strung out in demonstration—
We must tell him the hand
Has not changed, it is still
The malefactor's, and
It is alive. The pale
Tendons have reacquired
Occulted vigor, slipped
Back into place, and bathed

In blood again, that blood
Which in all innocence,
At freezing altitude,
Required the flier's glove
Of fur and swarthy leather.
Over the skies of Munich,
Through searchlights sweeping cloud
And flak flowers, that hand
Squeezed its release, and all
The fine grain of our shape
Graved deep into your blocks
Of oak, the arteries
Feeding back to the great
Aorta, *toti corpori*
vitalem spiritum—
All melted in the sudden
Flame—*naturalemque*
calorem.
This is the
Last glass, spinning its lees
To hellswirls out of Bosch
In silence, emptying
Its far end, tunnel of spirits,
Bosch's ascension panel—
Inexplicably yours,
Who wait there with the other
Suspect seekers for escort,
Angels handing you on
With your face passionless
And final toward the mouth
Of the high tunnel, till
You travel where the shapes
In little pairs waft lightward,
Mount through to the other side.
With us you leave these other
Figures, diagrams

Of unwilled ecstasy,
  Sinews drying to ink,
    This glass drying to stains
Of cider, while the autumn
  Milkweed lifts into air,
    Silk wrinkling in wind,
White inchworms draped from trees
  At loose in the loose wind,
    Fouling whatever moves,
Squandering transformation.

The Watcher

On the far edge of a plain,
As on white flats of Kirgiz,
A muzzy grey edge of men.

It moves in my direction
Through wind that sings.
An old anxiety
Relaxes, and I wait.

White-booted and white-coated
They approach over snow
That caves beneath them.
Their legs lift and plunge.

I am not seen as they near—
One speaks to another,
Confident, precise
Under white, fur-lugged headgear—
His language is alien
But I can see that he is
Confident, precise.

In my secrecy,
In my inaction,
I admire this.

Then with his trained eye
He turns, squinting above me
Into pines over my shoulder—
A flanking shaggèd wall
Over depths of forest.

His rifle goes up—
I follow its sighting
To a bird that perches, waxen
And with eye of dark berry.

As before, the wind that sings.
As before, a calm
Unaccountable, a moment
That continues to fill.

I do not ask, will it end;
But am aware of sky
As of scud over harbors—
Sheeted and stretched above
The snow poised on that bough.

The Ringers

One day ringing men will be a race gone,
But how to picture it, that day when the land's face

Lies wildered of belltowers, its thicket of belfries,
Walls of poured stone heaving the strike notes sharp for
   miles,

And older walls of brick, powdery bisque to the touch,
Soaking up and sweetening the spelled sound.

And those rooms beneath the bells, walls like fortresses
Around the cockpits, where upward, through the
  embrasure

Dangling the great ropes, hover the dark zeroes,
Huge mouths all silent round their clappers, waiting for
  sound.

One day those men will vanish into their sound, but now
The troops of ringers come, bands of far walkers, hale
  gatherers,

Seekers of good towers, composers and turkey drivers,
To lift arms in those rooms, rank and captain, in array

Down the long ropes, and feel the fur ball of the sally
Lifting against the palm like a dog startled.

Thus, it was all that Bunyan could do to tear himself
Away from ringing. At first he came back just to watch;

But quickly he perceived the bells poised overhead
Could fall and crush him. So, he sheltered under a beam.

But what if a bell should bounce off walls, squashing
  him!
So he retreated to the door, shouldering stone.

But, should the shuddering thick walls themselves give
  in,
That too would be the end of Bunyan. He fled the place.

One day these ringing men will be a race gone,
As sun-glare drifts in curves over old blazons,

Or knowledge disappears into its overtones,
Or mortar powders grain by grain between granites

Rocking to tenor over Bourdon—crumbles as white
As it first was, drying spidery on the hands

Of masons who would sing swatching its cool weight in.
Until then, we can wait, busy this side of silence,

Imagining how bells might ring their own passing.
It used to be, with passing bells, we would go down

To tell the bees, so they would not die. When they swarmed,
The village ran out banging scuttles and fire-irons

Like bells to bring them down. And once, when the sun went
Into eclipse at midday, ringers were at peals,

Ringing through changes when the light began to change,
The huge half-violet shadow stepping overland

With noiseless speed, swaddling us in altered air—
And through that calm rose the confused cries of birds,

While steadily, those pealing Stedman caters kept
Time with their own time, ringing for whatever reason.

The Spring Festival on the River

Crowd fear: blown paper and uprooted ferns,
Down newsreel streets, down spillways,
Hands at random over me, cold pork,

Sweat runneling down my back—
Then the bridge:
Like carpet bulging up, it heaved the bodies
Wedging above the river, over barges piled
With cargo to the edges of their curious roofs,
Hulls squatting low into the water, swaybacked,
While on the bridge the heads bobbed like balloons
Between shops perched on either side—
Women holding their children high
Out of the surge, awnings snapping.
Where have I seen that other ashen whirr of images?
The public stairs at Chungking, after the air raids, after
The stampede crush—mothers as if asleep upon
The wide stone steps, their clothes torn back about them
By panic force of feet, their arms
Serene over the tiny bodies.

I cannot reach you now, how shall I find you?
Out of the back windows of shops quick with hands
Burdock and mangoes spill, the looser tiles
Like pebbles tumble off the eaves, and no one hears
Their sputter as they splash. Then, unmistakable
As bowstring past the ear, the whuck
Of separating cable. Massively,
Swarming with rucksack figures stabbing with long
  poles,
A barge piles out along the wharf beneath us, heeling
Into the current, its bow sucking fast;
The polers thrust, their mouths go wide and wait for
  sound,
Their arms stiffen, their poles bend, their arms rise,
Water spins its tons under sharp snailshell eddies,
The fine lines of that ink, how wet, how ancient.
Craning off the bridge, whole torsos
Lean down, grabbing stupidly, with knothole mouths.

I cannot reach you. Now it is I watch, farther along
The bank between two hulls, some boy oblivious

Who hunkers down, playing in shallows with a stick,
Picking his nose, poking mud into clouds of acid.
Now it is that dust motes, boiling into light,
Spin heliographs, but to what date, what hour?
The hills beyond the city: was it them I saw,
Glancing and running? Red, then, they were,
And silent: the bright and the clear—
Slabs of jasper, crystals of mica.

Colophon for Lan-t'ing Hsiu-Hsi

(The Gathering at the Orchid Pavilion by Ch'ien Ku, 16th Century)

This is no poet's heaven
Where solitaries stroll the boulevards
Drunk with the power of transformation,
But a piece of earth near Shanyin
With a dragon-vein brook curving through it
And orchid, bamboo, pine, and one old ginkgo
Making a pavilion at Lan-t'ing.
Attendants glide along the bankside paths
Carrying salvers of fresh handscrolls
Tied up in fascicles
To figures ranged along the banks
Seated in lotus-fashion.
Other attendants settle cups of wine
On pads of lotus where the stream begins
And set them all adrift—
Each poet, with his stick,
Must capture one of these, drain off the cup,
And, as he may, submit thus to invention,
In solitude or conversation.
Those who can write no lines

Must drink off three whole cups
And place the empty vessels
On a tray, drying toward their glaze,
In a neat row set them down.
One man leans on his shoulder toward the stream
And vacantly regards the cups
Slide past him on the indolent current:
The wine tosses the same light
That the water tosses.
Others unroll their scrolls
And display to themselves
The white space that is theirs.
Framed in the keyhole of a tunnel rock
Another stares at the brook,
His hand extended in rhetorical stasis.
And so, down through the garden, each in place—
With their thin wands
They fish for cups and poems, or prod them past
The reach of their own hands.
One of them drinks, he rises into dance,
A dewlap bear in silks!
His hands hunt halfway up his fanning sleeves—
While on the other shore his neighbor
Squats in frustration.
And the last figure, who has drunk his three
Already, and need take no more,
Reaches to catch one cup that would float free—
For just at this point the pavilion ends,
The stream now widens and descends
Toward houses and sheaf-bearing men
Half-visible through trees or down ravines—
And all the undrunk poems, the chill wine,
Must be retrieved, and gathered on red trays.
And yet, beyond the farthest trees
And left edge of the painting with its seals,
Come poems themselves—
The ones composed that day, with all the names

Of those who failed,
Full thirty feet of scroll spilling
Downstream into the world—

For so it is with all men: a little while
In good talk or high feeling,
A little while
With no mind for our end.
But then sharply it comes
Back in upon us.
The dead felt as we do,
Read them:
Just so shall we be read.
Therefore my notes on this feast,
These poems,
I, Wang Hsi-chih.

STANLEY PLUMLY

Heron

I

You still sometimes sleep
inside that great bird,
flopped out,
one wing tucked,
the other slightly broken over my back.
You still fall asleep before I do.
You still wake up
in tears.

You have what is called *thin skin:*
if I put my ear to it
I can hear the wingbeat in your heart.
I can only imagine
how far down those long flights go.

II

Last night in my dream
about the heron
I stood at the edge
of water with a handful
of stones.
I was twelve, I think.
The heron perfect, still, kneedeep.
looking at himself.

Once he lifted his wings
in a mockery of flight.
For a moment I was inside you;

I could hear the heart.
I had stones in my hands.

Giraffe

The only head in the sky.
Buoyed like a bird's,
on bird legs too.
Moves in the slowmotion
of a ride
across the longlegged miles
of the same place.
Grazes in trees.
Bends like a bow
over water
in a shy sort of
spreadeagle.
Embarrassed by
such vulnerability,
often trembles, gathering
together
in a single moment
the whole loose
fragment of body
before the run downwind.
Will stand still
in a camouflage of kind
in a rare daylight
for hours,
the leaves spilling
one break of sun
into another,
listening to the lions.
Will, when dark comes

and the fields open
until there are
no fields,
turn in the length
of light
toward some calm
still part of a tree's
new shadow, part of the moon.
Will stand all night
so tall
the sun will rise.

Fungo

From pitch and catch
to this:
sometimes I feel I've waited
whole days, and only now
in the clarity
of any evening,
both our faces filled with the hours,
have you come to me
as from the other side
of something—grief, moonpiece,
a small clock of the single,
fixed star—to lie in this room
with me all night,
perhaps a day,
and nothing between us.

(The summer of nineteen sixty, more than once,
I drove all the way to the end of Long Island
to watch the whales.

Even eleven years ago
I waited and waited, but never saw one.

They should have loped
like great attenuated waves
in the animal waters
just off shore, just close enough
I could have watched
the one body
leave,
enter the other.)

Tonight the lighthouse scatters the light like snow
over the ocean

as I push out, cloud and oar,
over the dream of your pale body.
I have no hands for this:
they do not perform
miracles,
like fish out of water.

My body falls apart, layer after layer,
inside itself
like the underwater demolition of a fish.

I turn over and over
and what do I see but your forehead
fingerprinted like an underfin.

I want to come to you from a distance
of light years,
from the blind side,
as if this moment
were in perpetual motion.

I want you to come to me from the distance of those
  waters
that just make shore—
the light in the lighthouse filling you out like a moon.

In this one room
where I turn to you
in the dark,
lights in the shallow water on the wall
above us, I want nothing
empty.

Out-of-the-Body Travel

I

And then he would lift this finest
of furniture to his big left shoulder
and tuck it in and draw the bow
so carefully as to make the music

almost visible on the air. And play
and play until a whole roomful of the sad
relatives mourned. They knew this was
drawing of blood, threading and rethreading

the needle. They saw even in my father's
face how well he understood the pain
he put them to—his raw, red cheek
pressed against the cheek of the wood . . .

II

And in one stroke he brings the hammer
down, like mercy, so that the young bull's

legs suddenly fly out from under it . . .
While in the dream he is the good angel

in Chagall, the great ghost of his body
like light over the town. The violin
sustains him. It is pain remembered.
Either way, I know if I wake up cold,

and go out into the clear spring night,
still dark and precise with stars,
I will feel the wind coming down hard
like his hand, in fever, on my forehead.

The Iron Lung

So this is the dust that passes through porcelain,
so this is the unwashed glass left over from supper,
so this is the air in the attic, in August,
and this the down on the breath of the sleeper . . .

If we could fold our arms, but we can't.
If we could cross our legs, but we can't.
If we could put the mind to rest . . .
But our fathers have set this task before us.

My face moons in the mirror, weightless,
without air, my head propped like a penny.
I'm dressed in a shoe, ready to walk out
of here. I'm wearing my father's body.

I remember my mother standing in the doorway
trying to tell me something. The day is thick
with the heat rising from the road. I am
too far away. She looks like my sister.

And I am dreaming of my mother in a doorway
telling my father to die or go away.
It is the front door, and my drunken father falls
to the porch on his knees like one of his children.

It is precisely at this moment I realize
I have polio and will never walk again.
And I am in the road on my knees, like my father,
but as if I were growing into the ground

I can neither move nor rise.
The neighborhood is gathering, and now
my father is lifting me into the ambulance
among the faces of my family. His face is

a blur or a bruise and he holds me
as if I had just been born. When I wake
I am breathing out of all proportion to myself.
My whole body is a lung; I am floating

above a doorway or a grave. And I know
I am in this breathing room as one
who understands how breath is passed
from father to son and passed back again.

At night, when my father comes to talk,
I tell him we have shared this body long enough.
He nods, like the speaker in a dream.
He knows that I know we're only talking.

Once there was a machine for breathing.
It would embrace the body and make a kind of love.
And when it was finished it would rise
like nothing at all above the earth

to drift through the daylight silence.
But at dark, in deep summer, if you thought you heard

something like your mother's voice calling you home,
you could lie down where you were and listen to the dead.

After Grief

When you woke up among them,
when you rose,
when you got up and they asked you
what you were—*is it named?*—
and you in your new clothes
and face and body lined dry with newspaper,

when you climbed out of the coffin
and began to walk,
alive (*like a rainbow* one of them said),
without a word, in this place of skull and femur,
stone and the sounds of water, when you walked up
to the one talking, his face a face
of the moon, and started to speak, he said

no need, I know who you are.

All this recorded in the first book, The Dream,
The Book of the Dead, in the blessing
of the death of each day.

And tonight, bedded down,
the mind adrift, the body just a few feet
from the earth, it is written:

there is the river,
go wash yourself.
And you asked
what is this place? And the one

without a face answered
look around you, this is where you are.

I remember how even near the end
you would go out to your garden
just before dark, in the blue air,
and brood over the failures
of corn and cabbage
or the crooked row
but meaning the day had once more
failed for you.

I watched you as any son watches his father,
like prophecy.

And in my mind I counted the thousand
things to say.

And tonight, again, it is written
that the one talking said
Father, forgive everything.
leave these clothes, this body,
they are nothing.
lie down in the water.
be whole.

And having done so, you rose
among them, who are called The Bones,
without flesh or face.

All this recorded in the dream unending.

The first death was the death of the father.
And whosoever be reborn in sons
so shall they be also reborn.

In The Book of the Dead are names
the weight of the continents.
At each rising of the waters
shall the earth be washed:

this is the dream that holds the planet
in place.

And you, my anonymous father,
be with me when I wake.

LAWRENCE RAAB

The Assassin's Fatal Error

When in doubt have a man come through a door
with a gun in his hand.
—Raymond Chandler

He comes through the door,
the big gun in his fist. He says,
"Nobody's going anywhere."
Nobody was, nobody's
even here, except
me and this bottle of scotch,
and I'm used to waiting.

He tells me to explain
about the pearls, because he knows
ways to make me tell. However,
I know nothing about them,
nothing about Mr. R. or The Big Man,
and nothing about Oregon where I
have never lived at any time in my life.

Perhaps I'm lying, but he's convinced,
although he will shoot me anyway,
which I understand.

Perhaps I say, "What kept you?"
Probably I just finish the scotch,
which is third-rate but effective.

Mine, you understand, has been
a temporary disguise, which may or may not
be explained at a later time.
Its importance to the story

lies in the discovery of the body
by the detective, tomorrow.

I also turn up three chapters from the end
as a Doctor, where I can be trusted
even less than now, when I still have
this death to get through.

"There must be connections,"
I tell him. "There always are.
And it's smart to leave
the witness silent, get the job over
and get out of town."

The gun wanders around the room.
"Listen," I tell him. "Anything
can happen. But this could be
the fatal error. You don't know
any more than I do."

The long tube of the silencer turns toward me.
I consider the finger on the trigger,
the sound like somebody coughing
upstairs in an old building,
and now the single bullet
suspended in the air between us.

You could ask: But what did I expect?
And I would have to say: Only this.
Nothing but this.

Pastoral

Today in Peru, this first day of summer,
how easily another life
falls into your hands—marriage,

dreams, tables and chairs, and the same
incurable disease. Here
in this light you're
the handsome but dishonest
jungle doctor, happy to help the old man
to his grave, happy to find the daughter
beautiful, despondent, and anxious
for medication. *Today* you write
in your journal *in this helpless country*
I must pretend to overlook
the question of the inheritance. Likewise tomorrow
you will choose to ignore
reports of an army of ants
crossing the border into the nation.

Like the rest of us, in the other countries,
you've grown unwilling to accept
the madness of evidence, and so prefer
to walk until morning
beside the cold beds of night-blooming flowers,
considering the injuries of fog,
the small advances
of moonlight. Is it possible,
you wonder, she has not yet
noticed my affliction?

Evenings in Peru
twelve centuries of hoarded darkness
glitter in the faces
of the jewels she kept for herself.
Even the day of the wedding she would not
trust you. Nor would the servants
ever be your friends. *From that first afternoon*
the pulse of light in the foliage seemed
unnatural, and the thin music
of the jungle became too quickly the sound of trees
collapsing at a great distance.

No one is content,
in the country, in the middle of summer.
For weeks I have dreamt of waking up
on the table in the white surgery.
Back home in the winter
you'd tell your friends how the new life was like
the story of the doctor in Paris who knew
his work would never carry him
far enough and who said
at the end, "There's something here, but I can't
tell you what it is."

Once she had played for hours
Mozart on the harpsichord. It was the night
she left for good, taking the little purse
of diamonds, and all the silver—
forks and spoons—while you thought
the music was meant to say
everything had been revealed
when you were not watching. And you wrote:
But if she was that beautiful
it's no excuse, it never was.

Your plan remained
the same: leave the explanation
to the end or leave it out
altogether. Still, you could not help
but hear, each night, the muffled thud of your heart,
and of hers,
and the sound also of teeth
in the boards on the windows. Now

your house fills
with the paraphernalia of summer, as
the black swarm closes in—called
"the descent of spirits"—and after it
the famous yellow light

of autumn in Peru
drifts through the immaculate
bones of your fingers
and settles around you like
the finest gold of another distant country,
or a different season, or another life.

Voices Answering Back: The Vampires

Rising in lamplight dying at dawn
grim burials in sheds and cellars
the rats scuttling through holes
and the days following in their tracks
exiled here we named the hours
since you first forgot to be afraid
once departed we became
only ourselves
with the salt on our tongues
and the cold for company
so deft in escape so practiced in dying
you might have learned from us
but each time the easiest trick worked
the brandished cross the empty mirror
you could not see us our steps upon the stairs
and while you stumbled after bats in the garden
we climbed quietly
from the upstairs window down the drainpipe
and through all the parties
you never heard what we were saying
it was something about desire
what we had in common even then
in your silence you feared us
always winning at the end but do you think

nothing lingered past dawn
shadowed among the gathered elms
do not be mistaken
we heard you walking through our dreams
we felt death moving between your hands
now we are waking early
practicing with sunlight
now we pass unharmed beneath your terrible star
eyes covered hands in our pockets
for the rules have always said
if you stop believing in us
we inherit everything

Visiting the Oracle

It's dark on purpose
so just listen.

Maybe I inhabit a jar, maybe a pot,
maybe nothing. Only this
loose end of a voice
rising to meet you.
It sounds like water.
Don't think about that.

Let your servants climb back down the mountain
by themselves. I'll listen.
I'll tell you everything
I discover, but I can't
say what it means.

Someone will always
assure you of the best of fortunes,
but you know better.

And keep this in mind: The answer
reveals itself in time
like the clue that fits
perfectly and explains everything
after the crime has been solved.

Then you will say: *I should have known.*
It was there all along
and never even concealed,
like the story of the letter
overlooked by the thief because
it had not been hidden.
That's the trick, of course.

You don't need me.

Attack of the Crab Monsters

Even from the beach I could sense it—
lack of welcome, lack of abiding life,
like something in the air, a certain
lack of sound. Yesterday
there was a mountain out there.
Now it's gone. And look

at this radio, each tube neatly
sliced in half. Blow the place up!
That was my advice.
But after the storm and the earthquake,
after the tactic of the exploding plane,
and the strategy of the sinking boat, it looked

like fate and I wanted to say, "Don't you see?
So what if you're a famous biochemist!

Lost with all hands is an old story."
Sure, we're on the edge
of an important breakthrough, everyone
hearing voices, everyone falling

into caves, and you're out
wandering through the jungle
in the middle of the night in your negligee.
Yes, we're way out there
on the edge of science, while the rest
of the island continues to disappear until

nothing's left except this
cliff in the middle of the ocean,
and you, in your bathing suit,
crouched behind the scuba tanks.
I'd like to tell you
not to be afraid, but I've lost

my voice. I'm not used to all these
legs, these claws, these feelers.
It's the old story, predictable
as fallout—the rearrangement of molecules.
And everyone is surprised
and no one understands

why each man tries to kill
the thing he loves, when the change
comes over him. So now you know
what I never found the time to say.
Sweetheart, put down your flamethrower.
You know I always loved you.

JAMES REISS

The Breathers

Jeffrey Andrew Reiss—October 5, 1969

In Ohio, where these things happen,
we had been loving all winter.
By June you looked down and saw your belly
was soft as fresh bread.

In Florida, standing on the bathroom
scales, you were convinced—
and looked both ways for a full minute before crossing
Brickell Boulevard.

In Colorado you waited-out summer in a mountain
cabin, with Dr. Spock,
your stamps, and my poems in the faint
8000-foot air.

Listen, he had a perfect body,
right down to his testicles, which I counted.
The morning he dropped from your womb,
all rosy
as an apple in season, breathing the thick
fall air of Ohio, we thought good things
would happen.

Believe me, Dr. Salter and the nurses were
right:
he was small but feisty—they said he was
feisty. That afternoon in his respirator
when he urinated it was something to be
proud of.

Cyanotic by evening, he looked like a dark
rose.

Late that night you hear . . .

Think of the only possible twentieth-century
consolations:
Doris saying it might have been better this way;
think of brain damage, car crashes, dead soldiers.
Better seventeen hours than eighteen, twenty years
of half-life in Ohio where nothing happens.

Late that night you hear them
in the . . .

For, after all, we are young, traveling
at full speed into the bull's eye of the atom.
There's a Pepsi and hot dog stand in that bull's eye,
and babies of the future dancing around us.
Listen, the air is thick with our cries!

Late that night you hear them
in the nursery, the breathers.
Their tiny lungs go in and out like the air
bladder on an oxygen tank
or the rhythm of sex.
Asleep, your arms shoot towards that target
with a stretch that lifts you like a zombie,
wakes you to the deafening breathers.
And now you see them, crawling
rings around your bed, in blankets,
buntings, preemies in incubators circling
on casters, a few with cleft palates, heart trouble,
all feistily breathing, crawling
away from your rigidly outstretched arms—
breathing, robbing the air.

The Green Tree

Ever since my daughters started to walk
I have had increasing difficulty with my eyes.
I remember the day Wendy took her first steps, when
she said "bamboo" and waddled over to pat the rusty
  bumper

of a truck, I could barely make out the writing
scrawled in dirt on the trailer and had trouble focusing
as she stepped into its shadow.
The morning in Maine when she raced down the beach

and splashed into the ocean before I could reach her,
I actually mistook her for another little girl in pink
whom—I am sorry to say—I began leading slowly out of
  the water.
Then there is Jill: when she first walked I remember

looking at her and thinking, "I am a camera fading back,
  back."
Years later when she would go rollerskating with Wendy
my eyes were so bad I could no longer tell
where the sidewalks left off and my daughters began.

By now everything has faded into fine print. I
have been to a doctor who says he is also troubled,
but has sons. My only son died one day after
birth, weighing two pounds. His name was

Jeffrey, but I have always preferred to call him
  "Under-the-Earth"
or, especially on rainy days, "Under-the-Sod." In fact,
sometimes I catch myself repeating these words: "My
  only son,
Under-the-Sod, is playing over there by the green tree."

JAMES REISS

A Slight Confusion

A slight confusion has resulted in your office
phone number being the same as a brothel,
the Pleasant Street Rest Home.

Voices get you out of conference, asking,
Is this the Pleasant Street Rest Home? or spoil your
  afternoon
milk-break with, Hey Miss Belnap, how about a little
  meatball?

You decide to dial the Home, but since WA 7-
0204 is your number, too, you get a busy signal
with your own wheezing muffled underneath,
then nearly swallow your cough drop when you shout
into the receiver, Give me Miss Belnap
please! and the words echo back on themselves.

Meanwhile the operator is helpless, having determined
there is no record of a rest home with your number.
In fact, there is no record of a Pleasant Street in your
  city.
But Pleasant should be west of 13th near a playground
you went rollerskating in as a child: the wind would
  blow
between gray buildings, and skating would be best there.

So you drive out and find a deserted playground, but the
  riots
have left only brick-fields: no Pleasant Street, no rest
  home.
Surely something is wrong, you cry, surely there is
some confusion here! The wind begins to blow.

And then you see her cut across the playground
on rollerskates, a phonebook in one hand, a pillow

in the other: more like a queen than you
imagined, yet delicate and shy. Miss Belnap,
you whisper, at last I've found you!

On Hot Days

Remember those X-ray machines in shoe stores
where you put your feet under green light
and gazed at your foot bones like huge
    goldfish in an aquarium

and it was quiet and your mother looked on
with her Roosevelt button while the sweat-smelling
salesman with the Yiddish accent and the splotched
    face hovered like a giant

amoeba above you and grinned *Okay, sonny*
and your mother nudged you, because X-rays
could be dangerous, so you sat in the big
    chair by the window that faced

the El while the salesman lugged box after box
of fresh-smelling shoes from the back room,
lacing them to you like cool bags of water,
    and you squished to the mirror—

Captain Frogman with your swim
fins and rubber suit to protect you
from the icy terror of the deep green
    sea—so that when the salesman

grinned and turned off your X-ray vision you asked
for yet another cooler pair to swim in
and when he finally shook his shoehorn
    at you and frowned, his face

one fiery splotch of cordovan, your mother
winced and pulled you into the heat
of the street just as the El burst overhead
like a thunderclap.

¿Habla Usted Español?

The Spanish expression *Cuando yo era muchacho*
may be translated: when I was a boy,
as, for example, "When I was a boy I wanted to be
a train driver," or "When I was a boy I was completely
unaware of the flimsy orchid of life."
It is the kind of expression found in textbooks of the
blue breeze
and is more useful, really, than expressions like "Please
put the bananas on the table, Maria,"
or "Take it easy is the motto of the happy-go-lucky
Mexican."
When I was a boy the sun was a horse.
When I was a boy I sang "Rum and Coca-Cola."
When I was a boy my father told me the mountains
were the earth's sombreros.

KENNETH ROSEN

Girls

I said I'd get her a towel and ran
to a place where I maintained a stash
of towels and brought her two. She said
she liked the way I dried her and then
we began to talk of old times. "You're still
with—" "Oh, no. That only lasted
for six weeks." "But I thought, in Hawaii,
you—" "There have been so many others."
(My God, six years ago that was.) Now
her gold hair flashed in the sunlight, she sat
on the fender of my parked car, done with
the towels, waiting for me. "Before you go,
oh God, I want you to see Sebago Lake
at sunset, its turquoise, its pyramid
distances. In my car—" "Let's go!" she said,
and we were off, over the hills, between
the overhanging coolnesses of green; and yet
somehow we paused at what was apparently
a hospital and a farm, for as we passed
along a path with borders dense and over-
grown with weed and creeper, we overheard
a doctor explaining the goats to his patients.
They weren't goats. They were more like impala
or eland, horns like twisted baseball bats,
and they were after me. I seized a bucket
by the bailer, swung it at a goat, but its horn
ran through. Nor were they afraid to hear me
bang the bucket on the ground. At last
the doctor called them off. Without a word
we checked the punctures in the pail. What can
you do? We left, reached Sebago, sunset, and after all

these years, we fucked and fucked and fucked.
O oxygen, pinkness, protein, hair, and bone,
a stump in the meadow, river, and stone.

Confab

The men with ventilators of black straw
encircling their official hats, visors,
silver medals, signed my warrant and then
dove into grave discourse, my disposition
to destiny. "And how does he accept?"
"He won't believe." "And you told him
the fact." "I showed him a picture of
a crab and said the word: cancer. And
he said, 'Fuck you, snowflake.' And he
said, 'Fuck you, carcinoma. I ain't no
dancer.' And he ran into the forest. It
was dark, now. He tore his eyes out
on branches, tripped over creepers, and
his heart surged with glee and despair."
"How do you know that?" "Earth shuddered."
And I, giggling and weepy, passing fast,
reflect, in any prison men assert their
innocence, their significance as men.

Abstinence

At last I found the monastery. A young
brother or priest, named Harry, showed me
to my room. I was tired of changing rooms
and could not sleep, not in that empty bed,
on those clean sheets, yet Harry, his round

and Irish face, lank red hair around a native
tonsure, slept at ease, his chamber nearby.
Our doors were ajar, an ample hallway in between,
and in the late afternoon, or early morning,
I mean that casual, foreboding light, pretty
little Barbara found her way to my bedroom,
with her straight thin body, long fair hair,
terrible light and skyblue eyes, and made with her
arms, legs, and long hair enticing, inquisitive
triangles, so I showed her a secret of lambskin,
put it on, slipped it in, disregarding the leftover
little blue containers, the open door, Harry,
who might have been stepfather or administrator,
inform, indict, and banish me from this palace,
sanctuary. So now I feared the abbot, cook,
and in the morning, as I pursued ablutions
with the others, I saw I was different
in haircut, length of body, spirit of sadness,
marrow (she would be worshipped by outsiders,
strangers), and I saw on little boards of toast
huge slabs of corned beef hash adorned apiece
with golden yolks or crowns of eggs, sun wet
and intact, reduplicated in rows on trays, and I
went outdoors. Below me was a railroad track,
and a shelter surrounded by log palisades
across from that. Along came an engine and
a little car: foresters, and for a minute I wished
I was with them, one of them. Someone appeared
at my elbow and pointed out the cedar trees
of their concern, forked, truncated, three and four
feet off the ground. I knew what that meant,
high stumps, huge wood, wine red, so I descended
from the church's castle, crossed the tracks,
and checked the fire in the shelter. The floor
indoors was a little muddy from use, the soup
in a boil, the grill white with ashes of old shoes
and old clothes, but I could have eaten, lived there,

and went back mostly because of Barbara, but never
found her. Then began the real waiting, the real
abstaining, and after four days I returned to the
terrace asked my friend what he knew about her.
He told me of telephone calls to Harry, kissing
publicly, disappearing, emerging murmuring and
purring, and I, in new desolation, recalled the priests
with cowboy haircuts, masturbating in their chambers,
waiting, I guess, for me to bring them Barbara.

An Act

In an instant, by instinct, I apprehended
they were going to rob the bank. I seized
the gray bags of money from the unsuspecting
hands of the proper messenger, and racing the tile
hallways, slid them into the vault, locked it.
I was a caracole of action, under the desperate
circumstances of my prophecy, happy and exhausted.
It was too late to explain. By then the gang
was in the bank with everybody lying on the floor,
binding our wrists and ankles in rope of white
silk, taking special indecencies with the female
employees, binding their breasts, exposing
garter belts and snaps. Somebody, a little
old teller, panicked. They shot him in
the head, and on our polished pink granite walls
pieces of his gray cerebral matter splattered,
the calendar, the tiers of slips for withdrawal,
deposit, and special account, the clock. It's hard
to convey the shock of all this, my cheek
on the cold floor growing accustomed, little
clusters of dust becoming landmarks, my sense
of the whole room ascending to an airy dome,

gray skywells, people in black and white apparel,
suitcoats, ties, derby hats and businesslike
umbrellas, welded to the spot his brains adhered
like vomit, welded in rays. The gang, two men,
two women, were finishing their work. The men
wore black moustaches, the young one wished
to kill me, the old one stayed him. The women
wore frayed stockings, their greasy legs
bulged through the frays, their hair hung around
their heads like nests of hooks. Now, handkerchiefs
tied around their faces, trenchcoats belted, hats
in place, briefcases closed and latched, they aimed
their revolvers at us and toward the door backed.
The door sucked at them like a vacuum, plucked them
into the hurry of the back and forth, the angry,
frustrated traffic, the impatient horn. We untied
ourselves, sighed, and resumed putting the bank
in order for the day's routine. It began to appear
it wasn't money they were after, and my heroic dance
had spared the firm no losses, so it disappeared,
my act, in the onward press of business and
consequence.

MICHAEL RYAN

Barren Poem

for Marvin Bell

All night the blind entrance of the children.
Where are they coming from, smelling of boiled milk,
their bodies sliding beneath each other
like fish? Because my wife hears noise,
I go down to the cellar to look.
Nothing moves. The air is damp with sex.
Animals no one has named
live here, the ones who become children,
who eat each other's eyes in our dreams.
I can't find them.
I would hook one by the mouth, its nerves
crawling up my hand like hot worms,
and rake its brain until it talked roots.
Does their absence follow me,
hidden as breath in speech?

Once upstairs, I talk:
in my old room
there's a bed where I curl up
& one light that burns holes in closed eyes.
Each time I call my mother
I get smaller & she will not help.
My wife has heard it before.
She won't ask for a child
alive inside her
although she holds my mouth to her breast.
She prefers me beneath her.
Breathless, I pretend to enter her with knives.

Prothalamion

The love we define for ourselves
in terms of privacy, in suffering,
keeps each of us lonely as a fist,
but sometimes I might be arguing
with myself, you're that correct:
the hand inside me squeezes the word
intimacy until meaning a happy ending.
Perhaps this was also defined,
but driving at night, the shadows
on a drawn curtain meant terrible lives:
a father stuck in a job, his daughter
opening her blouse to strangers.

I'm afraid of marriage.
Your hands, for example, like a warm liquid
on my face don't evaporate
as you take them away.
Nor are those accidents silent,
the cut ones, or bodies crushed by trucks,
although we listen only in passing.
We're learning how to walk unlit streets,
to see threats instead of trees,
the right answer to a teenager
opening his knife. The answer is yes.
Always we couldn't do otherwise.

Speaking

I'm speaking again
as the invalid in a dark room.
I want to say thank you

out loud to no one.
I want to fold my hard arms in
on the sound, as the sound
dissolves slowly like a man living.

I'm honestly grateful there's breath
to make noise with, and many words
have meaning. I feel lucky
when hello doesn't hurt.
On a bus, I could love anyone.

It's not terrible to be alone.
Last night I talked to a person
so carefully I might have been looking
for a word that wouldn't change.
That made her ready for anything.

Really, I'm not being funny.

There are people everywhere sorry
for the pleasure that keeps them going,
although they circle that pleasure
like a herd around its dying leader.
This pleasure, for me, is in speaking,
as if words enclosed the secret
in myself that lasts after death.

Letter from an Institution: III

I have a garden here, shaped
like Marienbad, remember?,
I lose myself
in, it seems. They only look for me
sometimes. I don't like my dreams.

The nurses quarrel over where I am
hiding. I hear from inside
a bush. One is crisp
& cuts; one pinches. I'd like to push
them each somewhere.

They both think it's funny
here. The laughter sounds like diesels.
I won't move because I'm lazy.
You start to like the needles.
You start to want to crazy.

This Is a Poem for the Dead

fathers: naked, you stand for their big faces,
mouths stuffed flat, eyes weighted, your miserable dick
sticking out like a nose. Dressed, you're more
of a mother making dinner: those old dirt bags,
the lungs, sway inside your chest like tits
in a housedress. Perhaps you're frying liver
which shrinks like your father getting older.
You still smell him breathing all over
your skin. He drank himself to death.

Now each woman you meet is a giant.
You'd crawl up their legs & never come down.
Even when you think you're big enough
to touch them, his voice flies from under
your throat & "I love you" comes out
a drunk whimper. All you can do
is breathe louder. You're speaking
to the back of your mouth. Finally,
you admit you know nothing
about sex & drown the urge slowly
like a fat bird in oil.

Still, those wings inside you.
At the hot stove all day you feel yourself
rising, the kids wrapping themselves
around your legs oh it's sexual
this nourishing food for the family
your father stumbling through the door
calling to you Honey I'm home.

IRA SADOFF

A Concise History of the World

Columbus discovered America.
If you lived here before
him, you'd be sadly mistaken.

The same thing with Africa.
Before Diaz rounded the Cape, natives
provided background for the stars.

Edison, of course, harnessed light
into a tiny bulb. Everywhere else
around him had to be called dark.

Civilization is the clean sheet
on an empty bed. Before
marriage, no one made love.

All the Puritans really wanted
was freedom, the freedom to erase
the body before it spread to other places.

People in Red China want to take over
the world. We do not recognize them.
Yellow is really white not feeling

well. It is a little known fact
that people are not really poor:
they are just not hungry

enough to work. Let's face it:
anyone who is not me is mistaken
or my enemy. This is why we choose

up sides. On our side we have
truth. Your side is only human.
We will have to stamp you out.

My Father's Leaving

When I came back, he was gone.
My mother was in the bathroom
crying, my sister in her crib
restless but asleep. The sun
was shining in the bay window,
the grass had just been cut.
No one mentioned the other woman,
nights he spent in that stranger's house.

I sat at my desk and wrote him a note.
When my mother saw his name on the sheet
of paper, she asked me to leave the house.
When she spoke, her voice was like a whisper
to someone else, her hand a weight
on my arm I could not feel.

In the evening, though, I opened the door
and saw a thousand houses just like ours.
I thought I was the one who was leaving,
and behind me I heard my mother's voice
asking me to stay. But I was thirteen
and wishing I were a man I listened
to no one, and no words from a woman
I loved were strong enough to make me stop.

Poem After Apollinaire

I miss the peace and quiet of Chicago
that's the kind of guy I am
I've been to funerals where cigars
are the only monuments to the dead and lipstick
bleeds on the dead man's lips
I'm not afraid of death and I'm not afraid
of noise but when you take off your stockings
I hear moles tearing at the seams of the earth
field mice scurry into the depest holes
and a roar from the subway that could make me say
Yes Sir to the President who I hate

And if afterwards I should light a cigar
it has nothing to do with the movies
or having a good time it's just my way
of keeping my fingers busy
of burning your smell out of the room
I don't want to work I don't even want to smoke
I just need a few moments to recover

The Fifties

All day we walked the streets
of Toledo, lighting up cigarettes
& dreaming of the girls who passed us by
like stoplights late at night.
You remember the Good War, the one
where everyone died without weeping.
And I never had a woman like you
had, one who could clench her teeth
without coming. We listen in the corridors
for the sighs & moans

& wait for the fruits and nuts to jostle
into submission. We'd never kick a friend.

Meanwhile a hyped-up Ford glistens
in the distance. The radio won't stop
playing its three ugly tunes.
All day we can't wait for the daylight
to stop. At night it's never quite
bright enough. When the sun sets
over the tire plants, our old men
will strap us into rubber, all the while
we'll think of comparing welts. Let no one
tell you otherwise, we've never had it so good.

1928

We are sitting by the pool on a sunny day. You are wearing your white suit, holding a drink in one hand and shading your eyes from the sun with the other. Last night's party has just ended. There are splinters of broken glass gleaming in the sunlight, chaise lounges aslant, a spray of napkins spread over the lawn. Last night we went swimming in the pool with all our clothes on, it was the night you slept with the manufacturer's wife. We never met the host. Nothing could stop the band from playing our song over and over again. All night you talked about your work, how the market would go up and up, how there was nothing to lose no matter how great the risk. The women loved you for that. A strong wind blew in from the bay, but it did not so much as ruffle your hair. The wheels of the Chrysler spun freely in a ditch.

The ugliest men fell all over me. They could not keep their hands off my breasts. I could not count how many of their wives did not understand them, how many of their mistresses had not been faithful to them. I had nightmares of stillborn children and our house on the Cape burning into a small pile of ash. Still, it was comforting to wake up and find you were not beside me. And it was difficult to find you in such a big house: when I walked out of our room I saw a hundred men pacing on the balustrade in long white robes. The women had let their hair down but no one seemed to notice. The rustle of their nightgowns was like the gnawing of termites.

Now my red dress seems too harsh against the clear blue of the pool. We do not speak, but I know you are thinking it is a shame we cannot live this way—you do not have the means and I do not have the desire. You are a little bit sad because the party is over and we have nowhere to go. The women you love are lesbians, and everything you say rubs them the wrong way. The day you try to leave me I will take you for everything you have, I will let you know I never loved you, nothing you can ever do would hurt me.

DENNIS SCHMITZ

Goodwill, Inc.

caught at hanger's ends the limp
trousers suspended
from zippers like fish surprised
at what they carried
a king's ring or the genitals
that float like the air bladders
behind the fish's gills & take life
from the liquid where an alien heavy-

bodied animal may drown.
the belts, brassieres & galluses
with their elastic gone
in the orbits the bodies pulled
apart as they circled

each other. the big woman's
girdle broken
by buttocks that moved
like moons around her sex
till she strips
at night to that dark
reflected light a husband
sheds as he travels
in her stunning gravity.
Love, against your bin of odd
sizes I leaned last—
broken shoes, the borrowed old
man's digestion of a dead
wife who still travels the seamless
loneliness of his insides, or
that first love like a rare food
which went to fat about his loins.

in the dirty changing-room men &
women must share I assume other
men's clothes, as many as I can put
on of ever-larger sizes
till I stumble & weave

other richer lives on my own.

Chicago: Near West-Side Renewal

sleep was only a dream
Death had of us
I am afraid to touch
the wall that might be
too warm
the house that bore its gifts
through the night
till the wet sun lapped at the windows

what is the good news I should send
of the sealed landscapes, corners
remembered by light—
yesterday's body has travelled
over the same bones to the older
man who crawls

his young belly bare against the rug
he raises a hand suddenly dipped
in the sun's fresh golden
spoor who tried to wake only
in the empty lots, to recover his own
spoor before he woke

too late! the roads lick up
every kind of weather. inside my breath
returned, a tired rider,

hunter, wet with the sweat of his beast.
before the keyhole's half-
lit eye the humid dreams drift like
flawed glass showing the night

we dimly saw, the common death that
stirred under the small crown
of the gas-ring, the domestic sadness
in the wallpaper's distant
foliage. at night a man discards
the daytime face, the flat
map of his globular, primitive heart
he is at home & loneliness is the local
weather.

all night long we built this house
body by body
because after the flesh spreads
its natural foliage
after our roots will only pull
up pain & we refer
to ourselves in the plural
your bitterness becomes my bitterness

& it is not enough to nail
a wife in Sunday
love or if you are a woman drive
your teeth again & again
into the walls of widowhood
instead you are a day laborer
the Housing Authority hires
rural white, Southern black, planting

enormous blisters in the palms
you press to the old
walls papered with flowers rippling
under the wrecking ball's rusty sun
the bricks, worm-riddled joists

spineless linoleum & lintels
by which the living left
unused lengths of body preserved

in a permanent coat of fever:
this is our neighborhood broken
breath by breath
from our fathers. forty feet above
the broached foundation
only plumbing holds the bathroom
walls painted with the names
of the wrong loves, initials in the hearts
the graffiti a visitor
the lover who was a guest leaves.

The Mole

last of the poets, first of the undead
you must pound a pencil through his heart
before he bites the little seamstress
or gives her life eternal—

a poem patched together from calendars.
he detours through graves to kiss
our necks & nests in the intestines'

narrow tunnels: a penniless noble
without even a shadow to wear
out like the second in a two-
pants suit. how do I stop burrowing

into myself according to the legend,
blind. if I am dead I will be buried
with my toes around my neck
like a string of garlic.

this is the position for loving myself
I will die just once gnawing
the sober radish of the heart.

The California Phrasebook

west of the Sierras where
the central valley
drifts on its crusts of almond
orchards the fields
die in a holiday accident
the freeways snapping
back in the dust like severed
arteries while the accomplished
doctor of silence stitches the evening
closed with stoplights which
never hold. gardens go
on their knees to the sun
all summer turning
over the brief counterfeit the rain
leaves, looking for a real
coin. in the arbors the Italian
uncles sit stirring anise-flavored
coffees, red bandanas
over their knees pulsing
with the sweating
body's rhythm like an open
chest in which the transplanted
organ of the homeland has not yet
begun to function.

in East Bay beyond the valley
towns pore to pore
the children black & brown
press out a test pattern
of veins, their faces rigid with long

division. they stand
in front of the blackboards looking
for their features, refusing
to draw the white mark
of a dollar sign while the mayor
waits & all the examining
board of cops waits, the correction
texts trembling in their hands.
why must we repeat our lessons,
let us go. in the alleys we rehearse
the lonely patrol of hands
over each other's bodies.
if we unfold a woman's creases
we are afraid to read
the platitudes. the black
penis is the last piece
of the puzzle we put in place
before the streetlamps have slipped
away in the wet fingers of the April
night, before the pathways
through the asphalt gardens
disgorge the feathers of the black
angel.

you who arrive late
from some forgotten Kansas
laminated of wheat & the sweet
alfalfa wasted with incurable winter
take root in the familiar
flat valley where the only
winter is overweight with rain
again & again welling up in fallen
wet fruit an early unearned
bitterness like the bum who drowses
under the indelible azaleas scrawled
against the capitol's white
walls. his life too

is a fragrant perennial.
he is less foreign than you,
but you must learn his difficult
language full of inflections for another
self palpable as a stone in spoiled
fruit. another self! the cheap
foundations of love shift—
before you always built in the quake-
proof plains where small rivers
pillow their heads in poplar
roots & turn all night
in the drought's persistent
insomnia. the cellar was dirt
still alive with roots
from which your father cut
your life in rigid board walls
incredibly steady
on the rippling floor of yellow
grain. in California the cellarless
houses sway at the slightest
tremor.

Poke-Pole Fishing

at minus tide the music
is deeper, gruff
music the retreating
sea makes in the rocks callused

with mussels you break
open for bait. the short
cuttyhunk bobs with its weight

on the limber twelve
foot pole you poke in odd

sockets where eels
hold, tail in, to try whatever
the eclectic waves wash
through them. this music,
what more can you
catch, guess at, gummed down
by your small ration

of sense-news?
the pole is a parallel
to the horizon you lose as the opposite
earth pulls land from sea in fresh
creation. what custodian
fish will touch this index of another
world? you cannot reach the sea
by any step backward rigged

in clothes. the blenny eels imitate
kelp in its dwindling
from the land's foster-life.
tenant body, you too rehearse your
constituent parts, your intervals

of utter jubilee

The Name of Our Country

Our Generall called this Countrey
Nova Albion . . . because it might have
some affinitie with our Countrey
in name, which sometimes was so called.
—Hakluyt, *Voyages*

islands move inward
water-marked where the weathers
  unravel each level

till the true face shakes
  free & the islander aware
incredibly treads
  water. the ranger at Point
Reyes told the legend of Drake's
landing. how the cliffs that fall
  away a little every year
recalled the island home whose

wasting body Drake bore
in the liquid isolation where his own
  body fought the surface, eyes
shut that he might not spill
  a dissolving image. no one
drowns at first though the heart

fills with a weightless
  swaying & we are ready to turn
away the breath that crouches
like a wet animal
  in the mouth, preferring
for a moment the forms the moisture
  takes as it floats the coiled
insides that once worked

with their own currents.
a year's voyage looking back
  on a clear day from these cliffs
to the fog-bound Farallones
twenty-four miles distant though
a part of the present coast
  solid to the ocean
floor cleaned of whatever the waves
could carry away & later
  into another country throw

up suspended particles.

II

we came here for repairs
only. the long kiss of rust
   in the anchor-chains & cabin
metals, even mugs our lips print
   with tarnished love.
alone with what we live by,
   wedded to breath-
soaked wreckage, two-thirds water
we wander finger & arm
   into our flesh, land

in a seven-day world
its roof of birds & daily walls
   dividing our lives dried of sleep
as a sailor's dream. the first
   day we dig oysters, drag
stores up the estuary & pray

God dress the dilated
   solitude with proper beasts
tame as the breath we draw
in threads through this foreign
   tapestry. a devoted summer has closed

the ditches with bindweed & mends
   the crumpled bottomland
with bits of color. our melancholy
carpenter in tears trims firs
   for spars tries to memorize
the countersign this lands leaves
   in the drooling rings.

III

seals & indians suffer
   go wounded with the lost

harpoon scanning the dark skins
for the direction of the blood
  & the bones that move
out like sandbars in the shallow
waves of the skull:
  how long since the great

white gods landed & we
  listened unable to think what
we called ourselves. who blended
us soft as curd in the quivering
  pouch of the mother,

made the seal dog for our drowned
  brother, out of breath
& unable to hunt for himself.
how can we reply—your voice breaks
  off in our mouths when we repeat
your questions. flickering palm

is the sign for seal or fish
for man our hands are crippled
  with heavy secrets.
if we answer it will be with our eyes
  drifting like jellyfish
on the death-swell, self-stung
  for what they saw.

IV

a cupful to drink
from the uncovered eye. not the ocean
  its small solids that drain
away to the bottom when the memory
  bends to taste nor English

marshes weighed in place
with winter fogs & rank blooms

suffocating the sheep-folds
lip to lip over the laths
too much alive like tumors:
what can we pray to

who have evolved in this voyage
from the flesh & can't follow Drake
in his despair spreading
spare canvas every night to catch
dew when his new casks split
like saints' bodies with that excess
of another world. every day

the wind unravels
land-smells from the sailor's
nose until the lungs are caught
paired ancient animals the shut
Ark of his skull forced
to swim. the sea is our new country
& the senses crawl slowly
over the surface not heavy
enough to sink.

HUGH SEIDMAN

Tale of Genji

In Murasaki's time
they wept at the sunsets

It was easy

    If you were the Prince
    & in love

Calligraphy could do it

        The total life
        in the nuance of a line

& later

   The sun that had changed

The cold light defining shadow
Poetry leading nowhere

Occurrence made meaningless
The injustice of history

Not that it mattered

        Or the light
        they wept at

Science As Art

like the universe
if the universe could care

like dimensions
where you are, precise

like time is the fourth
and we don't know it
except by indirection

like Einstein when he's young
in the patent office
when the girl said
what do you do there

like gravity, like weight

Drop the Wires

How he thought
he could hold anything

the way a man will hold
what will kill him
unless he had the knack

what my father always said
electricians knew

and they say:
don't touch a dead man
one who has his hands on the wires

and it's not enough to know
you had to
I can hear my father saying

you had to let it go

The Great Nebula in Andromeda

That woman, vacuum in her mouth
arms extended, the stars
budding in her entrails
the last invasion
the ship's gantry gently
cracking in the windows
the alien secret of the breath
as the spine is kissed
and the serpent stirs
the sense of the infant's eyes
alive with light
and the women who have sung
of the silk dripping cunt

This is the hour when history starts
when the nipples are sucked
between my lips
and the Buddha winks and presses
his mouth to mine
in memory of the past
that he was confounded by
at the rim of the universe
when sight turns back
to the center of all things and this
my darling, my incredible angel
is the silence and the noise
I taste and know nothing of
gripping at my ears

The Making of Color

White

Parchment and paper left clean
or the lead, called white, or ceruse

The stack of vinegar and lead
embedded in tanbark or dung;
the temperature of fermentation,
moisture, carbon dioxide,
and the acid vapor of vinegar—
until a crust is formed on the coils of metal:
the white carbonate and hydroxide of lead

The metal may be wrapped in marc,
the refuse of grapes from the wine press,
or else in the waste from beer

The fundamental character is density,
opacity, and brilliant whiteness

Those who work this are warned of
the poisonous dust of this residue—
retained in the human system as
the body's tolerance incurably declines

There is the white of bone,
or of eggshell, or of oyster,
calcined and powdered,
or a pigment of chalk
to be mixed with orpiment

Black

Certain insects sting in oak
nodules called galls from which
tannic and gallic acids are soaked

Mixed with a salt of iron
to form a purple-black liquid
that blackens with age

The color of iron-inks
oxidized in the fibers
of parchment and paper

incaustum—burnt in

or less frequently
suspensions of graphite
or of lampblack

Red

Minium in the sense of cinnabar
the native red sulphide of mercury

Pliny reports
the excellent mines are in Spain
the property of the State

Forbidden to break up or refine
but sent under seal to Rome

Ten thousand pounds per year
the price sustained by law
seventy sesterces a pound

Liver-colored or occasionally scarlet
but a bright red when ground

Blue

Cloth dyed blue
licensed by the Crown

Ultramarine—lapis luzuli
pounded in a bronze mortar
Cennino relates

Eight ducats an ounce
for the patrons to purchase

Purple

The color of cheeks and the sea

Purpureus—the porphyry

The shellfish or the whelk

The murex—the purples of antiquity

Porphyrygenetos—born to the purple

A single drop from a skeleton

The stripes of the Roman togas
The purple of the ancient courts
The purple of Byzantium The purple
of the great codices written in gold
The purple ink of the Patriarch
in the letters to the Pope of Rome

Parchment dyed shellfish-purple
crimson, plum-color, black
and the true purple—rivaling gold

Gold

Sheet metal, foil the thickness of paper,
leaf that is thinner than tissue

Malleable but difficult to powder

Sawed or filed into coarse particles
ground with honey or salt and washed

Hardened with a base metal
filed and crushed and retrieved in acid

Brittle amalgams which are ground
mercury driven off by heat

The goldbeaters place a thin square
at the center of parchment and over this
more parchment and metal—hammered
until the gold spreads to the edges—
cut and the process repeated—
for the finest leaf, a sheet
of ox intestines—goldbeater's skin

One hundred and forty-five leaves
beaten from a ducat
Venetian—fifty-four troy grains

Powdered gold in suspension
chrysography
                    letters
on the reds and purples and blacks
of purple-dyed parchment
polished with a smooth hard stone
or with a tooth
                    the appearance
of filings of metallic gold

Fire

The pages are stained with purple

The letters are written in gold

The covers are encrusted with gems

St. Jerome remonstrates
The curling writhes
Molten gold on carbon
Ink burnt ash grey
Emerald into vapor
The book, the codex, the manuscript
The canvas, the panel, the wall
Conflagrant world against world

CHARLES SIMIC

Butcher Shop

Sometimes walking late at night
I stop before a closed butcher shop.
There is a single light in the store
Like the light in which the convict digs his tunnel.

An apron hangs on the hook:
The blood on it smeared into a map
Of the great continents of blood,
The great rivers and oceans of blood.

There are knives that glitter like altars
In a dark church
Where they bring the cripple and the imbecile
To be healed.

There is a wooden slab where bones are broken,
Scraped clean:—a river dried to its bed
Where I am fed,
Where deep in the night I hear a voice.

The Bird

A bird calls me
From an apple tree
In the midst of sleep.

Calls me from the pink twig of daylight,
From the top of a shadow with roots

That grow each night closer to my heart,
From the steeple of a white cloud.

I give her my sleep,
She dyes it red.
I give her my breath,
She turns it into rustling leaves.

In the throat of that unknown bird
There's a vowel of my name.

She calls me from the talons of the morning star,
She calls me from the nest of the morning mist,
That chirp, like a burning candle
On a windy threshold.

Bird, shaped
Like the insides
Of a yawning
Mouth.

Now your voice touches me even more tenderly,
Tracing its hushed trajectory
At five in the morning
When the sky turns cold and lucent
Like the water in which
They baptized a small child.

I started on the thread
Of the bird's whistle,
Naked,
Climbing like smoke.

The earth grew smaller underneath.
My bare feet touched
The chill coming from the north.

Later, I fell
In a field of nettles
And dreamt I had
The eyes of that bird,

Watching from the heights,
How the roads meet
And part once again.

Psalm

I

Old ones to the side.

If there's a tailor, let him sit
With his legs crossed.
My suit will arrive in a moment.

All priests into mouse-holes.
All merchants into pigs. We'll cut their throats later.

To the beggars a yawn,
We'll see how they'll climb into it.

To the one who thinks, to the one between yes and no,
A pound of onions to peel.

To the mad ones crowns, if they still want them.
To the soldier a manual to turn into a flea.

No one is to touch the children.
No one is to shovel out the dreamers.

II

I'm Joseph of the Joseph of the Joseph who rode on a
  donkey,
A windmill on the tongue humming with stars,
Columbus himself chained to a chair,
I'm anyone looking for a broom closet.

III

You must understand that I write this at night
Their sleep surrounds me like an ocean.
Her name is Mary, the most mysterious of all.
She's a forest, standing at the beginning of time.
I'm someone lying within it. This light is our sperm.
The forest is old, older than sleep,
Older than this psalm I'm singing right to the end.

Bestiary for the Fingers of My Right Hand

I

Thumb, loose tooth of a horse.
Rooster to his hens.
Horn of a devil. Fat worm
They have attached to my flesh
At the time of my birth.
It takes four to hold him down,
Bend him in half, until the bone
Begins to whimper.

Cut him off. He can take care
Of himself. Take root in the earth,
Or go hunting with wolves.

II

The second points the way.
True way. The path crosses the earth,
The moon and some stars.
Watch, he points further.
He points to himself.

III

The middle one has backache.
Stiff, still unaccustomed to this life;
An old man at birth. It's about something
That he had and lost,
That he looks for within my hand,
The way a dog looks
For fleas
With a sharp tooth.

IV

The fourth is mystery.
Sometimes as my hand
Rests on the table
He jumps by himself
As though someone called his name.

After each bone, finger,
I come to him, troubled.

V

Something stirs in the fifth
Something perpetually at the point
Of birth. Weak and submissive,
His touch is gentle.
It weighs a tear.
It takes the mote out of the eye.

Fork

This strange thing must have crept
Right out of hell.
It resembles a bird's foot
Worn around the cannibal's neck.

As you hold it in your hand,
As you stab with it into a piece of meat,
It is possible to imagine the rest of the bird:
Its head which like your fist
Is large, bald, beakless and blind.

Brooms

for Tomaz, Susan and George

I

Only brooms
Know the devil
Still exists,

That the snow grows whiter
After a crow has flown over it,
That a dark dusty corner
Is the place of dreamers and children,

That a broom is also a tree
In the orchard of the poor,
That a hanging roach there
Is a mute dove.

II

Brooms appear in dreambooks
As omens of approaching death.
This is their secret life.
In public, they act like flat-chested old maids
Preaching temperance.

They are sworn enemies of lyric poetry.
In prison they accompany the jailer,
Enter cells to hear confessions.
Their short-end comes down
When you least expect it.
Left alone behind a door
Of a condemned tenement,
They mutter to no one in particular,
Words like *virgin wind moon-eclipse,*
And that most sacred of all names:
Hieronymus Bosch.

III

In this and in no other manner
Was the first ancestral broom made:
Namely, they plucked all the arrows
From the bent back of Saint Sebastian.
They tied them with a rope
On which Judas hung himself.
Struck in the stilt
On which Copernicus
Touched the morning star . . .

Then the broom was ready
To leave the monastery.
The dust welcomed it—
That great pornographer
Immediately wanted to
Look under its skirt.

IV

The secret teaching of brooms
Excludes optimism, the consolation
Of laziness, the astonishing wonders
Of a glass of aged moonshine.

It says: the bones end up under the table.
Bread-crumbs have a mind of their own.
The milk is you-know-who's semen.
The mice have the last squeal.

As for the famous business
Of levitation, I suggest remembering:
There is only one God
And his prophet is Mohammed.

V

And then finally there's your grandmother
Sweeping the dust of the nineteenth century
Into the twentieth, and your grandfather plucking
A straw out of the broom to pick his teeth.

Long winter nights.
Dawns a thousand years deep.
Kitchen windows like heads
Bandaged for toothache.
The broom beyond them sweeping,
Tucking in the lucent grains of dust
Into neat pyramids,
That have tombs in them,

Already sacked by robbers,
Once, long ago.

ROBERTA SPEAR

A Sale of Smoke

As the swamp cooler breathes
into the room, the Chinese lamp
swings, bathing the girls' faces
with red half-moons. They wait
all night with sachets tucked
in their bras, skimming letters
or filing their toenails
into hearts. Through the grille
he points one out, one
unlike the others,
"I want that . . . She moves
like a snail." A half-moon
rises and follows him.

She can live in her own dark soil;
she can flip the sheets back
with one toe and lower her lids
like yellowed shades
against the heat. She can
give him what he wants.
For thirty cents, for thirty
beans . . . makes fifteen
for herself and fifteen
for mama, divided
like mice balls
and steamed to a mush. She can
live for another day.

Outside, in the city,
the day takes over. The vapor
lifts her lids again:

from the pool around the drinking post,
from the mush pots, and the clay jug
steeped with olive leaves
to get new men. An old whore
hikes her skirts, leaping
over the smoke twice,
and the one in bed feels
her pillow sink each time
the hag's feet hit the ground.
She squeezes the life
back into her nipples,
"when I dry up I'll break a jug
over the last fucker's head."
Her fire has already started.

The Bat

1

In autumn, the bats
steamed in their fur
like rotten eggs
stuffed under each shingle.
Following the shade,
we looked up—
the ladder shook
as the man pried their fists
loose with a crowbar.
In one burst
they shot deadeyed
into the thicket.

2

Bats never go away;
they settle nearby

on the darkest limbs
where they grow
and get uglier.
In a year's time
they wriggle back
into the beams and nests
of barnstraw, whispering.
The heifers wear out
their heels in the paddock;
people blow softly
into the currents of sleep,
leaving their hands
open at their sides.

3

Before lunch
I ease into sleep,
a quilt stretched
across my knees. A few words
crawl out, fanning
themselves: little-pallid,
pouch-winged, I am ready.
Leaf-nosed can't see
me coming and waits
on the last rib
for a slow moth. I steal
his edge on darkness.

4

Bluejay rams a cherry tree,
hummingbird rests its head
on the bar, asks for another,
the phoebe gives away
her drab wing, the wretched crow
gives up and begs for a field mouse,
who can't understand.

The answer is the bat
who finds life easy
to swallow. He drops here
like a hankie, but leaves
his song in the other world—
he too is a failure. Try again.

5

So you took
two clipped steps
toward the window, the curtain
swelled. He was asleep
and with each gust spread
like a burn over the white lace.
You opened a book
and closed it around his body,
tilting the binding
until he fell two floors
down to a bed of dahlias.
We assumed he was dead,
but we were wrong:
it was the beginning of sunlight
that bored the scalp
and got no warmer,
of a gust that kept insisting
and swept toward you.

August/Fresno 1973

Even the sun, still warm
and husky seems silly
as it searches the alley
for some loose fur. This is why

I take my time.
I pull the curtains when I wake
and stand naked in front of the cooler.
I don't try to fool myself:
it takes three seconds
to fill an ice tray, two hours
to make cubes, forty minutes
for the ice to melt and form
a lake that fruit flies skid across
when I leave the room.
Somewhere in this town
I have a perfect mate: not the one
who fucks to forget the heat,
but a young man
who patiently places a match
between each toe for every blond
that's left him. He ignites
the blue tips and when they go out
the snow settles on his shoulders.

Bringing Flowers

Alone for the evening
I settle for shadows, latch
a dozen hooks on the window screens.
In '62 he cut his way
through one in Marlene's bedroom
like a weasel
into a chicken coop. He raped,
then stabbed her
with a pair of scissors.

A man doesn't know
the feeling of that heavy voice

that falls on my bare shoulders;
the walls cut in
on my silent dance. I am tired
but force my eyes to open,
pull my legs in close
to my body. In a glass
on the table the snapdragons
loosen their tongues,
lapping the water around them.
From that corner
he comes towards me:
he's bringing a flower,
its purple mouth
opening in his hand . . .

Wanting to change the story
(I am alone, it is my right),
I will welcome the large warm body,
give him a rag to wipe
the sweat from his temples.
My coolness will melt him.
It will go on until morning
through a good breakfast
when he'll feel comfortable enough
to mop the loose yolk
in front of a stranger—
maybe laugh,
tell me how lucky I was.

KATHLEEN SPIVACK

Visions

Rilke, my river, I know your locked look of a poet:
how from your fingers spun threads
that suspended the universe,
the marionette angels curving and swaying,
sculptural, sermonal bodies.

You sought a shuddering, glorious silence
carved like a crèche; the shriek of a hare, inescapable,
fixing its mute-pooling eyes on a trapper
all hairy and heaving, hunting it down.
Everything holding its breath!

What can follow such terrible silence but salt?
In this ashland, I cup hands
to the Dark River, watch watery lovers,
eyesocketed, flow out of the mind
into a delta of touch.

I see women with blossoming bottoms,
hair like a thicket, flying up from their men
like firebrands, crying angrily "Now, now!"
The men watchful, their pupils dilating,
cougars at night as the brush takes flame.

Crouched under words is a flowering of panthers,
the exquisite jungle, reeking
of vaginal unguents. Green as crushed vine,
slit-eyed boas retwine, palpable,
growing into trees thick as thighs.

At each eyepoint a comet's gone crazy.
Breasts halve in the dark, blossoms
burst their dark nipples. The corners
fill up with bel canto. Camellias
devour the curve of the world—

genitalia unfolding, what secrets!
The brain, in its silence,
grows things behind its eyes.
Like a lily, like fingers, a stubborn root,
visions, narcissi, explode from their bulbs.

A Child's Visit to the Biology Lab

Stiff in a white coat,
dragged there by my mother,
I sulked through the laboratory
offices, the halls, the brass
cases, more gloomy than second grade.
My important tummy
strained in its white buttons, fingers
picked at things, sour and impatient as eyes.

Down the hall, the light was fine
as filtered lymph. The sodden chicks,
the unborn piglets swimming in their tears,
went round and round in jars;
the afternoon grew circular.

And babies too. Brine-flowers, their blind eyes
enclosed all specimens of coral.
Where their belly buttons grew
they floated, pink and new as toes.
They swam in a shield of arms.

I thought, that's where the changelings go;
prisoned forever, weeping, waiting for parents,
their arms upflung against knowing.
They have no souls, my mother said.
But I, whose seven years swelled in my eyes,
oh alter ego, fluttered at the glass.

Private Pain in Time of Trouble

How can I sustain
this troubled swelling:
my heart like an eggplant,

blackened, bulbous, grows too greedy:
bruised and sorrowful
it will not let its great loss go,

wanting to be pendulous with child.
Private pain in time of trouble
as the dark-eyed children burn.

They stretch out their small hands to me:
sparrows, and I do not hear.
It is a false spring this year.

But You, My Darling, Should Have Married the Prince

When we were children, clasping hands,
do you remember that moist circle, play?
How we were dancing and knew only the dandelions,
and the earth was livid with dandelions.

I see us now as in a photograph that never was:
hair like soapbubbles spun by nuns, the singing
raucous as starch. Our cries still echo
down the corridors of my ears: we,
rank and weedy, wanting to be old.

There were no secrets then
to prickle our knees.
No one hid in the closet.
Beards were friendly as forests of grass—
how we trembled, pretending to be lost,
caught in the chins of uncles.

We pared apples, made wishes,
and washed in the first dew of May.
Mother went through our laundry
and we didn't mind . . .
but how we wept when our cousin got married.
Home from the army, his six-month mustache
saluted both sides of his face.
Jealous as bridesmaids we watched
as he married the girl. She had apricot hair
and a cameo ring.
Look, now, how he takes her hand.
Never was it like that, picking scabs!
Peaches and morning were right for those two,
not for us, little pickles, fevered in bed, yanking
knots from our furious hair in the dark
and begging to be blonde.
Nights came. Net notching our chests,
thighs sticky, we went to the dances
and put up our hair.
You lost your virginity
in mother's garden
and finally I was kissed.

Now we are older. You are married.
Natashas both, we have grown up.
Those shivery wonderings lit from the street
are over; cousins put away in paper boxes.
Outside, the walnut trees
grow sticky as old tears
and I lie sweating in the dark.
The dusk comes swallow-winged;
the apples rot with wishes.
Where there is no magic, one stays a toad
and we who screamed to know it
know it, and grow old.

MAURA STANTON

Judith Recalls Holofernes

While he slept, I poured salt in his ears.
Yes, it was easy
until the wasps escaped from the first hole in his neck
to blind me with wings
settling iridescent on my arms while I hacked
fiercely into the spine.
When it was over, I kissed his lips
then thumbed the eyes open
looking for my reflection in the dark pupil.
Actually, it was my maid
wielding the sword with strong, anonymous fingers.
I hid in the sheets, imagining
how many soldiers in the mountains
north of Bethulia dreamed of me each night.
Excuse me, it's hard to remember:
the blue tent, the olives,
Holofernes leaning into my breasts
describing something called "snow."
Did he have a beard or was that Anchior?
Perhaps I poisoned him first, yes, of course.
He drank greedily, his muscles
rippling silver in the light while he pulled
my left earlobe in fun.
Let me try out your sword, I said.

His wife writes me sad letters, asking for detail.
Did he eat well? Or catch cold?
Judith, you're the heroine, she says, I can't complain
about history, but didn't he call
my name in his sleep?

I write back: I'm not sure, I think the sword
flew by itself, a miracle, into his throat.
I'm not responsible for God.

This is our shipwrecked anniversary
which I celebrate by lighting a candle
inside his skull above the town gate
except, this year, they've torn it down.
Listen, his heart simply burst—
he was singing, he was so lonely
he stuffed flowers in his mouth
just to entertain me a moment longer.
Why did he hang his sword on the bedpost?
No, I don't remember.
Something is buzzing in my head,
something that sounds like a thousand
transparent wings rising behind my eyes.

Letter to Kafka

Your closed eyes bulge like mushrooms.
While you sleep, I carve maps on your skin,
asking forgiveness with awkward kisses,
asking, do you understand theft, how I need
your white sperm? The fiancée
in her lace dress, jilted, arranging her mouth—
is really me—wearing a shawl of razors.
I tilt my head, telling the waistcoated suitor:
"Of course I believe in friendship!" I believe in whales.
I believe in the magic of water on the brain,
your illness, my teeth, our postponed death.
All those letters in your vest, the good wishes
scribbled by me & other eager women—
they're only ransom notes, knives at our throats.

If you mumble about your father
what can I say? Here is mine—
a whole childhood of frown & circumference
locked on a prairie without history,
without oracular words like "Prague" or "Jew."
Of course you want nothing from me. You are salt.
You fly in my wounds when I wake up
blind in the darkness, calling for a thesaurus
to explain sex in all its musical failure.

The All-Night Waitress

for Gail Fischer

To tell the truth, I really *am*
a balloon, I'm only rubber, shapeless,
smelly on the inside . . .
I'm growing almost invisible.
Even the truckers admire my fine
indistinctiveness, shoving their fat hands
through my heart as they cry,
"Hey, baby! You're really weird!"
Two things may happen: if the gas
explodes at the grill some night,
I'll burst through the greasy ceiling
into black, high air,
a white something children point at
from the bathroom window at 3 a.m.
Or I'll simply deflate.
Sweeping up, the day shift will find
a blob of white substance
under my uniform by the door.
"Look," they'll say, "what a strange
unnatural egg; who wants to touch it?"
Actually, I wonder how I'd

really like being locked into orbit
around the earth, watching
blue, shifting land forever—
Or how it would feel to disappear
unaccountable in the arms of some welder
who might burst into tears
& keep my rubbery guts inside his lunch box
to caress on breaks, to sing to . . .
Still it would mean escape
into a snail's consciousness, that muscular
foot which glides a steep shell
over a rocky landscape, recording passage
on a brain so small how could it hurt?

Extracts: from the Journal of Elisa Lynch

note: *Elisa Lynch was the Irish mistress of Francisco Solano Lopez, dictator of Paraguay from 1862–1870. She was a colonel in his army during the war with Argentina, Brazil and Uruguay in which Lopez and her oldest son were killed. She died in Paris.*

I *May, 1866*

Distance doesn't matter, Francisco,
nothing matters, not cigars, yerba maté,
brandy staunching the pain of black teeth.
The violent garden was always lush soil.
The Guaraní girl, naked & mad in the shrubs
is really me tugging at your genitals.
Let's put away detail, your height, my hair
limned grey at the nape & all language
stuffed manic into song or thesaurus.
Skin is the only safe country; defies

even my nightmare of beached whales
rotted to white ghost ships on the Chaco.
The route across anywhere is scrub forest
gaudy with snakes & headhunters. How could
we survive alone? No trails, no water,
no mapped skies, instinct or destination.

II *December, 1868*

The donkeys bray in the ditches, legs broken,
straw twisted in their eyes: I killed two men
yesterday; I am not changed into a lizard
although the Guaraní have a wooden cage, two thin
mice for my dinner. They look at my fingers for scales
or the green mold which sprouts from my heart.
Last night, Francisco, wasn't my skin odd
under your fingers? My words gagged me,
feathers, feathers . . . you said I was Lot's salt
wife, immobile except for a brain like blue light.
So death is boring. See, it comes rigid-lipped,
too small for hell, celebrated by these blind
donkeys who gnaw their riders. "A woman who kills
will eat sand like the lizard." Isn't my throat
dry? Do you believe my knees are fattening?
A lizard crawls on the battlefield, alive
& blinking over rocks, over the hands of soldiers.

III *March, 1870*

Horseback. Over the Chaco.
Yesterday we found the mining-
engineer haphazard in sand.
A hundred gaudy butterflies
sucked & swirled on his skin.
I said, Francisco, those flowers . . .
Today the mistress of Paraguay

lost grey gloves, her firstborn,
Pancho. A silver pain—
clean as any compass needle
jabbed through the heart of a mutineer.
Already landscape grows internal.
Asunción tilts on its hill, off-angle,
fragil as cigar-paper. Lopez
they mock me: Madame General!
My nipples hum under linen.
My bastard children claw
for the enemy's Argentine sugarcane.
Look, already their eyes burrow.
I want to tell them secrets,
whisper magic words for keepsakes
until we all disappear. These lessons
grow difficult, the map not parchment
& blotted ink but our own soil,
the firstborn's heart open, flowery—
(the Indian-women, cleverer,
ate their husband's sperm & intentions.)
Lizards flick, usual over flat rock.
The war subsides. Madame General
breakfasts on spoiled avocado,
counting her children like lemmings.
How do I teach erratic geography,
sudden snow in the ruined vineyards?
Nothing to make it worth telling, only
roots in a damp cellar gone berserk
through the walls for our oxygen.

IV *March, 1870*

Jungle encroaches on the veranda,
monkey-weed smelling of piss & rotten
soldiers left for the general burial.
Paraguay collapses into straw & arson.
The guards boil jacaranda with lizard
& pork salt. I tear old cloth,

dream I am hidden in mesquite
with all my silver hairbrushes & children,
straw hampers, beef, & your photograph.
Still no word. Maybe you are blind,
raving for me on bloody ankles
screaming, "O Muerte! O Muerte!
O Muerte!" I want to bandage my eyes.
Mad dogs ravage the hills. They watch
our throats, quiver, aware of civilizations,
how they end with shard & survivors.

V *November, 1875*

I'm afraid of the bones swimming up
through my children's skin, the white sheen
on their lips as they gobble from tin
plates: In exile I haggle over the *ficelle*
or *petit pain,* wrap my stunned head
in vinegar cloth. Francisco, in dreams now
I bring water for your black tongue, I touch
your cheek until the silver maggots run.
Your grimace bristles in stone at Notre Dame
where I force the children to chant Guaraní
prayers to the lizard at a side altar.
Squinting at needles in dark rooms,
I blanch like a toad, thumbs flat & sore
as an old crone in a fairy tale.
No proper death, Francisco, no bullet
smashing my angry heart into shock;
only the usual butcher's crablike mouth
gnawing mine, mumbling, "You love it! Admit
you love it!" A woman's face disappears
in adversity, going under like battle
terrain with a few scrub pine left blooming,
my eyes, frightening the children on nights
when I tear off my nightgown, crying
"Look at me! Look at your mother!"

DAVID ST. JOHN

Poem

for Georg Trakl

Your face,
so pale now it is blue.
And in the icy, dead moons
of your eyes, the things you
loved are trembling; all
utterly blue—

The small, soft breasts
of your sister. Vienna's night—alone;
frosted stairways. Blue sonata, blue rosary
of morning, blue sun. The river, and the sleek
angel stepping from its waters, offering
a robe of woven larkspur.

And the azure pearls
of opium, asleep in your palms—
as if, from the glazed balcony
of your cheeks, blue tears
had fallen.

For Lerida

Clove, salmon knocking
in the pot; flames waking
off blue wood. A bottle
of Spanish wine squats on
the table. The sad radio

talks of herons rising out
of the Capital, of pianos
blown to dice, of trains
ticking across the borders,
towards this city. I touch
the bruises, shadowed pink
with makeup, around her eyes.
She tells her dream: a street
like milk, painted with new
snow. Of a house where it is
always winter; her sister
fluttering down hallways like
a paper corsage. The spoons
her mother ties to her dresses
spilling always with a pale
dust, or heroin. Her lover
in a blond raincoat, slipping
thin, quiet fingers into her
rings; and leaving.—Outside,
the river is howling its prayers.
A last moon is packing its bags.

Slow Dance

It's like the riddle Tolstoy
Put to his son, pacing off the long fields
Deepening in ice. Or the little song
Of Anna's heels, knocking
Through the cold ballroom. It's the relief
A rain enters in a diary, left open under the sky.
The night releases
Its stars, & the birds the new morning. It is an act of
grace
& disgust. A gesture of light:
The lamp turned low in the window, the harvest

Fire across the far warp of the land. The somber
Cadence of boots returns. A village
Pocked with soldiers, the dishes rattling in the cupboard
As an old serving woman carries a huge, silver spoon
Into the room & as she polishes she holds it just
So in the light, & the fat
Of her jowls
Goes taut in the reflection. It's what shapes
The sag of those cheeks, & has
Nothing to do with death though it is as simple, &
insistent.
Like a coat too tight at the shoulders, or a bedroom
Weary of its single guest. At last, a body
Is spent by sleep: A dream stealing the arms, the legs.
A lover who has left you
Walking constantly away, beyond that stand
Of bare, autumnal trees: Vague, & loose. Yet, it's only
The dirt that consoles the root. You must begin
Again to move, towards the icy sill. A small
Girl behind a hedge of snow
Working a stick puppet so furiously the passersby bump
Into one another, watching the stiff arms
Fling out to either side, & the nervous goose step, the
dances
Going on, & on
Though the girl is growing cold in her thin coat & silver
Leotard. She lays her cheek to the frozen bank
& lets the puppet sprawl upon her,
Across her face, & a single man is left twirling very
Slowly, until the street
Is empty of everything but snow. The snow
Falling, & the puppet. *That girl.* You close the window,
& for the night's affair slip on the gloves
Sewn of the delicate
Hides of mice. They are like the redemption
Of a drastic weather: Your boat
Put out too soon to sea,

Come back. Like the last testimony, & trace of desire.
Or,
How your blouse considers your breasts,
How your lips preface your tongue, & how a man
Assigns a silence to his words. We know lovers who quarrel
At a party stay in the cool trajectory
Of the other's glance,
Spinning through pockets of conversation, sliding in & out
Of the little gaps between us until they brush or stand at last
Back to back, & the one hooks
An ankle around the other's foot. Even the woman
Undressing to music on a stage & the man going home the longest
Way after a night of drinking remember
The brave lyric of a heel-&-toe. As we remember the young
Acolyte tipping
The flame to the farthest candle, & turning
To the congregation, twirling his gold & white satin
Skirts so that everyone can see his woolen socks & rough shoes
Thick as the hunter's boots that disappear & rise
Again in the tall rice
Of the marsh. The dogs, the heavy musk of duck. How the leaves
Introduce us to the tree. How the tree signals
The season, & we begin
Once more to move: Place to place. Hand
To smoother, & more lovely hand. A slow dance. To get along.
You toss your corsage onto the waters turning
Under the fountain, & walk back
To the haze of men & women, the lazy amber & pink lanterns

Where you will wait for nothing more than the slight
  gesture
Of a hand, asking
For this slow dance, & another thick & breathless night.
Yet, you want none of it. Only, to return
To the countryside. The fields & long grasses:
The scent of your son's hair, & his face
Against your side,
As the cattle knock against the walls of the barn
Like the awkward dancers in this room
That you must leave, knowing the leaving as the casual
& careful betrayal of what comes
Too easily, but not without its cost, like an old white
Wine out of its bottle, or the pages
Sliding from a worn hymnal. At home, you walk
With your son under your arm, asking of his day, & how
It went, & he begins the story
How he balanced on the sheer hem of a rock, to pick
  that shock
Of aster nodding in the vase, in the hall. You pull him
  closer,
& turn your back to any other life. You want
Only the peace of walking in the first light of morning,
As the petals of ice bunch one
Upon another at the lip of the iron pump & soon a
  whole blossom
Hangs above the trough, a crowd of children teasing it
With sticks until the pale neck snaps, & flakes spray
  everyone,
& everyone simply dances away.

TERRY STOKES

All Morning

All morning a wren has been building
a nest in my ear. I will shelter anyone

who needs it, it's always been
my problem, & who can resist small

birds? They cannot hurt you,
even their tail feathers

twitching like soft razor blades,
my friend, oh, my friend.

Crimes Of Passion: The Slasher

What I like most is when
the hemline rises
& they place the high heel,
usually the right,
onto the first step of the bus,
then, they grasp the small
rod, & pull themselves up. The nylons
flare like hot butter, & as that
thigh bulges slightly, & then
taut, I gently nudge her
& with the razor blade, one side
taped, as if a finger
were lovingly running from the back

of the knee toward the buttocks.
She will sometimes turn & smile,
feeling some part of herself freed,
only hours later does she learn
how deep my passion runs, the thick
blood of birth drips silently
to some cold floor,
& in that pool, my face returns
the wonderful smile, & then, I think,
she probably screams. She will dream of me,
& that is all
anyone can ever ask.

Crimes of Passion: The Phone Caller

No, no, don't, please,
oh my warm chicken, do
not be upset, & do not
hang up, what I wish to
say can only be spoken
in low tones, no, tonight
I won't groan, I groan
only when I am unhappy, do
you understand? If I throw
a kiss into your ears, who
knows? & who cares? That is
the problem, what you learn
of loneliness, I teach, & I
teach it slowly, so you will
understand fully. I am chewing
on a carrot, & I am thinking of
nothing but you, I am thinking
of you quietly, putting out

tomorrow's clothes, tomorrow
you will wear the red sweater
which causes your breasts to be
like carrots. & you will come
down the stairs at 7:46, & you
will squint & put on your purple
oval sunglasses, & trying to
appear quite casual, you will
look up the street, you will
look down the street, you will
pause one second, & sigh, &
when that look of relief covers
your face, I will step out of
the morning, drag you into the warm
alley, & there with what's left
of this carrot, I will hurt you
very badly, but of course I will
kiss you ever so gently first,
with all my heart.

Travis, The Kid Was All Heart

You watched out for him or
you got your mouth messed up.

Orthodontist was not a word he
hauled around behind his mauler's
eyes. He liked to fuck sheep &

eat spiders. When he slept, he
farted toads. In those games of touch

football, his feet would send your balls
back where they belonged. A friendly
slap on the ass was "fag stuff." He'd

goose you forever with everything he had,
Coke bottles, brooms, or his rough nose.

In the huddle he'd call for plays involving
several pubescent girls, electric toothbrushes,
multiple vitamins, & honey. We'd lap

it all up. The rubbers in our wallets
wobbled like failed field goal attempts.

Downfield, he always caught the pass on his
fingertips. Defensive ends, guards, & backs
humped the earth for him.

Some teeth raked the fur of his calves, some
teeth crunched having found themselves

trapped in his simple sidestep. He cut
roses all the way to the wounded moon
lying on her back waiting, fuck yes, waiting.

A Man All Grown Up Is Supposed To

The anger rises with metal filings &
I will not see the ground as rock &
the stones will not carry my rubber spirit.
I have hit nothing in months & the candle
stuffed in my stomach flaps fire, flaps
smoke, goes out. I have no money, I am
very sorry about that, it would make things
easier, I suppose. A man all grown up is
supposed to have a pocket full wherever he
is, & feed his woman & kiss the teeth of

the fire & dance with the trucks & pitch
pennies with the soft children.

When his anger collected he found the dog's
rubber bone, he chewed on it in the corner,
growling at the cat, the children, the night
of impetigo. She took it away, saying, come
inside. It's cold out there, come inside
before you catch your death of cold, he knew
what she meant, he knew & tore the hair off
her head, the moon was harmless & so pale.

He sighed with the moths, & asked the
linoleum, for god's sake, forgive, his
fingers rolled around in the sink under
the hard water, & her eyes were a deer
carcass out in the woods, no one around,
no one ever there when you need them.

BRIAN SWANN

Quiet

I'm quiet as an old leather belt lapped snakewise
tail in tongue
over the antique wicker chair
where the window looks down on another yellow
  window
set low in the white frame of the house next door
Quiet as the man who rests on his hoe
and watches a wedge of swans fly some legend
over a torrent still with fullness
hears the long breath of their whistle
and the distant drag of the weir
like a thousand feet scuffing

Quiet with a woman who came when I didn't expect
a dark woman from tea leaves to sit on my knee
as I faced rigidly front
whose face goes back in phases to a child moved
over seas and continents to one place
not to be moved

There had been a turkey carcass feathered tight as if
  glued
empty and vaulted
A child waited patiently for eggs in the straw
I hunkered and explained
gave him two from pocket
smiling

          That's also why I'm quiet
as an old shoe

happily wrinkled

Paradigms of Fire

knuckles over the flame
over the host's head
over the limits of his hearing
crackling in sharp bursts
like gunfire or lightning
a crisp discharge of goats
leaping the night from
crest to crest and dying
in the chasms they created
sides speckled and tawny
smooth and vellum-scraped
tapped with stars and the long
spasm of a comet
cracking at the outer
limits of air
habitable worlds

The fingers have many hands
rubbing to a fine powder
where the mind has been
whatever it has cut and folded
whatever soot and ochre
it has blown over the
mutilated hand its missing
fingers alongside the wounded bison
and the leaping stag
Starting again from dry
moss and nursed flame
near the skin suckled
with breath and the new air
that slid over seaweed
danced with dry sticks and
wisps of skate-purses over
sand steps had shaped with
cool heels and measure

There are fine birds on the nails
rising from the flames with
white half-moon wings
that soar out of sight while
we are staring at them and still
staring present and disappear
the eye lifted where it can
never recover the child's eye
taking on primeness and the new
age of things the paradigms
cool hearts giving off coolness
like heat like anemonies like
an invitation to the hand like
daughters of the wind
disobedience the coin
of insight lucidity
of burnt skin

Whenever it is time to go
it is time to return for
the outward journey is the
inward lake with green lemons
tempting lemons of water
and the ash fruit we grasp in the
echo of the chill-fired fruit
we cannot grasp

In cupped hands the fire
of skin the broken interdiction
of touch

Year of the Bird

Dead scents I couldn't bear bore
  fruit
and filled earth full of small cuts

Prows split thin ice-gusts
and downwind dropped
opal gardens
spice patches

The birds come
in colter waves
Their wings tatter the straight
They loosen
hot pleats of earth
unfurl them
in loam skies where
harvests wave wide as the sunsets
whose winds churn the land
past farmhouse and field
to wild oats and barley
ancestral grasses that
shoulder stones and root

The birds bring sky in their
  claws and clay
Where they settle ears are shaken
  free
then cast again in gold
They have come from nowhere
and are going everywhere
Each place is discovery
retrieval
a feather from their breasts

Desert in the Sea

My urine smells of smoke
Smoke & the whiteness
Of a blind eyeball

How had time the groundswell
Swamped these inland caves
And scratched high-water even on the flames

The sunflower has recourse
To affidavits and the thumbprint
On the mackerel's flank

Is the saint's mark to ensure
The sea is alive
The cloud over the scarp

Is the last ash before it
Recoups and refuels
No sky but self

The following of birds
The clods whistle with wings
The oaks

With burn scars in our heads
Look less solid than pointillism
Hummingbirds suck at the window

And the air sprinkles dots
Winds flow between in minute eddies
Cutting corners who needs eyes

Or who would believe
The inside could combust
With such slow smoulder

Between the hard palms
Of fisherman or shepherd
Cupped round the volcanic thistle

The tent is just flap
The body heat
The earth the corner we turn

That comes trailing horizons
And verticals from its horns
The eye is visible but cannot see itself

It can hear better than see
Seeing is better done with the skin
For it has no distractions

No doctor would
Diagnose your urine
As smoke nor your blindness

As ear infection so
It is time to up tent
And seek shelter in the open plain

Where mirage and duster
Wrap tides fish and birds
In the total cloth of restitution

Tides birds and fish
Smoke and all the vivid lazy colors
Caught in the

Tricky strip of rawhide
Thin blueprint for the new
City raised within sight of the sea

This is no trick but infinity
Though the desire still remains
To sip through the glass the wide choice of horizon

Here there is cleanness in the desert
No haste to complete and all sweetness
Tinged with the virtue of salt

The oars we spent years to learn
Push air by us in tight bundles

JAMES TATE

The Soup of Venus

This soup is cold
and it needs something,
you probably didn't follow
the recipe, you were
in a hurry and wanted
to surprise me.
That was sweet of you
but you forgot
that I don't like
cold soup.
You might try adding
one bay leaf
while you are in there.
The salt is on the table
and I will experiment
with that myself.
The parsley doesn't
taste much but it
does improve
the appearance.
You used to make
such good soup.
I always bragged
about your soup.
I think that's what
originally attracted me
to you, that hot soup
you used to make.
I loved that soup.
Do you still have

that recipe?
Well, this tastes
a little better now,
lukewarm soup
is my second favorite.

Coda

Love is not worth so much;
I regret everything.
Now on our backs
in Fayetteville, Arkansas,
the stars are falling
into our cracked eyes.

With my good arm
I reach for the sky,
and let the air out of the moon.
It goes whizzing off
to shrivel and sink
in the ocean.

You cannot weep;
I cannot do anything
that once held an ounce
of meaning for us.
I cover you
with pine needles.

When morning comes,
I will build a cathedral
around our bodies.
And the crickets,
who sing with their knees,

will come there
in the night to be sad,
when they can sing no more.

The Blue Booby

The blue booby lives
on the bare rocks
of Galápagos
and fears nothing.
It is a simple life:
they live on fish,
and there are few predators.
Also, the males do not
make fools of themselves
chasing after the young
ladies. Rather,
they gather the blue
objects of the world
and construct from them

a nest—an occasional
Gaulois package,
a string of beads,
a piece of cloth from
a sailor's suit. This
replaces the need for
dazzling plumage;
in fact, in the past
fifty million years
the male has grown
considerably duller,
nor can he sing well.
The female, though,

asks little of him—
the blue satisfies her
completely, has
a magical effect
on her. When she returns
from her day of
gossip and shopping,
she sees he has found her
a new shred of blue foil:
for this she rewards him
with her dark body,
the stars turn slowly
in the blue foil beside them
like the eyes of a mild savior.

Deaf Girl Playing

This is where I once saw a deaf girl playing in a field. Because I did not know how to approach her without startling her, or how I would explain my presence, I hid. I felt so disgusting, I might as well have raped the child, a grown man on his belly in a field watching a deaf girl play. My suit was stained by the grass and I was an hour late for dinner. I was forced to discard my suit for lack of a reasonable explanation to my wife, a hundred dollar suit! We're not rich people, not at all. So there I was, left to my wool suit in the heat of summer, soaked through by noon each day. I was an embarrassment to the entire firm: it is not good for the morale of the fellow worker to flaunt one's poverty. After several weeks of crippling tension, my superior finally called me into his office. Rather than humiliate myself by telling him the truth, I told him I would wear whatever damned suit I pleased, a suit of armor if I fancied. It was the first time I had challenged his authority. And it was the last. I was dismissed. Given my pay. On the way home I thought, I'll tell her the truth, yes, why not! Tell her the simple truth, she'll love me for it. What a touching story. Well, I didn't. I don't know what happened, a loss of courage, I suppose. I told her a mistake I had made had cost the company several thousand dollars, and that, not only was I dismissed, I would also somehow have to find the money to repay them the sum of my error. She wept, she beat me, she accused me of everything from malice to impotency. I helped her pack and drove her to the bus station. It was too late to explain. She would never believe me now. How cold the house was without her. How silent. Each plate I dropped was like tearing the very flesh from a living animal. When all were shattered, I knelt in a corner and tried to imagine what I would say to her, the girl in the field.

The Distant Orgasm

I am reading:

" 'Huh! promising me a hundred children.' Then she waits for the God to show what he can do, and Siva (but it can't be Siva) is touched, and forced by her faith, resuscitates the husband."

And as I am reading
I hear a cry: Oooooooo!
O God, the heart fails
I know it
it can happen next door
(see *Musée des Beaux Arts*)
while you are reading

"What I am telling here is the story according to the expression of the group. But the Hindus do not know how to paint, still less how to carve natural expressions. That is why I am inclined to think that the woman's attitude should be a little more respectful."

What can I do
but lunge from bed
                the telephone . . .
no the moments spent
dialing may be her last
the kiss of life
how does it go?
Once I had to try it
on a boy he
was not dying he was
only a cub scout
but he could die
and I could if
I would
save him if
I was not timid
and I was
how *does* it go!
splayed out
in the bathroom she
was stepping
from the shower she
had no history
her heart was free
of history
I would stay with her
hammer the kiss of life
onto her
hold a mirror
over her lips
                Ooooooooo!
She cries again
I am slow closing
the book

"The Hindu does not rush. He is never elliptic. He does not stand out from the group. He is the exact opposite of the climax. He never bowls you over. In the 125,000 verses of the Ramayanas, in the 250,000 of the Mahabharata there is not a flash."

I saw her once only
she was not
attractive
no one would call her
beautiful
I hear her music at night
Haydn
she plays when she is alone
as she is most nights
a working woman
up at seven
I hear the alarm
I hear her hum
as the coffee perks
as the bath runs
as the radio
softly conveys the news
that has occurred
in her sleep
and now she is going
she has been called
as my grandmother would say
she is crossing over
as the spiritualists say
                    Oooooooooo!
a third time she cries
it must be terrible
it did not show mercy
with swiftness
I have heard that cry
I "respond" to that cry
as if it were caught
in my throat
                    Ooooooo yes
she says Ooooooo yes

I am in the doorway
with one foot raised
the foot stays raised
through the next cry
and the next cry
the foot is becoming
aware of something
the awareness moves
up through the ankle
into the calves
the knees and into the thighs
the thighs say
this neighbor of mine
is not dying
no she is not dying
the foot lowers itself
to the ground
one foot follows the other
back into the bedroom
the hands pick up
the book
the eyes are shy now
they feel foolish
but they must read
to the end.

Someone must think
she is beautiful.

DIANE WAKOSKI

The Mechanic

to T.W.

Most men use
their eyes
like metronomes
clicking off the beats
of a woman's walk,
how her hips press
against the cloth, as figs just before
they split their purple skins
on the tree,
measuring how much of her walk
goes into bed at night,
the jar of the sky
being filled with the Milky Way
glittering for every time
she moves her lips

but of course
the secrets
are not the obvious beats
in the song
that even a bad drummer can play

hearing the speed of the motor
—it too made up of beats—
so fast,
subtle, I suppose,
they register
as continuous sound
or the heart which of course
beats without any fan belt to keep it
cool,

it is a test,
a rhythm,
they could not see
with those measuring eyes
though perhaps there are some
whose fingers and ears
are so close to the motors
with clean oil passing through their ears
and draining properly into the brain pan,
perhaps a few . . .

who can tell
what the secret bleeding of a woman
is all about

As a woman
with oily stars sticking
on all the tip points
of my skin
I could never
trust a man
who wasn't a mechanic,
a man who uses his
eyes,
his hands,
listens to
the
heart.

Justice Is Reason Enough

He, who once was my brother, is dead by his own hand.
Even now, years later, I see his thin form lying on the
sand

where the sheltered sea washes against those cliffs
he chose to die from. Mother took me back there every
  day for
over a year and asked me, in her whining way, why it
  had to happen

over and over again—until I wanted
never to hear of David any more. How
could I tell her of his dream about the gull beating its
  wings
effortlessly together until they drew blood?

Would it explain anything, and how can I tell
anyone here about the great form and its beating wings.
  How it
swoops down and covers me, and the dark tension leaves

me with blood on my mouth and thighs. But it was that
  dream,
you must know, that brought my tight, sullen little

brother to my room that night and pushed his whole
  taut body
right over mine until I yielded, and together we yielded
  to the dark tension.
Over a thousand passing years, I will never forget
him, who was my brother, who is dead. Mother asked
  me why
every day for a year; and I told her justice. Justice is
reason enough for anything ugly. It balances the beauty
  in the world.

Wind Secrets

I like the wind
with its puffed cheeks and closed eyes.

Nice wind.
I like its gentle sounds
and fierce bites.
When I was little
I used to sit by the black, potbellied stove and stare
at a spot on the ceiling,
while the wind breathed and blew
outside.
"Nice wind,"
I murmured to myself.

I would ask mother when she kneeled to tie my shoes
what the wind said.

Mother knew.

And the wind whistled and roared outside
while the coals opened their eyes in anger
at me.
I would hear mother crying under the wind.
"Nice wind," I said,
But my heart leapt like a darting fish.
I remember the wind better than any sound.
It was the first thing I heard
with blazing ears,
a sound that didn't murmur and coo,
and the sounds wrapped round my head
and huffed open my eyes.
It was the first thing I heard
besides my father beating my mother.
The sounds slashed at my ears like scissors.
Nice wind.

The wind blows
while the glowing coals from the stove look at me
with angry eyes.
Nice wind.

Nice wind.
Oh, close your eyes.
There was nothing I could do.

Smudging

Smudging is the term used for lighting small oil fires in the orange groves at night when the temperatures are too low, to keep the leaves and fruit warm, so as not to lose the crop.

I come out of a California orange grove
the way a meteor might be
plucked out of an Arizona desert. The icy origins
of genes
could easily be
flaming ones
                              And in my head
those red-hot rocks
shake down into a bed of
coals, oranges roll off the shelves,
amber sticks on the roof of my mouth,
honey glistens in glass jars, the combs full of music,
—all in the back of my head / the gold
of the small loops in my ears
is the sound of a king cobra crossing the rocks,
tigers walk across my lips / the gold is
in my head. It is the honeysuckle of an island.
This gold is in your house;
I sleep in your bed at night
and love you,
                              but the firelight from those smudging
                                 pots flickers
against my eyes, burned by the eclipse this year,
and reminds me:
        When I was five years old, we lived on the

edge of Orange County, in an orange grove,
in a small two-room house with a sagging
screened porch. Outside the kitchen at
night when it was near frosting, the
immigrant laborers would build fires in the
smudge pots to keep the trees from freezing.
The poetry of dew-points would be on the
news each night, and after we went to bed,
the flickering of these fires would embroider
the windows, and the sounds of voices
talking in Spanish and laughing over their
tequila bottles would wander into the
windows like turning lawn sprinklers.
Our doors had locks that opened with
skeleton keys. You could purchase them in
dime stores. The flimsy jambs and lintels
could have been pushed down by children, and
my mother was not at all secure in her
plain whiteness. Those voices frightened
her. My father was never home. I was a
child with a father who was a sailor, a
child who did not even know what a fishing
rod looked like. My mother stood up in
agony, all night, in the dark, every night
there was smudging and the Chicanos were
sitting on our steps laughing, drinking, or
under the kitchen window, talking.

Orange groves in California
are the boundaries
of my childhood.
Nights
when the temperatures hovered
near the mouth of frost
on the thermometer /
pots of glowing oil
tended by dark Mexicans
on dark nights

in the dark rows of the dark-leaved trees. Each orange
  shining
like a cold sour gold anger
on the bushy tough arms
of the tree.
                I remember those hard knots
of light
that turned into the fruit
for dew-soaked breakfasts.
But it was the smudge pots
burning
like old lamps in a dim room,
warming the trees
glowing in the orchards
as I passed on asphalt highways
unable to talk
that reminded me
of my own unripe sour tight
globular fruit
hopefully ripening,
hopefully not killed off
by a frost.
Even now,
my leaves like toes
reach out
for warmth. Cold
nights and city
streets
have no glowing smudge pots
to leave traces
of soot
on the leaves and golden finally-ripe
oranges.
You are
the man with big hands,
the man whose brain
numbers every piece of hardware,

and who knows how to use any tool. A mechanic
you always come home dirty,
as if some flame had
been smudging you,
keeping your tender leaves from
low temperatures,
and I who grew up in a little house
frightened of soot and angry
at the voices of men in the night,
long for you
with all the mystery of my childhood.
You threw me out once
for a whole year,
and I felt that all the masculinity I knew about was
gone:
saw blades humming through stiff wood,
the hand that threaded wire into place and made
light,
the soaking parts of motorcycles and cars which
were sloshed free of old dirt and put meticulously
back
into now running
machines,
the hands and mind which could fix the shower
or the furnace if either
didn't work.
That year
I sought sunshine,
looked for men who could work in a foundry,
who were not afraid to touch hot metal.
And I was the orange
who began to love the dark groves at night,
the dewy shake of the leaves,
and who believed these burnings in the night
were part of a ritual
that might someday be understood.

And from the little girl who read fairy tales,
I have grown into the woman
in them, the one who steps magically out
of those fragrant orange peels,
into your house,
next to your side. I sort your dirty smudged work
  clothes
for the laudromat and long for the sun.
You are the voices in those dark nights, laughing on the
  front steps
into that clear fiery tequila;
and always there will be part of the child shivering in
  me
inside, knowing my mother feared something
that I must also fear,
her husband who left her alone for the salty ocean.
My father who walked away from me;
and then there is the part of me, that golden fruit
  growing on
the orange tree outside in the orchard,
searching for the warmth of the smudge pot,
and it is that part of me that takes your hand confidently
as we walk down the street and listens to your deep
  voice telling
stories.
Thank god for our visions.
That in our heads
we play many roles. There is part of me that trembles,
and part of me that reaches for warmth,
and part of me that breaks open
like mythic fruit,
the golden orange every prince will fight
to own.

ALICE WALKER

Expect Nothing

Expect nothing. Live frugally
On surprise.
Become a stranger
To need of pity
Or, if compassion be freely
Given out
Take only enough.
Stop short of urge to plead
Then purge away the need.

Wish for nothing larger
Than your own small heart
Or greater than a star;
Tame wild disappointment
With caress unmoved and cold.
Make of it a parka
For your soul.

Discover the reason why
So tiny human midget
Exists at all
So scared unwise.
But expect nothing. Live frugally
On surprise.

Burial

I

They have fenced in the dirt road
that once led to Wards Chapel
A.M.E. church,
and cows graze
among the stones that
mark my family's graves.
The massive oak is gone
from out the churchyard,
but the giant space is left
unfilled;
despite the two-lane blacktop
that slides across
the old, unalterable
roots.

II

Today I bring my own child here;
to this place where my father's
grandmother rests undisturbed
beneath the Georgia sun,
above her the neatstepping hooves
of cattle.
Here the graves soon grow back into the land.
Have been known to sink. To drop open without
warning. To cover themselves with wild ivy,
blackberries. Bittersweet and sage.
No one knows why. No one asks.
When Burning Off Day comes, as it does
some years,
the graves are haphazardly cleared and snakes
hacked to death and burned sizzling

in the brush . . . The odor of smoke, oak
leaves, honeysuckle.
Forgetful of geographic resolutions as birds,
the farflung young fly South to bury
the old dead.

III

The old women move quietly up
and touch Sis Rachel's face.
"Tell Jesus I'm coming," they say.
"Tell Him I ain't goin' to *be*
long."

My grandfather turns his creaking head
away from the lavender box.
He does not cry. But looks afraid.
For years he called her "Woman";
shortened over the decades to
" 'Oman."
On the cut stone for " 'Oman's" grave
he did not notice
they had misspelled her name.
(The stone reads *Racher Walker*—not "Rachel"—
Loving Wife, Devoted Mother.)

IV

As a young woman, who had known her? Tripping
eagerly, "loving wife," to my grandfather's
bed. Not pretty, but serviceable. A hard
worker, with rough, moist hands. Her own two
babies dead before she came.
Came to seven children.
To aprons and sweat.
Came to quiltmaking.
Came to canning and vegetable gardens
big as fields.
Came to fields to plow.

Cotton to chop.
Potatoes to dig.
Came to multiple measles, chickenpox,
and croup.
Came to water from springs.
Came to leaning houses one story high.
Came to rivalries. Saturday night battles.
Came to straightened hair, Noxzema, and
feet washing at the Hardshell Baptist church.
Came to zinnias around the woodpile.
Came to grandchildren not of her blood
whom she taught to dip snuff without
sneezing.

—

Came to death blank, forgetful of it all.

When he called her " 'Oman" she no longer
listened. Or heard, or knew, or felt.

V

It is not until I see my first-grade teacher
review her body that I cry.
Not for the dead, but for the gray in my
first-grade teacher's hair. For memories
of before I was born, when teacher and
grandmother loved each other; and later
above the ducks made of soap and the orange-
legged chicks Miss Reynolds drew over
my own small hand
on paper with wide blue lines.

VI

Not for the dead, but for memories. None of
them sad. But seen from the angle of her
death.

Black Mail

Stick the finger inside
the chink;
nail long and sharp.
Wriggle it,
jugg,
until it draws blood.
Lick it in your mouth,
savor the taste;
and know your diet
has changed.

Be the first at the crucifixion.
Stand me (and them and her and him)
where once we each together
stood.
Find it plausible now
to jeer,
escaped within your armor.
There never was a crucifixion
of a completely armored man.

Imagine this: a suit of mail,
of metal plate;
no place to press the dagger in.
Nothing but the eyes
to stick
with narrow truth.
Burning sharp,
burning bright;
burning righteous,
but burning blind.

ROGER WEINGARTEN

Ethan Boldt

In canary grass insects
fly around my head like quicksilver. I'm a pony-
express rider balancing a message
on foot, through weeds, over the sagging
barbed wire fence and a creek
to a graveyard.

I came West before I understood wild plants;
my reasons were good: twenty-three, leaning against
a brick warehouse, I saw the sky reflected
in the veins of my forearms, a rider paddling
a canoe through clouds, dark clouds. Father named me

Ethan after a book he never read; Benjamin
for the father of electricity: Mother sold
undergarments in a dry-goods store. She left
the eighteenth year in our stone house, her bosom
stuffed with cash, with a man who sold bone meal and
bitters.

Doctor broke the bag of waters. Father stood
timing her contractions as she exhaled and sucked air
to get rid of me. Her belly folded. My brewing done,
father laughed while I thundered

in his arms. I ate my food
with a little dirt, built my wife a shelter
by the Hocking River, left her
with a knife and blanket;
came back in the rain to a garden dug

with a clamshell, a son, and a wife about to die; grateful
I built the lean-to, our family

eating the skin of the wild turkey baked in mud;
I hate gardens, rivers are for fish. Bathe
in the rain when your body gets smoky! Outside
my bedroll in the weeds, my arms
paddle into a field of lightning.

Blue Bog Children

The remains of blue bog children
are fast clouds and no water; fat
trees without sap or bark; potato whistles
for the parson to pipe on—abrupt
and erupting—empty cisterns
of withered leaves breaking into light,

pornography read aloud in a wood known
for blue mosquitoes, blossoms that sail
and press under the shoes of children,
as the sleeves of a bridesmaid catch
on the pew. On red moss under ice, a bluebell

bog child, asleep, outside
a river town in western Illinois. His eyes
the size of fists, his wrists wound with briar,
banished by a storm that overflowed the river
for a fling with the shrubs. Strike the child

for kindling and hand him to a winter fire
to climb like field mice fingered in the hollow
of a tree, ashes poured into a wooden bowl,
the approach of a coffin on the horizon

of a trail, whispering children
riding to burial on their father's sled.

Her apron through the trees

of the Elmira Wood
is a path overgrown
with gooseberry, King
Solomon's Gold, the dry

skin of the shagbark hickory.
It's late fall, late morning,
and we duck the cold
the way a slug fingers its way

into the gills of a honey mushroom.
Above ground the brown leaves
and furry shafts of poison ivy
won't bruise your hands. Hand me

that hickory nut, her hard breast,
and everywhere we step the butternuts
are the stillborn spread around the jack-
in-the-pulpit, upon

the wet carpeting of the Elmira Wood.
Beneath stinkhorns a woman spins
the brown threads of the nineteenth
century; because of the ministry
of corn spiders, a few trees, and our walk,

she's not dead: we clean our fingernails
on her webs, the morning dew rising
from her wash bowl. A stonecutter, in 1858,

chiseled a pig into her stone. She died
"of malaria." Elmira would.

These Obituaries of Rattlesnakes Being Eaten by the Hogs

1

The arthritic farmer and a calf watch Dr. Graves
punch a needle into the jugular
of a cow with milkfever, and feed
calcium salts from a jar into a surgical tube. I wonder
at the flat maroon afterbirth of the night before, the
 farmer's
tobacco pouch, and the brown saliva of 6 A.M. on his lip.

In a booth at The Grill I order wheat
cakes and tea, the vet
a waffle and a tuna-fish sandwich. He shouldn't
tell me this but every time he looks up at the cookie-
punched tin ceiling he sees the farmer, his child
 stumbling
into the bailer, how he found her leg sticking out of the
 hay,
went home for his scattergun, and blew his brains into a
 burlap bag.

Standing in a manure gutter holding a heifer by the ears
over the wood slats of a manger, a farmer's wife, with
 sour
cream on her breath, asks what's my name, my business
in life, tells me that all this must be very
inspiring, and when the heifer's nose, clamped and tied
 to a beam, starts

to pull away from her face, I pass the tattooer, the syringe,
and the ink to the vet and say it is, Mrs. Hochstetler, it is.
"Then why don't you get out of the light so he can write the bill."

About two instruments with funny names: the twitch and White's
improved emasculator. The twitch is a bat with a loop tied at one end
you twist around a horse's nose that hypnotizes
while you run a lubricated tube down a nostril into the belly. Pump wormer
into the tube, warm water, and air. I
hold the twitch, while Doc tells his fingers, red from the cold
and white from the wormer, that horses
bring out the steel in women.

2

Chili and coffee at The Grill, and a walk through the Lower
Deer Creek Cemetery, granite table lamps, pink marble
urns, epitaphs with Old Testament first names, and bestial icons
get the Doc wondering if the Christians around here aren't a little
too much like the Egyptians and the Jews. He powders
their heads and tosses
testicles into a long glove that I hold open for our supper.
Horns and scrotums get lost in the straw, and barn cats
risk being trampled for a meal. Dr. Graves, after a twelve-
hour day, packing a testicle into a snowball that breaks against

the barn, tells me that the branches of a walnut tree in winter
are like the legs of a woman on a mattress of twigs, that dehorning
a bull sounds like cobs breaking.
That he once lay down with a woman under the axletree
of a cart just outside Lancaster, Pennsylvania, and when
we got home, if I would kindly peel the tunic
off the tripes, he could pour us a sly drink from the cider jug.

JAMES WELCH

Visit

I come alone. To surprise you
I leave no sign, my name
shucked at the familiar gate.

Your name is implied in exile.
I bring meat for your memory,
wine for the skinning of muskrats.

I leave this wood, not much,
but enough to streak your face
a winter red despair.

Why no songs, no ceremony?
Set your traps to catch my one
last track, the peculiar scent,

goodbyes creaking in the pines.

In My First Hard Springtime

Those red men you offended were my brothers.
Town drinkers, Buckles Pipe, Star Boy,
Billy Fox, were blood to bison. Albert Heavy Runner
was never civic. You are white and common.

Record trout in Willow Creek chose me
to deify. My horse, Centaur, part Cayuse,
was fast and mad and black. Dandy in flat hat
and buckskin, I rode the town and called it mine.

A slow hot wind tumbled dust against my door.
Fed and fair, you mocked my philosophic nose,
my badger hair. I rolled your deference
in the hay and named it love and lasting.

Starved to visions, famous cronies top Mount Chief
for names to give respect to Blackfeet streets.
I could deny them in my first hard springtime,
but choose amazed to ride you down with hunger.

Plea to Those Who Matter

You don't know I pretend my dumb.
My songs often wise, my bells could chase
the snow across these whistle-black plains.
Celebrate. The days are grim. Call your winds
to blast these bundled streets and patronize
my past of poverty and 4-day feasts.

Don't ignore me. I'll build my face a different way,
a way to make you know that I am no longer
proud, my name not strong enough to stand alone.
If I lie and say you took me for a friend,
patched together in my thin bones,
will you help me be cunning and noisy as the wind?

I have plans to burn my drum, move out
and civilize this hair. See my nose? I smash it
straight for you. These teeth? I scrub my teeth
away with stones. I know you help me now I matter.
And I—I come to you, head down, bleeding from my
smile,
happy for the snow clean hands of you, my friends.

The Only Bar in Dixon

These Indians once imitated life.
Whatever made them warm
they called wine, song or sleep,
a lucky number on the tribal roll.

Now the stores have gone the gray
of this November sky. Cars
whistle by, chrome wind, knowing
something lethal in the dust.

A man could build a reputation here.
Take that redhead at the bar—
she knows we're thugs, killers
on a fishing trip with luck.

No luck. No room for those
sensitive enough to know they're beat.
Even the Flathead turns away,
a river thick with bodies,

Indians on their way to Canada.
Take the redhead—yours for just a word,
a promise that the wind will warm
and all the saints come back for laughs.

Lady in a Distant Face

The odd way you comb your hair,
those big hands drawing circles in a room
and a Mormon background—you become
the Sunday all-day Scotch friend
who needs a friend to keep these mountains back.

We came upcountry, not knowing
your Paris days, the summer-wide search
for Frenchmen with wild hair
and eyes that made for easy lies.
No life is chilly as your own
when time makes parents foreign and brothers
come to mock you when you're drunk.

Summer was no lifetime. It rolled with games
and play on sand with sullen kings.
Bikinis fit you then; you fit the beaches
with your famous boys—life so shallow
you could end it with a kiss.

What bird could go alone this unnoticed?
On those beaches—did you fly for seven years,
then drop, exhausted, in the sea?
The fishermen—they knew you for a fraud,
rescued you with words that meant go home.

Home. The steamer edged you
from that scene of what is nice, the Paris days
of sun and mortgaged gold.
And now, here, in these mountains
that hold you from yourself, the wind
blowing down your final face,
you tell us what we know: Time is clean
and brief for girls in a wild time,
past for ladies up like smoke in narrow wind.

PETER WILD

Dog Hospital

Riding by there every day
surrounded by eucalyptuses and palms
I hear them barking behind the whitewashed adobe
fence,
see from my bicycle the ladies going in carrying
the loved ones in their arms—
in fact have been there myself
met the receptionist smiling beneath her cap,
read the magazines on training waiting
for the nodding Japanese man
who tries to pet her as he gives her shots,
gets bitten on the hand. nevertheless
days later she comes out smiling, refreshed
as she jumps into my arms and he almost
bowing winks. though riding by now
there are stories of those others calling
over the walls, that they are left to starve,
given other brains, arms
sewn to their necks, and
some are locked in cannisters,
lowered down polished tubes
into caves where there is no light
except the candle in their heads,
and the shadows around them that they
seeing now bark at.

Riding Double

You think they might come
tandem, swinging buckets,
their fishermen's coats on;
the vines let go, ashes from the screen
seeking wells, burning roots
into the hours of the afternoon

one has a mask on
showing only her eyes
and the teeth sticking out
parallel to the ground;
she stares at you,
body a bag of pumping muscle.
behind, all buckskin, he whirls his thunder rod;
they stand still.

and the trees begin their wheels
spiked with birds,
ribbons and a thousand whistles;
these cut across your nose:
those two going off in a smoke,
a grinning salad.
and instead of the sun
an iron ship glides into the deserted horizon.

Thomas and Charlie

Here where the parrots come down
out of the morning fog,
out of the fog that hangs along the river
to flash through the bamboo

tearing out the night's shoots
or sit on a cow's back
and eat raw hamburger from a waiter's hand
you wake having travelled all night through
the sweat of your friends,
the dusty comics
sick farmers by the road
and the peaks
jumping out of the clouds into the moon,
to see the buttocks of the fat busdriver where
he rolled from his hammock drunk
and slept
hearing over the hill the morning traffic—
you know where you are
and breaking the dust from your lids
breaking your back
climb up the veranda
still slick and dripping dew
to be the first one
to hear the farmers singing
off in their lost valleys,
to see again the innkeeper's thirteen
mythical daughters
that make you famous,
tight in Levi's through the smoke of your coffee,
here where the llamas could be gold spindles
where you could wear a gold ring in your ear,
and the adventuresome tourist
taking his black veins in his teeth
drives with his wife locked behind
in the trailer for fear
for weeks through the spiralling mountains,
to reach the top and see
they have slipped away into the mists . . .

Snakes

The rattlesnakes have begun to come out,
into the gardens,
out of the mountains,
from the parched fields,
after water it is said,
after mice;
the papers have announced it,
we find warnings
tacked to our doors—
I think one gardener,
a faithful servant,
has been bit, stooping
to tend a marigold,
and a child reported
her hand horribly mangled—
the citizens have been armed,
mothers keep their
brooms by the door,
police carrying shotguns . . .
I have seen none. walking
barefoot through the beds,
checking the mulch
behind lattices,
even rabbit burrows . . .
I have never been harmed;
but last night fidgeting
I awoke dizzy to sweet music;
outside on the lawn, the road,
the housetops, our flowerbeds
were full of them, almost erect,
their thin necks
swaying toward the moon,
humming, smiling,
sensuously

drinking in the light;
while others sped
back and forth on great
rice-paper wings,
carrying messages
across the cloudless night . . .

CHARLES WRIGHT

Chinoiserie

Why not? The mouths of the ginger blooms slide open,
The willows drag their knuckles across the earth;
Each year has its fields that no one tends.

Our days, unlike the long gasps of the wind,
Stay half in love with the rushes, and half with the
  water reeds.
Outside the body, all things are encumbrances.

The Fever Toy

The arms seem clumsy at first,
Outsize, the eyes detached; at odd angles,
The wrists respond to no touch;
Rickety, flat-veined, the legs
Push out like stems from their bulbous feet;
The fingers repeat themselves.

What pleasure this gives, this sure
Mating of parts, this slip and catch
Of bone to bone, of stiff flesh
To socket and joint, this gift
You give yourself in advance.
Instructions are not enclosed, and yet

How well you assemble it,
How well you insert yourself in each
Corner and crevice of its wrong arms:

Its breath caresses your eyes,
Its lips—like larvae—explore your face,
Its lashes become your own.

And this is how it begins.
This is the way your true name
Returns and returns again,
Your sorrow becoming a foreign tongue,
Your body becoming a foreign tongue,
Blue idiom, blue embrace.

Yellow

Yellow is for regret, the distal, the second hand:
The grasshopper's wing, that yellow, the slur of dust;
Back light, the yellow of loneliness;
The yellow of animals, their yellow eyes;
The holy yellow of death;
Intuitive yellow, the yellow of air;
The double yellow, telling who comes and who goes;
The yellow of yellowhammers, one drop of the devil's
  blood;
The yellow of what is past;
Yellow of wormwood, yellow of straw;
The yellow of circuits, the yellow beneath the skin;
The yellow of pencils, their black veins;
Amaranth yellow, bright bloom;
The yellow of sulfur, the finger, the road home.

Dog Creek Mainline

Dog Creek: cat track and bird splay,
Spindrift and windfall; woodrot;

Odor of muscadine, the blue creep
Of king snake and copperhead;
Nightweed; frog spit and floating heart,
Backwash and snag pool: Dog Creek

Starts in the leaf reach and shoal run of the blood;
Starts in the falling light just back
Of the fingertips; starts
Forever in the black throat
You ask redemption of, in wants
You waken to, the odd door:

Its sky, old empty valise,
Stands open, departure in mind; its three streets,
Y-shaped and brown,
Go up the hills like a fever;
Its houses link and deploy
—This ointment, false flesh in another color.

*

Five cutouts, five silhouettes
Against the American twilight; the year
Is 1941; remembered names
—Rosendale, Perry and Smith—
Rise like dust in the deaf air;
The tops spin, the poison swells in the arm:

The trees in their jade death-suits,
The birds with their opal feet,
Shimmer and weave on the shoreline;
The moths, like forget-me-nots, blow
Up from the earth, their wet teeth
Breaking the dark, the raw grain;

The lake in its cradle hums
The old songs: out of its ooze, their heads
Like tomahawks, the turtles ascend
And settle back, leaving their chill breath

In blisters along the bank;
Locked in their wide drawer, the pike lie still as knives.

*

Hard freight. It's hard freight
From Ducktown to Copper Hill, from Six
To Piled High: Dog Creek is on this line,
Indigent spur; cross-tie by cross-tie it takes
You back, the red wind
Caught at your neck like a prize:

(The heart is a hieroglyph;
The fingers, like praying mantises, poise
Over what they have once loved;
The ear, cold cave, is an absence,
Tapping its own thin wires;
The eye turns in on itself.

The tongue is a white water.
In its slick ceremonies the light
Gathers, and is refracted, and moves
Outward, over the lips,
Over the dry skin of the world.
The tongue is a white water.).

Delta Traveller

MWW, 1910–1964

Born in the quarter night, brash
Tongue on the tongueless ward, the moon down,
The lake rising on schedule and Dr Hurt
Already across the water, and headed home—
And so I came sailing out, first child,
A stream with no bed to lie in,
A root with no branch to leaf,

The black balloon of promise tied to your wrist,
One inch of pain and an inch of light.

*

No wonder the children stand by those moist graves.
And produce is spread on the cobbled streets,
And portraits are carried out, and horns play.
And women, in single file, untangle
Corn from the storage bins, and soft cheese.
I shield my eyes against the sunlight,
Holding, in one hand, a death's-head,
Spun sugar and marzipan. I call it Love,
And shield my eyes against the sunlight.

*

I lie down with you, I rise up with you.
If a grain turns in my eye,
I know it is you, entering, leaving,
Your name like a lozenge upon my tongue.
You drift through the antilife,
Scrim and snow-scud, fluff stem, hair
And tendril. You bloom in your own throat,
Frost flame in the frost dust,
One scratch on the slipstream, a closed mouth.

*

High necked and high collared, slumped and creased,
A dress sits in a chair. Your dress,
Or your mother's dress, a dress
On a wooden chair in a cold room, a room
With no windows and no doors, full of the east wind.
The dress gets up, windbone and windskin,
To open the window. It is not there.
It goes to the door. It is not there.
The dress goes back and sits down. The dress gets
up . . .

*

Three teeth and a thumbnail, white, white; four
Fingers that cradle a black chin;
Outline of eye-hole and nose-hole. This skull
And its one hand float up from the tar
And lime pit of dreams, night after slick night,
To lodge in the fork of the gum tree,
Its three teeth in the leaflight,
Its thumbnail in flash and foil,
Its mouth-hole a nothing I need to know.

*

Cat's-eye and cloud, you survive.
The porcelain corridors
That glide forever beneath your feet,
The armed lawn chair you sit in,
Your bones like paint, your skin the wrong color—
All this you survive, and hold on,
A way of remembering, a pulse
That comes and goes in the night,
Match-flare and wink, that comes and goes in the night.

*

If the wafer of light offends me,
If the split tongue in the snake's mouth offends me,
I am not listening. They make the sound,
Which is the same sound, of the ant hill,
The hollow trunk, the fruit of the tree.
It is the Echo, the one transmitter of things:
Transcendent and inescapable,
It is the cloud, the mosquito's buzz,
The trickle of water across the leaf's vein.

*

And so with the dead, the rock dead and the dust:
Worm and worm-fill, pearl, milk-eye

And light in the earth, the dead are brought
Back to us, piece by piece—
Under the sponged log, inside the stump,
They shine with their secret lives, and grow
Big with their messages, wings
Beginning to stir, paths fixed and hearts clocked,
Rising and falling back and rising.

DAVID YOUNG

The Boxcar Poem

The boxcars drift by
clanking

they have their own
speech on scored
wood their own
calligraphy
Soo Line
they say in meadows
Lackawanna quick at crossings
Northern Pacific, a
nightmurmur, Northern
Pacific

even empty
they carry
in dark corners
among smells of wood and sacking
the brown wrappings of sorrow
the rank straw of revolution
the persistence of war

and often
as they roll past
like weathered obedient
angels you can see
right through them
to yourself
in a bright

field, a crow
on either shoulder.

August at the Lake

Shall we sit here some more
On old lawnchairs, while the wind
Settles across our fingers?

Maybe the purple martins
Have already reached the tropics;

But we aren't migratory birds.
We have too much to pack.

So we sit here, our faces
Working, while the red evening
Climbs the fence and is gone.

Thoughts of Chairman Mao

1

Holding black whips
the rulers rode
in the blue hills.

But the peasants were everywhere and nowhere,
a soft avalanche, gathering
courage; in famines
we ate the mules, tasting vinegar,

lived among rocks above the passes,
and gradually became an army
red flags snapping in the wind
and I wrote of "a forest of rifles,"
and of heroes strolling home
against a smoky
sunset.

2

Wars merge like seasons;
sometimes over hot wine
the old campaigners try to remember
who we were fighting that winter
on this plateau, that plain,
and whether we won.

It blurs . . .
miles in boxcars
doors wedged open
miles across blue-shadowed snow.
Hungry evening.

Artillery at the river
bodies in the rice fields
a black truck on its side
burning . . .

At night we could hear the gibbons
calling each other up the valley.
When there was a rest or a vista
someone would write a poem.
It blends and blurs:
conferences melonseeds sabotage
dungfires treaties mosquitoes
my great red army on the march
blinking in the sunshine.

3

Now it is changed.
I am the giant in the pageant,
toothy, androgynous, quilted.

To the slow roll of drums
my effigy speaks to the people
of harvests, steelmills, stars.

In the puppetshows I battle
enemies of the state
sometimes with blows and curses
sometimes with love and flowers
while Marx pops up to hug me
and Lenin takes my arm.

I would have done it
with poems! Instead
I have come to be
a red book, a pumped-up myth,
from Long March to Big Swim
surfacing, always surfacing:
said to have gone
miles through golden water
wrestled the Yangtze and won,
water god, flower king, rice prince;

the current takes me on
and it is no small thing
riding these tides, wave upon
wave of love; smiling, unspeaking,
ten thousand miles of mountains and water,
a chanting race, a skin on history,

until the people rise and go,
dispersing me.

4

At the end I enter a small room.

Stalin is standing there alone
hands behind his back
gazing out the window.

We link arms. We merge.

And the rulers ride the blue hills
holding their black whips high.

Mandelstam

He had difficulty breathing . . . Osip breathed heavily; he was catching air with his lips.
—Anna Akhmatova

1 *At the camp*

Hell freezing over. To keep sane
he studies the tiniest sensations
such as the touch of a necklace
of dry dead bees around a woman's neck.
Having said that, he can mention
honey, then speak of sunlight.
He studies his hands. Stalin's a swine.
Nadezhda's head is a beehive, full of poems.
He licks his lips to whisper one.
They're chapped. His breath is smoke.
His ears stick out, as if to catch
even the noise of a candleflame.
Frostbite will get them first.
A sledge goes past, stacked high.
Better not look. Ice lies in piles,

shoals, hummocks. Memories of Warsaw,
Paris, Petersburg, the warm Crimea,
keep their distance, Northern Lights,
or the swords of half-drunk cossacks
whirling through stupid dances.
He lives on garbage, is never warm, will die.

2 *The tear, 1938*

A tear is floating over Moscow
swollen, seeking a home, a mirror.

Tear, take my advice, get lost.
Those onion domes don't want you

the rivers are solid glass
the earth's a cake of permafrost

even those women wrapped in shawls
would gulp you like a drop of vodka.

Better go east, better follow
that long railway to Asia;

you can survive, little crystal,
in the glossy eye of a reindeer

on the bear's nose as he sleeps
dreaming sun into honey

in the fur of the wolf who runs
through the endless, falling snow.

3 *Nadezhda writes a letter*

Nonchalant, the sun goes off
and then returns. You won't
Except in dreams, old films

flickering, buzzing when
your lips whisper, catching air,
making poems, soundtracks, and
I reach to touch you in the dark.

You left in a hurry, shrugging,
framed by policemen.
And your journey? The camps,
the cattlecars, beatings, stinks—
I see your forehead wrinkle, tongue thicken,
I turn away. Tears sting.
Maybe we should have jumped
hand in hand through the window!

It's warm in the Kremlin, there's music.
Stalin's small eyes glitter
his mustache is greasy with shashlik
he drinks, smashing his glass:
if the universe
makes any sense
how did we get from those fine-drawn
Petersburg afternoons
through the bonfires and rifleshots
of that marvelous revolution
to *this?*

But listen, Osip,
the joke's on them. Poems survive.
Your costly whispers carry.
They coexist with the state
like sunlight.
                        I can
still hear you, Osip;
catching air, your highstrung voice
speaks for the frozen and forgotten
saying, it *was* their earth, it was
their earth. Purges don't change that!

Though that's dim comfort tonight
as I sit with my bread and soup
and the wind off the wrinkled plains
howls like a man without a tongue.
Brave man, who shredded the death warrants
of a leather-jacketed terrorist
and then ran wild through the Russian cold,
my warm sun, shrunk to a star,
it's a stiff, black world
you left behind.

The Death of the Novel

1

As she shook her little fist
her filmy gown
swung open.
"*Sacre bleu!*" he gasped.
"Shall we seal this pact
as only a man and woman can?"

Outside the jungle chattered in the dawn.

2

Claude paused to wipe his brow.
The tractor sputtered, idling;
a cow stared from a nearby field.

What had his father meant?
How would he ever get
to college? It
all seemed out of joint, and yet . . .

3

Because he took her everywhere
in his old droshky, they made a stir
in all the villages that summer
while she grew to like, then to adore
his very pawkiness, his air
of staggering kindness. Love flared,
kindling her cheeks. She picked a flower.

4

And now the glade
where Stan was sprawled
grew still. A bird
twittered, insects drowsed.

And then
a shrill scream came
from the middle distance,
came again, and Stan's
heart jumped. The noon
express! Would Anne, or Kim,
be on that train?

5

Bertram rattled the door, a wild
glare on his face, teeth clenched:
"What have you done with my manuscript?"
The undertaker smiled.

Notes on the Poets

AI (1947) was born Florence Anthony in the Southwest. Her father was in the army, and she spent much of her early life moving about the country. She received her B.A. in Oriental Studies from the University of Arizona in 1969. In 1971 she received her M.F.A. in Creative Writing from the University of California at Irvine. She taught one semester at the Pima Junior College in Tucson, Arizona, and has been a costume model.

Cruelty. Houghton Mifflin, 1973

JON ANDERSON (1940) was born and raised in Lexington, Massachusetts. After graduating from the Writers' Workshop at The University of Iowa, he taught in the English department at the University of Portland. He now teaches at the University of Pittsburgh and lives on a small farm near the city with his wife, three large dogs, and a horse.

In Sepia. University of Pittsburgh Press, 1974
Counting the Days. Penumbra Press, 1974
Death & Friends. University of Pittsburgh Press, 1970
Looking for Jonathan. University of Pittsburgh Press, 1968

MARVIN BELL (1937), born in New York City, grew up among potato farmers, duck farmers, and fishermen in Center Moriches, on the south shore of Long Island. He attended Alfred University, Syracuse University, the University of Chicago and The University of Iowa, where he now teaches. His poems have received the Lamont Award from The Academy of American Poets, the Bess Hokin Award from *Poetry,* and an Emily Clark Balch Prize from *The Virginia Quarterly Review.* Since 1958 he has lived in upstate New York, Chicago, Indianapolis, California, Vermont, Mexico, Spain, and Iowa City.

Residue of Song. Atheneum, 1974
Woo Havoc. The Barn Dream Press, 1971
The Escape Into You. Atheneum, 1971
A Probable Volume of Dreams. Atheneum, 1969
Things We Dreamt We Died For. The Stone Wall Press, 1966
Poems for Nathan and Saul. The Hillside Press, 1966

MICHAEL BENEDIKT (1937) was born in New York City and attended New York University and Columbia University, where he received an M.A. in Comparative Literature, writing his thesis on Baudelaire and Wallace Stevens. He has worked as an editor at a publishing house, and between 1963 and 1972 was an Editorial Associate for *Art News* magazines. Between 1965 and 1967 he was the New York correspondent for *Art International.* His interests range from theatre and cinema to musical composition and criticism. He has taught at Bennington College, Sarah Lawrence College, and is now at Hampshire College in Amherst. He is the poetry editor of *The Paris Review.*

Mole Notes. Wesleyan University Press, 1971
Sky. Wesleyan University Press, 1970
The Body. Wesleyan University Press, 1968
Changes. The New Fresco, Inc., 1961

FRANK BIDART (1939) was born in Bakersfield, California. He attended the University of California at Riverside, and Harvard University. He now lives in Cambridge, Massachusetts, and teaches at Wellesley College.

Golden State. George Braziller, 1973

MICHAEL DENNIS BROWNE (1940) was born in Walton-on-Thames, England. He attended Hull University and Oxford University, then lived a year in France and a year in Finland. He came to the United States in 1965 and received his M.A. in English at The University of Iowa two years later. He has taught at The University of Iowa, Columbia University, Bennington College, and since 1971, the University of Minnesota.

Fox. Knife River Press, 1975
The Wife of Winter. Scribner's, 1970

LUCILLE CLIFTON (1936) was born in Depew, New York, and attended Howard University and Fredonia State Teachers College. She now lives in Baltimore with her husband and their six children. Her work has appeared in numerous publications, and in 1961 she won the YMHA Discovery Award. She has also written three children's books.

An Ordinary Woman, Random House, 1974
Good News About the Earth, Random House, 1972
Good Times, Random House, 1969

CONYUS (1942) was born in Detroit, Michigan. His work has appeared in such publications as *Ramparts*, *Scanlan's*, *The Black Scholar*, and *Black Dialogue*. He is included in the anthologies *Dices or Black Bones* (1970), and *New Black Voices* (1972). He makes his home in San Francisco, where he is "studying, looking, listening, and singing when there is a song, within."

PETER COOLEY (1940) was born in Detroit and, except for a year spent in France, has lived all his life in the Midwest. He received his M.A. in art and literature from the University of Chicago and in 1970 a Ph.D in Modern Letters from The University of Iowa, where he was a student in the Writers' Workshop. Since 1970 he has been poetry editor for *The North American Review*. He presently lives in Green Bay, Wisconsin, where he is an Associate Professor of Humanism and Cultural Change in the College of Creative Communication at the University of Wisconsin. He has published widely in literary magazines.

PHILIP DACEY (1939) was born in St. Louis, Missouri. He received a Catholic education: eight years from nuns and eight years from Jesuits. He has a B.A. from St. Louis University, an M.A. from Stanford, where he was a Woodrow Wilson Fellow in 1961–62, and an M.F.A. degree from The University of Iowa. He has taught at Miles College in Alabama, the University of Missouri, and as a Peace Corps Volunteer in Nigeria. He now teaches at Southwest Minnesota State College, where he is coordinator of the creative writing program. In 1974 he received a National Endowment for the Arts Fellowship and was one of the winners of the YMHA Discovery Award.

RITA DOVE (1952) was born in Akron, Ohio, and received her B.A. from Miami University in Oxford, Ohio. In 1973 she attended Bread Loaf Writers' Conference on a scholarship. She is currently studying German literature at the University of Tubingen on a Fulbright Scholarship, and playing cello in a string quartet. Her poems have appeared in *Antaeus*, *Prairie Schooner*, *Intro 6* and *Eating the Menu*.

PHILIP DOW (1937) was born in Santa Fe and moved to Vallejo, California, where he grew up. He attended Napa College and took a degree at San Francisco State, where he taught. He has also held teaching positions at Reed College and, currently, the State University of New York at Binghamton.

NORMAN DUBIE (1945), born outside Websterville, Vermont, has lived most of his life in the north country of New England. He received his B.A. from Goddard College and his M.F.A. from The University of Iowa, where he taught for four years. His poems have appeared in numerous magazines, including *The American Review, The American Poetry Review, Antaeus, The New Yorker* and *The Quarterly Review of Literature.* He lives in Athens, Ohio, where he teaches English at Ohio University.

> *In the Dead of the Night.* University of Pittsburgh Press, 1975
> *The Prayers of the North American Martyrs.* Penumbra Press, 1974
> *The Alehouse Sonnets.* University of Pittsburgh Press, 1971

STEPHEN DUNN (1939) was born in Forest Hills, New York, and went through Hofstra University on a basketball scholarship. After a period of semiprofessional basketball and various odd jobs, he went to Spain to write for a year. When he returned he enrolled in the Graduate Writing Program at Syracuse University. He won the Academy of American Poets Award there, and in 1971 was a winner of YMHA Discovery Award. In 1973 he received a National Endowment for the Arts Fellowship. He has taught at Southwest Minnesota State College, Syracuse University, and is presently at Stockton State College in New Jersey.

> *Looking for Holes in the Ceiling.* University of Massachusetts Press, 1974
> *5 Impersonations.* Ox Head Press, 1971

RUSSELL EDSON (1935) writes, "The only thing worth saying about the author, in my view, is what he has given to be public, all the rest being the generalized personal, which is mere confusion and finally dust." He received a Guggenheim Fellowship for 1974–1975.

> *The Clam Theater.* Wesleyan University Press, 1973
> *The Childhood of an Equestrian.* Harper & Row, 1973
> *What A Man Can See.* The Jargon Society, 1969

The Brain Kitchen. Thing Press, 1965
The Bound(a)ry. Thing Press, 1964
The Very Thing That Happens. New Directions, 1964
A Stone Is Nobody's. Thing Press, 1961
Appearances. Thing Press, 1961

SUSAN FELDMAN (1950) was born and grew up in Brooklyn. She attended Simmons College in Boston and received a B.A. in English in 1971. She received her M.A. in Creative Writing from Boston University, where she studied with Anne Sexton, John Malcolm Brinnin and Donald Barthelme. She is presently living and writing in Boston, and working as the assistant to an editor of a Boston publisher.

CAROLYN FORCHÉ (1950) was born in Detroit, the oldest daughter of a Slovak-American family, and grew up in the farm country of southern Oakland county. Her work has appeared in *Antaeus, Poetry Now, Mademoiselle* and other literary magazines.

KATHLEEN FRASER (1937) was born in Oklahoma and graduated from Occidental College. She taught for two years at The University of Iowa Writers' Workshop, has been Writer-in-Residence at Reed College, and now teaches at San Francisco State College, where she is Director of the Poetry Center.

What I Want. Harper & Row, 1974
Little Notes To You From Lucas Street. Penumbra Press, 1972
In Defiance of the Rains. Kayak Books, 1969
Change of Address. Kayak Books, 1966

TESS GALLAGHER (1943) was born and raised in the Pacific Northwest near the Olympic Mountain Range and The Straits of Juan de Fuoa. She was a member of the last class Theodore Roethke taught at the University of Washington. She went to the Writers' Workshop at The University of Iowa, where she wrote and made films. She currently teaches at St. Lawrence University in Canton, New York.

Stepping Outside. Penumbra Press, 1974

GARY GILDNER (1938) was born in northern Michigan. He went to Michigan State University intending to play basketball, but started writing stories instead. His poems and stories have been printed in a number of anthologies and magazines. He has been a Robert Frost Fellow at Bread Loaf, received a National Endowment for the Arts Fellowship, and has read his poems in schools throughout the country.

Nails. University of Pittsburgh Press, 1975
Digging for Indians. University of Pittsburgh Press, 1971
First Practice. University of Pittsburgh Press, 1969

LOUISE GLÜCK (1943) was born in New York City and raised on Long Island. Her awards include grants from the Rockefeller Foundation and the National Endowment for the Arts. Her work is represented in such anthologies as *The New Yorker Book of Poems, Contemporary American Poets* and *New Voices in American Poetry.* She has taught at Goddard College, the University of North Carolina, the University of Virginia, and is a member of the visiting staff of the Fine Arts Work Center in Provincetown, Massachusetts. She lives in Plainfield, Vermont.

The House on Marshland. The Ecco Press, 1975
Firstborn. New American Library, 1969

LINDA GREGG (1942) has lived most of her life among the hills north of San Francisco, but has traveled extensively in Europe. She has studied dance since she was ten and written poetry for the past twelve years.

MARILYN HACKER (1942) was educated in New York City and then lived for three years in San Francisco, where she co-edited *City,* a poetry magazine, through five issues, and, with Samuel Delaney, *Quark,* a speculative fiction quarterly, through four issues. She lives in London, where she is an antiquarian book dealer. Her first book *Presentation Piece.* won the Lamont Award for 1973, and the 1974 National Book Award.

Presentation Piece. The Viking Press, 1973

DANIEL HALPERN (1945) was born in Syracuse and grew up in Los Angeles and Seattle. He spent two years living in Tangier, Morocco where he began the literary magazine *Antaeus.* He has received various awards, including the YMHA Discovery Award in 1971, the Great Lakes Colleges National Book Award for his first book of poems, National Endowment for the Arts Fellowships, and was a Robert Frost Fellow at Bread Loaf. He is the editor of The American Poetry Series for The Ecco Press, and teaches at Princeton University and The New School for Social Research.

Street Fire. The Viking Press, 1975
The Lady Knife-Thrower. The Bellevue Press, 1975
Traveling on Credit. The Viking Press, 1972

MICHAEL S. HARPER (1938) was born in Brooklyn, New York. His earliest artistic influence was jazz and the blues—Billie Holiday played piano in his family's house when he was twelve. He moved to the west coast when he was thirteen, and later played collegiate and professional football under an assumed name. He earned M.A. degrees from The University of Iowa, Los Angeles State College, and has taught at various schools around the country, including Lewis and Clark College, Reed College and, since 1970, Brown University. For his poetry he has received awards from the Black Academy of Arts and Letters, as well as the American Academy/National Institute of Arts and Letters.

Nightmare Begins Responsibility, University of Illinois Press, 1974
Debridement, Doubleday, 1973
Song: I Want a Witness, University of Pittsburgh Press, 1972
History As Apple Tree, Scarab Press, 1972
History Is Your Own Heartbeat, University of Illinois Press, 1971
Dear John, Dear Coltrane, University of Pittsburgh Press, 1970

JIM HARRISON (1937) lives on a farm in northern Michigan and makes his living as a writer (novels, poetry, journalism). In recent years he has traveled to South America, Russia, Europe, and Africa. He has received a National Endowment for the Arts Fellowship and a Guggenheim Fellowship. He is a regular contributor to *Sports Illustrated.*

Letters to Yesenin, Sumac Press, 1974
Outlyer & Ghazals, Simon & Schuster, 1971
Walking, Pym-Randall, 1968
Locations, W. W. Norton, 1968
Plain Song, W. W. Norton, 1965

ROBERT HASS (1941) was born and raised in San Francisco, and studied at St. Mary's College in Oakland and at Stanford University. He has taught in the English Department at SUNY at Buffalo, and currently at St. Mary's College. His first book, *Field Guide,* won the 1973 Yale Series of Younger Poets Award.

Field Guide, Yale University Press, 1973

WILLIAM HEYEN (1940) was born in Brooklyn and educated at SUNY at Brockport and Ohio University, where he received a Ph.D. in English in 1967. He is now a Professor of English at Brockport. From 1970–71 he was a Senior Fulbright Lecturer in American Literature in Germany. He was also given an National Endowment for the Arts Fellowship for 1974–75. In addition to his books, he has reviewed widely and written essays on American poets for numerous periodicals.

Noise in the Trees: Poems and a Memoir, The Vanguard Press, 1974
Depth of Field, Louisiana State University Press, 1970

LAWSON FUSAO INADA (1938) was born a Sansei (third-generation Japanese American) in Fresno, California. He lived through the war with his family in "evacuation camps," resettling afterward in the Black and Latin section of Fresno. In this musical environment he developed a talent and enthusiasm for the bass. He has studied writing at Fresno State College, the University of California at Berkeley, the State University of Iowa, and the University of Oregon. He is now on the faculty of Southern Oregon College at Ashland.

Before the War. William Morrow, 1971

THOMAS JAMES (1946–1973) was born in Joliet, Illinois, and graduated from North Illinois University in 1968 with a degree in English and theater. After teaching English in a public school, he moved to Chicago, where he worked as employment counselor for the state of Illinois. He published in various literary magazines and was the winner of the Theodore Roethke Prize from *Poetry Northwest* in 1969. His novel, *Picture Me Asleep,* was dramatized by an experimental theater in the Chicago area. He committed suicide soon after the publication of his first book of poems.

Letters to a Stranger. Houghton Mifflin, 1973

LAURA JENSEN (1948) was born in Tacoma, Washington, where she worked part-time at the local library before graduating from high school. She completed her undergraduate work at The University of Washington, and received an M.F.A. from The University of Iowa in 1974.

After I Have Voted. Gemini Press, 1973

ERICA JONG (1942) was born Erica Mann in New York City, where she grew up on the Upper West Side. She was educated at Barnard College and Columbia University and has taught at various schools. Her poetry and fiction have won numerous prizes, including *Poetry* magazine's Bess Hokin Award, a National Endowment for the Arts Fellowship and a Creative Artists Public Service grant. She is the author of *Fear of Flying* and is at work on a new novel, *How to Save Your Own Life.*

Loveroot. Holt, Rinehart & Winston, 1975
Here Comes & Other Poems. New American Library, 1975
Half-Lives. Holt, Rinehart & Winston, 1973
Fruits & Vegetables. Holt, Rinehart & Winston, 1971

PETER KLAPPERT (1942) was educated at Cornell University and The University of Iowa. He has taught at Rollins College, New College (Sarasota), and Harvard University. His first book of poems won the Yale Series of Younger Poets Award in 1971.

Lugging Vegetables to Nantucket. Yale University Press, 1971

JUDITH KROLL (1943) was born in Brooklyn and moved to Queens when she was eight. She attended Ithaca College, Smith College and Yale University, where she received her Ph.D in English in 1974. Since 1968 she has taught at Vassar. She recently completed a study of Sylvia Plath, *Chapters in a Mythology: The Poetry of Sylvia Plath.*

In the Temperate Zone. Scribner's, 1973

GREG KUZMA (1944) was born in Rome, New York. He received an M.A. from Syracuse University in 1967 and is now conducting poetry workshops at the University of Nebraska. He edits the magazine *Pebble* and runs The Best Cellar Press; he is also a contributing editor to *Prairie Schooner.* His poems have appeared in many publications.

Good News. The Viking Press, 1973
What Friends Are For. The Best Cellar Press, 1973

Song for Someone Going Away. Ithaca House, 1971
The Bosporus. Hellric Publications, 1971
Harry's Things. Apple, 1971
Eleven Poems. Portfolio 2, 1971
Sitting Around. Lillabulero, 1969
Something At Last Visible. Zeitgeist, 1969

AL LEE (1938) was born in Louisville, Kentucky, and educated at Yale College and The University of Iowa Writers' Workshop. He spent two years with the Peace Corps in Ghana, and the following year in Paris. He is the editor of *The Major Young Poets,* and currently teaches English at Newark College of Engineering.

Time. The Ecco Press, 1974

FRED LEVINSON (1936) was born in a small Wisconsin farm town, and now lives in North Hollywood, California. He has attended numerous schools but has received no degrees. Until 1974 he made his living as a director of adolescent psychiatric treatment programs.

LARRY LEVIS (1946) was born on a farm near Fresno, California. He studied with Philip Levine at Fresno State College and went on to Syracuse University for an M.A. in creative writing. In 1971 he won the U.S. Award of the International Poetry Forum. He has taught at Los Angeles State College, The University of Iowa, and teaches presently at the University of Missouri.

The Rain's Witness. Southwick Press, 1975
Wrecking Crew. University of Pittsburgh Press, 1972

ELIZABETH LIBBEY (1947) was born in Washington, D.C., and grew up in Maryland. She received a B.A. degree at the University of Montana, where she studied with Richard Hugo. She received her M.F.A. from The University of Iowa in 1973, and is now working as a cook at a motel in Iowa City.

THOMAS LUX (1946) was born and raised in Massachusetts on a dairy farm. He received a B.A. in English Literature from Emerson College, and co-founded the Barn Dream Press. In 1971 he began teaching creative writing at Emerson College and spent the following year in the Writers' Workshop at The University of Iowa, where he worked as Managing Editor of *The Iowa Review.* He left Iowa without an M.F.A. degree to return to Boston and Emerson College as Poet-in-Residence. He is currently teaching at Oberlin College, where he is an Associate Editor of *Field.*

Almost Dancing. Pym-Randall Press, 1975
Memory's Handgrenade. Pym-Randall Press, 1972
The Land Sighted. Pym-Randall Press, 1970

WILLIAM MATTHEWS (1942) was born in Cincinnati. He took a B.A. from Yale University, and an M.A. from the University of North Carolina at Chapel Hill, where he founded, with friends, Lillabulero Press and its magazine, *Lillabulero.* He has been Advisory Editor of the *Tennessee Poetry Journal,* a member of the editorial board for poetry at Wesleyan University Press, and has taught at Wells College, Cornell University, Emerson College, Sarah Lawrence College, and teaches currently at the University of Colorado.

An Oar in the Old Water. Stone Press, 1974
Without a Mouth. Penyeach Press, 1973
Sleek for the Long Flight. Random House, 1972
The Cloud. Barn Dream Press, 1971
Ruining the New Road. Random House, 1970
Broken Syllables. Lillabulero Press, 1969

ANGELA McCABE (1951) was born on a small farm in Nebraska. She has been employed as an artist's model in New York City and a waitress in a New Mexico cafe.

The Keeper of Height. Barlenmir House, 1974

DAVID McELROY (1941) was born in Milwaukee and raised on a dairy farm till the age of fifteen. He studied forestry and English at the University of Minnesota, and poetry with Richard Hugo at the University of Montana. In 1966 he received a creative writing award from the National Council on the Arts and Humanities. He has worked as a smokejumper in Montana and Alaska, and in 1967 authored *The History of Forest Fires in Alaska.* He now works as a bush pilot in Juneau, Alaska.

Making It Simple. The Ecco Press, 1975

HEATHER McHUGH (1948) received her B.A. from Radcliffe College in 1969 and her M.A. from the University of Denver in 1972. Her work has received numerous awards, including the Academy of American Poets Prize and a National Endowment for the Arts Fellowship. She lives in Tyringham, Massachusetts.

JAMES McMICHAEL (1939) was born in Pasadena, California and went to school at the University of California at Santa Barbara and Stanford University. He is the co-editor of *Just What the Country Needs, Another Poetry Anthology,* and *The Style of the Short Poem.* He teaches in The Writing Center at the University of California at Irvine.

Against the Falling Evil. Swallow Press, 1971

SANDRA McPHERSON (1943), after doing graduate work at the University of Washington for two quarters, worked as a technical writer at Honeywell, Inc., and was a member of the Forum studying individuality for the White House Conference on Children. She has also edited issues of *Poetry Northwest* and *The Iowa Review.* She spent the 1974–75 school year as Visiting Lecturer at The University of Iowa's Writers' Workshop. She has won grants from the National Endowment for the Arts and the Ingram Merrill Foundation. She was raised in California, but her permanent residence is now the Northwest.

Radiation. The Ecco Press, 1973
Elegies for the Hot Season. Indiana University Press, 1970

ROBERT MEZEY (1935) was born in Philadelphia, Pennsylvania. He was educated at Kenyon College and The University of Iowa, and has taught at several universities. He lives with his wife and children in the Sierra Nevadas. With Stephen Berg, he edited the anthology *Naked Poetry.*

The Door Standing Open. Houghton Mifflin, 1970
A Book of Dying. Kavak Books, 1970
Favors. (privately printed), 1968

The Mercy of Sorrow. Three People Press, 1966
White Blossoms. The Cummington Press, 1965
The Lovemaker. The Cummington Press, 1961

PAUL MONETTE (1945) was born in Lawrence, Massachusetts, and educated at Andover College and Yale University. He lives in Cambridge, Massachusetts, where he is an instructor in English at Milton Academy.

The Carpenter at the Asylum. Little Brown, 1975
Sarah. David Scharr, 1970

CAROL MUSKE (1945) was born in St. Paul, Minnesota, and received an M.A. in creative writing at San Francisco State College in 1970. In 1973 she won the Dylan Thomas Poetry Award at The New School. She is currently running a writing center at the Women's House of Detention on Riker's Island called "Free Space," which is funded by the National Endowment for the Arts and Poets and Writers, organizing the poetry series for the Bronx Council on the Arts, as well as reviewing and writing articles for various magazines. She is Assistant Editor of *Antaeus.*

Camouflage. University of Pittsburgh Press, 1975

JACK MYERS (1941) was born in Winthrop, Massachusetts. At various times he has been a news editor, lobsterman, French chef, mailman, teacher, animal keeper and secretary. From 1970–1972 he attended the Writers' Workshop at The University of Iowa, where he received his M.F.A. For the past three years he has been painting houses.

Will It Burn (with David Akiba). Falcon Publishing, 1974
Black Sun Abraxas. Halcyone Press, 1970

GREGORY ORR (1947) was born in Albany, New York, and grew up in the rural Hudson River Valley in upstate New York. He lived in Haiti for a year while his father served as a doctor at the Hospital Albert Schweitzer. He attended Hamilton College for two years, then transferred to Antioch College, where he received a B.A. in 1969, and in 1972 an M.F.A. from Columbia University, where he won an Academy of American Poets Prize and the YMHA Discovery

Award. From 1972–1975 he lived in Ann Arbor, Michigan, as a Junior Fellow of the University of Michigan Society of Fellows.

Gathering the Bones Together. Harper & Row, 1975
Burning the Empty Nests. Harper & Row, 1973

GREG PAPE (1947) was born in Eureka, California. By the time he was twelve he had lived in Ohio, New York, California, Arizona, Florida, and Mexico. He received an M.A. from Fresno State College, where he studied with Philip Levine, Robert Mezey, Peter Everwine, and others. In 1974 he received an M.F.A. in writing from the University of Arizona. At present, he is living and writing on Cape Cod with the assistance of The Fine Arts Work Center in Provincetown.

JOHN PECK (1941) comes from the river valleys of Pittsburgh, where his family drove trains, sold fish, and designed furnaces for the metal foundries. He attended Allegheny College, Stanford University, and has been teaching in the writing program at Princeton University. He writes, "In the manner of the commentator, alas, or the gnomes who hammer gold for Alberich, I have written on Ezra Pound." He has also made random translations, including versions of those Yu-Vu songs which the Na-khi shepherds of Tibet have improvised about suicide pacts between lovers.

Shagbark. Bobbs-Merrill, 1972

STANLEY PLUMLY (1939) was born in Barnesville, Ohio, and grew up in the lumber and farming regions of Virginia and Ohio. He received a B.A. from Wilmington College and an M.A. from Ohio University. He has taught at Ohio University, Louisiana State University, and most recently, at The University of Iowa as a visiting lecturer. *In the Outer Dark* won the Delmore Schwartz Memorial Award, and he held a Guggenheim Fellowship in poetry for 1973–74.

Giraffe. Louisiana State University, 1974
How the Plains Indians Got Horses. Best Cellar Press, 1973
In the Outer Dark. Louisiana State University Press, 1970

LAWRENCE RAAB (1946) was born in Pittsfield, Massachusetts and received his B.A. from Middlebury College, where he studied writing with Robert Pack, and his M.A. from Syracuse University. Mr. Raab's poems have appeared in a number of magazines, and he has received several awards for his work—Book-of-the-Month Club Creative Writing Fellowship, a Fulbright Fellowship offer in 1968, a grant from the National Endowment for the Arts and a three-year Junior Fellowship in the Michigan Society of Fellows in 1973. He was the Robert Frost Fellow at Bread Loaf Writers Conference in 1973, and has taught writing at The American University in Washington, D.C., and the University of Michigan.

Mysteries of the Horizon. Doubleday, 1972

JAMES REISS (1941) was born in New York City and grew up in Washington Heights. He took two degrees, and won two Academy of American Poets' Prizes, at the University of Chicago. In 1974 he won a National Endowment for the Arts Fellowship, and the YMHA Discovery Award. He is the co-editor of *Self-Interviews* by James Dickey. Since 1965 he has taught at Miami University in Ohio and is the regular poetry critic for the Cleveland *Plain Dealer.*

The Breathers. The Ecco Press, 1974

KENNETH ROSEN (1940) was born in Boston and attended Pennsylvania State University. He received his M.F.A. degree from The University of Iowa in 1964 and since then has taught at the University of Maine, Portland-Gorham.

Whole Horse. George Braziller, 1973

MICHAEL RYAN (1946) grew up in Pennsylvania, studied at three universities and earned four degrees. He spent four years at The University of Iowa, where he was a student, an editor of *The Iowa Review,* and a teacher. His book *Threats Instead of Trees* won the Yale Series of Younger Poets Award in 1973.

Threats Instead of Trees. Yale University Press, 1974

IRA SADOFF (1945) was born in New York City and graduated from Cornell University. He then took his M.F.A. degree at the University of Oregon, where his thesis was a collection of short stories. His first teaching job was at Hobart & William Smith Colleges, where he started the literary magazine *The Seneca Review.* He has been a Fellow at both the Bread Loaf Writers' Conference and the Squaw Valley Community of Writers. In the fall of 1974 he was appointed poetry editor of *The Antioch Review.*

Settling Down. Houghton Mifflin, 1975

DENNIS SCHMITZ (1937) was born in Dubuque, Iowa. He was educated at Loras College and the University of Chicago, and now teaches at Sacramento State College in California. He will have a new book published by The Ecco Press in the spring of 1976, entitled *Goodwill, Inc.*

Double Exposures. Triskelion Press, 1971
We Weep for Our Strangeness. Follett Publishing Co., 1969
Monstrous Pictures of Whales. Big Table/Follett, 1969

HUGH SEIDMAN (1940) was born in Brooklyn. He holds undergraduate degrees in science and an M.F.A. from Columbia University. His first book, *Collecting Evidence,* won the Yale Series of Younger Poets Award. He has taught writing workshops in secondary schools, at Yale University, and currently at the City College of CUNY in New York City. His awards include grants from the National Endowment for the Arts and the Creative Artists Public Service program.

Blood Lord. Doubleday, 1974
Collecting Evidence. Yale University Press, 1970

CHARLES SIMIC (1938), who teaches at the University of New Hampshire, was born in Yugoslavia and educated at New York University. He has published various volumes of his own poetry, as well as numerous translations of French, Russian, and Yugoslav poetry. He and Mark Strand have completed a collection of translations, entitled *Another Republic,* to be published soon by The Ecco Press.

Return to a Place Lit by a Glass of Milk. George Braziller, 1974
White. New Rivers Press, 1972
Dismantling the Silence. George Braziller, 1971
Somewhere Among Us a Stone is Taking Notes. Kayak Press, 1969
What the Grass Says. Kayak Press, 1967

ROBERTA SPEAR (1948) was born and raised in Hanford, California, a small farming community in the San Joaquin Valley.

She attended four colleges, including University of California at Irvine, and Fresno State College, where she received an M.A. in creative writing.

KATHLEEN SPIVACK (1938) was brought up in North Bennington, Vermont, and Montclair, New Jersey. She attended Oberlin College, holds an M.A. degree from Boston University and has been the recipient of a fellowship from the Radcliffe Institute. In 1972 she was a winner of the YMHA Discovery Award.

The Jane Poems. Doubleday, 1974
Flying Inland. Doubleday, 1973

MAURA STANTON (1946) was born in Evanston, Illinois. She received her B.A. from the University of Minnesota and an M.F.A. from The University of Iowa. She presently teaches creative writing at the University of Richmond, Virginia. Her first book, *Snow on Snow,* won the Yale Series of Younger Poets Award for 1974. She also received a National Endowment for the Arts Fellowship for 1974–1975.

Snow on Snow. Yale University Press, 1975

DAVID ST. JOHN (1949) grew up in California's San Joaquin Valley. He studied with Philip Levine at Fresno State College and The University of Iowa. During 1974 he worked as a poetry editor for *The Iowa Review.*

This. The Cassiopeia Press, 1975
For Lerida. The Penumbra Press, 1973

TERRY STOKES (1943) was born in Flushing, New York and baptized by Norman Vincent Peale. He grew up in Colebrook, Connecticut, and went to the University of Hartford, where he earned a B.A. in English, and The University of Iowa, where he received an M.F.A. in writing. He has taught at Western Michigan University and the University of Hartford, and in 1973 won a Creative Artists Public Service grant.

Boning the Dreamer. Alfred Knopf, 1975
Crimes of Passion. Alfred Knopf, 1973

Punching In, Punching Out. Burning Deck Press, 1973
A Season of Lost Voices. Baby John Press, 1973
Natural Disasters. New York University Press, 1971
Living Around Other People. Westigan Review Press, 1971
The Satanic American Flag. Cat's Pajamas Press, 1970
The Night Ed Sullivan Slapped One of the Kessler Twins Right On the Ass in the Middle of Show, & Their Song & Dance. Burning Deck Press, 1970
The Lady Poems. Runcible Spoon, 1969
Balancing Out. Runcible Spoon, 1968

BRIAN SWANN (1940) was born in Northumberland, England and came to America in 1964. He received a B.A. and an M.A. from Queens' College, Cambridge, and a Ph.D. from Princeton University. He has taught at Princeton University, Rutgers University, and The Cooper Union. His poems, essays, translations, and fictions have appeared in many journals. He is the co-editor and co-translator of four books of translations.

The Whale's Scars. New Rivers Press, 1974

JAMES TATE (1943) was born in Kansas City, Missouri. His first book, *The Lost Pilot,* won the Yale Series of Younger Poets Award in 1966. He has taught poetry at the University of California at Berkeley, Columbia University, Emerson College and the University of Massachusetts. He has given poetry readings at scores of colleges throughout the country, and has lived in Sweden, Ireland, and England. In 1974 he was awarded the National Institute for Arts and Letters Award for Poetry.

Hottentot Ossuary. Temple Bar Press, 1974
Absences. Atlantic, Little-Brown, 1972
Hints to Pilgrims. Halty Ferguson Press, 1971
Are You Ready Mary Baker Eddy (in collaboration with Bill Knott), Cloud Marauder Press, 1970
The Oblivion Ha-Ha. Atlantic, Little-Brown, 1970
Shepherds of the Mist. Black Sparrow Press, 1969
Row With Your Hair. Kayak Press, 1969
The Torches. Unicorn Press, 1968
Notes of Woe. Stone Wall Press, 1968
The Lost Pilot. Yale University Press, 1967

DIANE WAKOSKI (1937) grew up in Southern California and graduated from the University of California at Berkeley in 1960. She went east that year and began publishing in magazines around the country. She was awarded a Guggenheim Fellowship for 1972–73.

Virtuoso Literature for Two and Four Hands. Doubleday, 1975
Trilogy. Doubleday, 1974
Dancing on the Grave of a Son of a Bitch. Black Sparrow Press, 1973
Greed: Parts 8, 9, & 11. Black Sparrow Press, 1973
Smudging. Black Sparrow Press, 1972
The Motorcycle Betrayal Poems. Simon & Schuster, 1971
Greed: Parts 5–7. Black Sparrow Press, 1971
The Magellanic Clouds. Black Sparrow Press, 1970
Greed: Parts 3 & 4. Black Sparrow Press, 1969
Inside the Blood Factory. Doubleday, 1968
Greed: Parts 1 & 2. Black Sparrow Press, 1968
The George Washington Poems. riverrun press, 1967
Discrepancies and Apparitions. Doubleday, 1966
Coins & Coffins. Hawk's Well Press, 1962

ALICE WALKER (1944) was born in Eatonton, Georgia. She attended Spelman College for two years and received a B.A. from Sarah Lawrence College. She has worked in voter registration in Georgia, in welfare rights, and in the New York City Welfare Department. She has lived in Kenya, Uganda, and the Soviet Union, and is the author of a novel, *The Third Life of Grange Copeland,* and a collection of stories. She has taught at Wellesley College and the University of Massachusetts.

Revolutionary Petunias. Harcourt Brace Jovanovich, 1973
Once. Harcourt, Brace & World, 1968

ROGER WEINGARTEN (1945) was educated at the Goddard Seminary in Barre, Vermont, and The University of Iowa. In 1973 he received a National Endowment for the Arts Fellowship, and now lives in East Montpelier, Vermont.

Ethan Benjamin Boldt. Alfred Knopf, 1975
What Are Birds Worth. Cummington Press, 1975

JAMES WELCH (1940) was born in Browning, Montana, and lived in several different parts of the Northwest during his early years. He attended the University of Minnesota and Northern Montana College. After two years of working at various jobs in various places, he completed his undergraduate studies at the University of Montana and then worked in the M.F.A. program there. He is the author of the novel *Winter in the Blood.*

Riding the Earthboy 40. World, 1971

PETER WILD (1940) was born in Easthampton, Massachusetts, and did his undergraduate and graduate work at the University of Arizona. In 1963–65 he served a term with the U.S. Army in Heidelberg, West Germany, with the task of replying to correspondence from members of Congress and other high government officials. He received an M.F.A. in writing from the University of California at Irvine in 1969, and has since then received numerous awards for his work. He is an Associate Professor of English at the University of Arizona.

The Cloning. Doubleday, 1974
Tumacacori. Twowindows Press, 1974
Cochise. Doubleday, 1973
New and Selected Poems. New Rivers Press, 1973
Wild's Magical Book of Cranial Effusions. New Rivers Press, 1971
Peligros. Ithaca House, 1971
Grace. The Stone Press, 1971
Dilemma: Being an Account of the Wind That Blows the Ship of the Tongue. Back Door Press, 1971
Terms and Renewals. Twowindows Press, 1970
Fat Man Poems. Hellric Publications, 1970
Love Poems. Lillabulero Press, 1969
The Afternoon in Dismay. The Art Association of Cincinnati, 1968
Mica Mountain Poems. Lillabulero Press, 1968
Sonnets. Cranium Press, 1967
The Good Fox. The Goodly Company, 1967

CHARLES WRIGHT (1935) was born in Pickwick Dam, Tennessee, and spent the first twenty-one years of his life in Tennessee and North Carolina. He graduated from Davidson College in 1957 and spent the next four years in the U.S. Army Intelligence Service.

After he received his M.F.A. from The University of Iowa in 1963, he went to live in Rome for two years as a Fulbright Scholar, and spent an additional year in Rome translating *La Bufera,* by Eugeno Montale. He has taught at the University of Padua, the Writers' Workshop at The University of Iowa, and teaches currently at the University of California, Irvine.

Bloodlines. Wesleyan University Press, 1975
Hard Freight. Wesleyan University Press, 1973
The Venice Notebook. Barn Dream Press, 1971
The Grave of the Right Hand. Wesleyan University Press, 1970
The Dream Animal. House of Anansi Press, 1968

DAVID YOUNG (1936) grew up in the Midwest, mostly in Omaha, Nebraska. He was educated at Carleton College and at Yale University. Since 1961 he has taught at Oberlin College and is the editor of *Field.* He has translated from the Italian, Chinese, and German, his most recent effort being a new translation of Rilke's *Duino Elegies.* His literary criticism includes work on Wallace Stevens, and a book-length study of Shakespeare's pastoral plays, *The Heart's Forest.* His poems appear in a number of anthologies, and magazines.

Boxcars. The Ecco Press, 1973
Sweating Out the Winter. University of Pittsburgh Press, 1968